What The Church Won't Talk About

Real Questions From Real People About
Raw, Gritty, Everyday Faith

- Revised and Updated -

J.S. Park

Copyright © 2014, 2015 by J.S. Park
Publisher: The Way Everlasting Ministry
Published September 2014, Updated 2015

All rights reserved.
Printed in the United States of America.

This book or any portion thereof may not be reproduced, stored in a retrieval system, transmitted, or used in any manner whatsoever without the express written permission of the author except for the use of brief quotations in a book review or study/presentation material.

The scanning, uploading, and distribution of this book via the Internet or via any other means without the permission of the publisher is illegal and punishable by law. Please purchase only authorized electronic editions, and do not participate in or encourage electronic piracy of copyrighted materials.

Scripture quotations are from the Holy Bible, New International Version®, NIV®.
Copyright © 1973, 1978, 1984, 2011, by International Bible Society. All rights reserved worldwide. Used by permission of Zondervan. The "NIV" and "New International Version" are trademarks registered in the United States Patent and Trademark Office by Biblica, Inc.™

Cover art by Rob Connelly.
http://heyitsrob.com

All quoted Scripture is from the New International Version 1984, and is also God-breathed and useful for teaching, rebuking, correcting, and training in righteousness.

Park, J.S., author.
    What the church won't talk about: real questions from real people about raw, gritty, everyday faith / J.S. Park.—First edition.
    Includes bibliographical references.

ISBN 978-0692499528
    1. Christian Life—Spiritual Growth 2. Christian Life—Devotional
    3. Religion & Spirituality—Worship & Devotion

Printed in the United States of America.
10 9 8 7 6 5 4 3 2 1

Citation Information:
J.S. Park, *What The Church Won't Talk About* (Florida: The Way Everlasting Ministry, 2015 Revised)

Also the author of:
Mad About God
The Life of King David
The Christianese Dating Culture
Cutting It Off

Join me in the journey of faith.

Wordpress. http://jsparkblog.com
Facebook. http://facebook.com/pastorjspark
Tumblr. http://jspark3000.tumblr.com
Podcast. http://thewayeverlasting.libsyn.com
Twitter. http://twitter.com/pastorjs3000
YouTube. http://youtube.com/user/jsparkblog

Dedicated

To my wonderful lady, J.Y. We're in this, together.

To my amazing family: Mom, Dad, & Brother.

To my second family: Beloved fellow bloggers and Planet Tumblr.

To the many wonderful advance readers who cheered me on.

To my ninth grade English teacher,

who told me to keep writing.

To my first pastor: you challenged me to be.

To Yeshi:

I tried harder to do, and in my place, you said, *It is done*.

A Note About The Revised Edition

This edition has been expanded with all new content and questions, totaling about an extra 16,000 words. I cover a few new topics, including racism, career, ministry, and some recent headlines. These have been added to the end of every chapter, so the original content remains the same. I've also added four new interludes between chapters: one about marriage, since I've gotten married after the publication of the first edition, one about justice and social media, and the last two to encourage the discouraged. There are also some general corrections and formatting changes.

—J.S.

The Coffee Table of Contents

Foreword, by T.B. LaBerge: A Better Place For You. 1

Preface 1: Honesty, Grace, Wide Open Space. 3

Preface 2: You Can Stop Reading After This. 7

Chapter 1 — Struggling With Struggling:
The Frustrating, Messy, Uphill Journey of Faith. 11

Chapter 1.5 — Interlude: A Letter To The Tenuous Christian Who Has Left Church And Is Hanging On By A Thread. 37

Chapter 2 — Everyone's Doing It:
Sex, Dating, the L-Word, and the F-Word. 39

Chapter 2.5 — Interlude: Three Lessons I Learned Instantly In My First Week of Marriage (That I'll Need For Life). 75

Chapter 3 — Confrontation And Conflict: Dealing With *People*. 79

Chapter 3.5 — Interlude: When You're Too Quick To Dismiss That Guy, You Can't See What God Is Doing. 123

Chapter 4 — The Deep End of Icky Awkward Issues:
Sexuality, Society, and Politics. 125

Chapter 4.5 — Interlude: The One Thing We're Not Doing About Injustice. 149

Chapter 5 — Why (Me) God? Doctrine on Disasters, Death, and Staring Down The Devil. 151

Chapter 5.5 — Interlude: Around The Corner, A Second Wind. 179

Chapter 6 — Extreme Trauma: Stressed, Depressed, & Stuck. 181

Chapter 6.5 — Interlude: Mistakes Don't Say Everything About You, And It's Okay To Make Them. 225

Chapter 6 and ¾ — Interlude: Forgetting How To Be, Reclaiming How To Breathe. 229

Chapter 7 — Heaven, Hell, Heresies, and
The Hairy Mess of Religious Objections. 231

Chapter 7.5 — Interlude: Everyone's Screwed Up, Busted Up, and Catching Up, and That's Okay. 277

Conclusion — The Final Authority: Why This Book Doesn't Matter. 281

＊What The Church Won't Talk About＊

Foreword:
A Better Place For You

In the day and age of the internet, I find it interesting how many people have so many answers at their fingertips, but still, they are seeking a genuine response that has been lost in our era of "connectedness." The gospel is still relevant in a time where the world seeks to extinguish its flame, and one of the carriers of this flame is my dear brother Joon.

The first time I ever encountered Joon, it was from a post he wrote about brothers in Christ encouraging each other. Little did I know how much of an encouragement he became to me. How he would reach out and offer to pray for me, how he would be humble and ask for prayer in return.

The heart of Christ is one that is inviting, and few are as inviting as J. He has a way of showing the love of God that blankets you; it covers you up and keeps you warm in a world that is so frigid. Joon does with his words what Christ did with His; he says, "Come, there is a better place for you, a place where you are welcomed," and that is a call that so many are starving to hear, longing to take part in.

What you are about to take part with in this book is a conversation that has taken place since the beginning of the world, the conversation of humanity and its place with God. The story of Christ and His grand love for us, how it calls us to leave what we think is good for what Jesus knows is holy. Each question comes from a real person, with a real story, and Joon speaks from the heart of a real God who is telling a real story.

Grace, upon grace, upon grace, this is what we are to do, whether it is for ourselves or for our neighbor, we must be brave enough to share this great love, and that is what this book is drenched in. It is a reminder that God is still with us, that He has not forgotten our tears, and He will wipe them away someday.

I pray that each word speaks to you, I pray that your search may be one of many blessings, I pray that you are filled with a love the must be poured out. I pray that J.S. Park is continued to be used, because the vessel that says, "Send me, Lord!" will be used and used and used again, until all the world has returned to its first Love. May you have a heart that is ignited by the gospel, may you come to an understanding of what it means to live like Christ.

I know Joon has spoken volumes into my life. I believe he will into yours as well.

May the glory of our Father be most evident with each word that is said, so that His kingdom may come, and the wounds of this earth be healed.

— **T.B. LaBerge** of tblaberge.tumblr.com

Preface 1:
Honesty, Grace, Wide Open Space

Hello there, fellow traveler and dear friend.

Over the last seven years as a pastor, blogger, and professional rambler, I've been asked thousands of questions through my blog that have absolutely punched me in the gut. Over and over, my heart was broken for such wonderful, struggling, fellow travelers.

From sex, dating, sexuality, doubts, depression, pornography, abortion, apologetics, to family drama, these were questions that I've always wanted to ask in church, *but was too afraid to ask out of fear of judgment, stirring the status quo, and getting another Sunday School lesson-bomb.*

I felt ill-prepared to answer them too, because I was so often in the same boat. I'm not qualified. I wrestled with faith just as much as everyone else who was asking me about it.

But I found we all had something in common.

We wanted to talk about these things

with **honesty**,

expecting **grace**,

out in the **open**,

and we all wanted the kind of church where we didn't have to be afraid of the hard questions.

We wanted authentic truth, no sugarcoating, no watered down theology, yet with a gentle reassuring hand that there was a way forward from the occasional mess of life. I began to answer with excitement. I was electrified because maybe I wasn't alone in this, maybe we've all been shot down in church when we earnestly sought the truth, and maybe all of us smart-sounding church-attenders were the same insecure people scratching for a summit of vulnerability.

Soon I found, *so many of us were in the same place, clawing for air, looking for space.*

We were enduring the consequences of poorly made decisions. We had no idea how to help our friends go through their terrible trials. We were disappointed weekly by the church's avoidance of tough topics, or the black-and-white binary boxes. The church gave us cat-poster clichés or pulpit-pounding guilt-trips. So we adopted the self-improvement techniques of culture, which turned out to be self-improvisation, and it only made us worse.

It's not that we needed the universal binding theory of reality. We were all looking for the *What-now?* We wanted theology that would endure the heat of the moment, that would make it past Monday in rush hour traffic, in between the panic of bills and conflicts and a wrecked up home. We need something more for the raw, gritty, everyday lived-out faith.

I found that much of our Churchianity only works in theoretical abstracts or within the safe confines of Christianese Sunday subculture. People neck-deep in the dirt of life find it hard to pull Heaven into the heartache. In the throes of anger or despair: our carefully constructed theology goes out the window. It only takes a single emergency to expose the shallowness of our propped-up faith.

I don't mean to badmouth the church. In fact: *I wish we could turn to our church first when we encounter the hard questions.* But the church doesn't make this easy, because we go for the quick formulas and the neat three-point sermons. We like our sugary ocean-wallpaper Instagram slogans and Jeremiah 29:11 (but not verses 12-13). And they all fall apart just as fast as we do, because our seams cannot be held by sound-bites and surface-level confessions.

I don't know more than you. I just want to meet you there, in the middle of that gritty gray-space where there is no bullet-point formula to fix our lives overnight.

I want to meet you there in that long walk between the back door of your church and the door of your car, where we shake off the sermon and re-enter real life, back to nine-to-five and hospital bills and family turmoil, back into the daily grind.

Most Christians can't help but live a double-life because we're not sure how our faith fits into daily living. We don't feel safe to ask those sticky embarrassing questions. But I sense that *we do want* Jesus in our whirlwind of deadlines and demands. We sense the church might not have been very good at affirming that God is ready for our honesty.

So here we are, in that sacred space: where honesty is okay.

I've compiled seven chapters with seven different topics, each with five to ten of the toughest, most viral questions I've been asked through my blog. The book is designed to be like a pull-down menu, so please feel free to skip around. There might just be one or two questions you're interested in, or you'll go front to back, or maybe there are a few topics you've always wondered how to answer to a friend. And if we don't see eye-to-eye on these, that's okay. I still wrestle with these questions, and God is really okay with our constant seeking, learning, and re-learning.

I can't promise I'll have the "answers." I won't get it right every time. You might discern a different way, a better way. I won't always cover every angle or hit every base. And none of this is anything to memorize or formulize. My hope is that it'll start a conversation, or start off your next Bible Study, or your next prayer item, or a reflection for a long-night-drive. It could even change the path you're on. But the important thing to know is that *we're not alone in our questions*. Living our faith in the middle of the fire can feel crazy sometimes, and we wonder how Jesus makes sense in the mess.

But my dear friend, he does.

In the crooked question mark of my heart, He was the only one there.

Preface 2:
You Can Stop Reading After This

Even when I don't say it with bells and italics and all caps, the bottom line is always Jesus.

Once, a young lady in college approached me after my sermon and she had the look I've grown to recognize. Discouraged, scared, fidgety, unsure, a mess. She pulled me aside and said, *"I need your help. I'm so screwed up right now. But I don't want you to say anything about God. I don't want you to do that pastor thing where you pray for me after we talk. I just want the advice. Don't tell me about Jesus."*

I did exactly as she asked. I gave her smart tips, effective habits, a couple analogies, some good examples. I didn't bring up the Bible or Jesus or anything about faith, at all. When she moved to leave, I didn't pray for her, and she was relieved.

I didn't hear from her for a long time. Months later, I checked on her through social media and I saw she was the same exact person as months before, but no longer had the conviction to change. It was like she and I had never talked, like she had never reached out to me in such desperation.

I don't mean to demonize this young lady. Really. I can't judge her; she is not any lesser than me or anyone else for choosing her own way. There's no guarantee that she would've been different if I brought in Scripture or the Gospel. But partially, I had failed her, because I was too ashamed to talk about the Only One who can really create life-long change. I told her how to grow and adapt and survive, but I never told her about getting a new heart. I never spoke up about the one relationship that truly transforms everything. If anything, she probably tried to follow these "good principles" but was eventually imprisoned by them, and she could no longer endure the shackling weight of such morality.

If you're brand new to Christianity or you're finding it more and more distant and irrelevant, I understand how we all got here. I know that the church hasn't always been thoughtful or articulate about what really matters, and we tend to live inside a suffocating bubble of secret keywords and snobby hierarchy. We've either watered it down to pop-psychology or we've weaponized it into a sledgehammer. It's probably hard to imagine becoming a Christian or staying one when a handful of Christians down the street were so red-faced angry and too busy fighting each other, or when you were offered nothing more than spiritual cotton candy.

But I'm really hoping you would know that the Christian faith has a deep, rich, profound thoughtfulness about life, because I believe it comes from the one who has healed the universe. I know this isn't so obvious from all the Christians you see in the news. Yet if you can forget, even for a moment, all the baggage tied with the name "Jesus," and for a time call him *Yeshi* or Teacher or Healer or Truth, then maybe it would be worth considering that he not only said really wonderful, powerful, relevant things, but also offers the grace to embrace them. I believe this is not just advice, but a living, breathing, dynamic heartbeat, which you can trace back to the Author of *Ta Hera Gramata,* or what we call the Holy Scriptures.

I truly believe that none of our advice makes sense until we know the Jesus who purchased us out of sin-bound slavery on a criminal's cross and rightfully brings us into himself. He is owed the glory and credit and thanks for all there is, because God gave us everything — Himself — when He owed us nothing. You might have heard that a million times, but it's no less true and glorious. He gave us life, and more.

There's no point in answering anything if it ultimately does not point to Christ. There's plenty of practical advice coming up and you can run with it, but *advice without Christ is living without life*. If you don't believe that, that's okay. It's hard to believe for even the most veteran of Christians. But by witnessing how the Christian faith can be so pulsating and thriving and true for us today, we can see how alive that Jesus is for us, too. I trace back my thirst to the fountain.

I believe that God's Word is absolute authority, not just because it's the Word of God, but because it actually *works*. I believe the Bible has timeless wisdom for issues big and small, hairy and tall, today and tomorrow. When the Word is funneled through experience, logic, and sound interpretation, we travel this journey of faith with the stirring of *joy*.

One day, I believe our questions will dissolve before the presence of God. That'll be an awesome day for the faithful few: the clarity, the wiping of tears, the melting of pain, the face-palm for all our tiny human flailing. We'll stand before the One who breathes stars in His nostrils, and we'll be like ants trying to wave down a helicopter. Jesus will be the answer to everything. When I say Jesus is the answer, I don't mean that in an abstract, ethereal way. I actually mean it. He's the Alpha and Omega, the Galaxy-Sculptor, the lover of busted up hearts.

While I can give you tips and application and insight and Ten Steps and How-To, I can't promise you purpose or meaning or soul. Only Jesus can, and does.

He is life. Without him, none of this matters.

I know that until we see him in fully revealed glory: we're in the fight, the fray, the frustration. Things get tough, fast. Saying "Jesus" for everything or throwing around Bible verses doesn't always do it for you. We want to be armed for the daily grind. Our concerns are real. And despite how the church culture might have made it so distant, it's here that God speaks with force, gentleness, and truth. There's an unbelievable wealth of wisdom when you get with Him.

As G.K. Chesterton said,

"The Christian ideal has not been tried and found wanting. It has been found difficult; and left untried."

So let's talk. We can be honest here.

Chapter 1 —
Struggling With Struggling:
The Frustrating, Messy, Uphill Journey of Faith

A preacher might have convinced you that faith is a one-time, one-chance, one-shot thing, or *it's over, man.*

"You're either in or you're out. You're committed or not. Are you for real or what?"

I understand the passion behind this. It's possible that the preacher preaches this way because he was taught this way, too. But so much of it is supported by the shaky scaffolding of guilt, fear, and shame, which are lazy tactics that cannot feed a sustainable faith. No one in the history of anywhere has ever been successfully shamed into change.

When we have doubts, questions, and confusion, the church culture often responds:

"You have unconfessed sin. You're not praying enough. You need to faith harder."

In other words, we tend to stack on more religious duty, more fervency, and more dedication. This always leads to moral exhaustion, because conforming your behavior is like stacking bricks instead of healing a soul. You can make a lot of neat stuff with bricks but they will never grow. We are more like plants pushing through the dirt, waiting for the sun, hoping for new breath and chain-breaking freedom.

So can we be free to be real about our journey?

Can we confess that there are dry seasons and silent periods of not hearing from God?

Can we be free to talk about doubt?

1. My Faith Is Up & Down & All Over The Place

"Hey Pastor. I guess I'm just wondering if I'm the only Christian who blows hot and cold. I'm terrible about reading my Bible or even praying. I tend to go in phases where I'll do really well and be on it every day and then I hit a spot where I go weeks without cracking open my Bible once, and then I just sort of feel guilty so I keep staying away. Sometimes I second guess myself and wonder if I'm even saved, because if I was, wouldn't I love Christ enough to give Him that time? I know that I am born again, and I also know that Christ has enough grace even for this, even though it's the same thing over and over, and I know that I am the one shaming myself. I guess I'm just wondering if you've ever struggled with this yourself, and if you have advice on how to combat it?"

My dear friend: You're not the only one who feels this way.

Most Christians are shocked that they can't maintain a certain level of excitement and discipline in their spiritual walk, but I'm wondering where we got all these spiritual parameters from. Maybe it's our emphasis on an over-hyped Sunday rock show. Or it's the way the preacher keeps guilt-bombing with, *"When was the last time you really read your Bible and sang from the bottom of your heart?"* (Not last week or the week before, when you asked the same thing.) It could be the Westernized ideology of performance and competition. Or it's just our own self-criticism. Or just life.

But please allow me to give you a little grace and freedom here.

Not every day of your marriage can be like your wedding. No one is expected to duplicate the first feelings of chemistry into their fifth decade of a relationship. No one is meant to be on-fire a mile high all the time.

Faith is a tough, messy, muddy, organic sort of thing, slipping and crawling up the mountain. I know that's probably a hipster thing to say.

But so long as we live between a perfectly loving God and this hostile fallen world, we'll have trouble believing the unseen eternal.[1]

Your spiritual walk is not an isolated, vacuum-wrapped package that is untouched by the realities of your shifting soul. You'll get worn down sometimes, you'll feel alone in faith, you'll have ups and downs like everyone else, and there will be dry spells, cold seasons, and endless second-guessing. Because you're human. We fall into a rut, and it's all about how we respond to these things.

Think of where you obtained your spiritual awakening. Most people come to faith in a church setting, a retreat, a revival, a conference, with many other Christians. The first few months of your journey, you're on fire because you're in this new world of amazing people with a well-constructed church culture. **But no real faith is ever lived out in ideal circumstances.** When the real world catches up to us and the flames get dampened, we tend to blame ourselves. We think we've done something wrong. We think feeling distant from God means that God is gone.

Really all that's changed is you're now trying to make sense of how God is alive in all the areas of your life and how He breathes life in them. Sometimes, churches don't provide help for this. They're trying to collect people instead of getting into their real daily walk. I don't mean to bash the church here because I *love* the church. But you know what I mean. We are usually ill-prepared for the eventualities of life, and more than that, how God speaks to us through them.

I'm with you on this. Having been an atheist, I default to doubt very easily. There are entire seasons I'm not sure He's real and I'm ready to throw the Bible in the trash. Maybe that's too candid, but I look at our "Bible heroes," and they often skated the edge, too. Their victories were interspersed with so many valleys.

---

[1] 1 John 3:2

But you know, I keep serving anyway. I keep acting like God exists. I keep loving people. I keep obeying His commands, as far-away as they feel. I force myself into the church community. I put my tiny little shred of faith into His Son. I pray, even if it's a few words at night. I read Scripture, my heavy head on a pillow as the app shines its tiny little screen into the darkness. And most days, that meager little mustard-seed-faith is just enough.

It sounds like legalism, but *effort is not legalism*. It's only legalistic to presume that God's law can save, which leads to self-righteousness. **I don't believe merely following God's law will save me. I believe following His law will lead me back to the heart who made me.** As C.S. Lewis said, I'm trying to trace the sunbeam back to the sun.[2] The days I succeed, I praise God. The days I fail, which are many, I continue on by the bare skin of my teeth.

I'm learning this is okay. I'm learning we are works in progress looking towards the work finished, Jesus.

I'm not endorsing a shriveled up faith. Certainly I commend a robust, vibrant, out-loud faith that declares God in everything. Of course, if there is an old pattern of life you need to leave, then seek help and cut it off, today. I'm not ever promoting the language of "struggle" as a permission slip to disobey God. I just grew weary of comparing myself to other on-fire Christians.

My faith burns slower, more methodical, seated in the back, plagued with questions, desperate in prayer, trusting those rare moments when Christ is fully visible.

My friend, keep going anyway. Get plugged in, talk it out with other mature Christians, bug your pastor, get into places where you know there's a chance you can encounter Jesus.

---

[2] C.S. Lewis, *Letters to Malcolm: Chiefly on Prayer* (NY: Harcourt, 1992), pp. 89-90

God absolutely loves you, right now, even in your most downward spiral of doubt and frustration. Tell Him how you feel. He will love you through that. He won't bite your head off. And when you feel the guilt, simply take your eyes off yourself and look to the cross. It was there he took on even the guilt you would feel of feeling far away.

"I read once that when a person falls in love the brain creates a chemical that bonds the person to their love interest. Sadly, after two years, that chemical subsides and another chemical is created that continues the bond (if nurtured and protected) but the bond is less passionate, less energetic and more thoughtful and familial. I suppose that's how I feel about Jesus now. I feel like He's family. Or, more appropriately, I feel like I'm in His family. It's almost like we once had a passionate thing and now we're just kind of growing old together. Often, when people try to get me worked up about Jesus, zealous and emotional, I don't necessarily feel like it fits me. I'd have to fake it if I acted that way. To me, faith is about maintaining and protecting a solid relationship in which there is now about fifteen years of history, too many memories to name, lots of great, slow work to do and plenty of other people to introduce Jesus to so they can start their relationship as well."
— Donald Miller

2. I'm A Lying Cussing Smoking Sinner — Am I Still Saved?

"Hi. I know you get this a lot. Am I saved? I faced my sinful life and confessed to God. I know and believe Christ is God, came in flesh to fulfill the Law and atone for my (and everyone's) sin. He died, rose again, and ascended. It is finished. My faith is an unmerited gift of His Grace. I want more than fire insurance. I want to know and feel Him, and do those 'greater works.' But sh*t, I keep cussing, lying, lusting, smoking, gossiping. Help!"

Please allow me to share a quick childhood story. When I was a kid, I had to breathe on a medical machine for a certain amount of time every day. I was a sickly child and my lungs were not fully developed. I had bouts of asthma and chronic bronchitis and was near death a few times. The machine kept me just functioning.

My dad, being a ninth degree black belt, kicked my butt to exercise and eat right. Eventually I got off the breathing machine and started winning trophies at tournaments. Today I'm a fifth degree black belt, I can jump kick over your head, and I can kill you in two moves. But occasionally, I'm still short of breath and I get sick very easily. I have never run over a mile in my life. And I'm allergic to almost everything.

Sometimes people tell me, "Why do you get sick so much? Why are you so allergic to everything?" And I tell them, "You should've seen where I used to be." I talk about the breathing machine, the asthma, the trophies, and my two-move exploding throat technique. From where I was to where I am — it's a pretty big leap.

You must know that every blip and spurt of righteousness in your life is nothing short of a supernatural God-made miracle, because naturally in our own fleshly skin, we're incapable of True Good. The very fact that you're questioning your own faith is a good thing, because you care. We can rejoice in that, because that wasn't even there before.

Before you met Jesus, even our desire to feed the homeless and save the rainforest and memorize the Bible was motivated by self-promotion, image maintenance, and Darwinian survival. It's human nature to trick our hearts by beating ourselves up into upstanding citizens, or "I don't want to be like my snobby neighbor down the street." I'm either scared or smug about being a *good person,* and so my reason to be "good" is motivated by external appearances and a pat on the head.

But after Jesus, we have the reason of No-Reason, because now we're lit up by a Person who dared to die in our place on the cross by his own initiated love. He put His Spirit in us to live out our true calling: to love Him and love others without expecting anything back. You're recreated with a new heart to care about what God cares about, and the Father is proud even of your stumbles. *So any step forward into your purpose is like the birth of a new life: it is momentous, surprising, awesome, and worth celebrating.*

I know at some point this will sound like "soft theology," like I'm enabling or pampering or coddling you somehow. Please know that I would never promote some kind of halfway faith that doesn't take God seriously, because we do have a mission and commandments and a vision that He has cast over us. God does care about holiness and purity and steering clear of "worldly ways." We do want to avoid harmful behavior, because some things do kill us, and we need to quit them.

Yet — *What's the motivation? Why quit at all? Where does the power come from?*

One type of motivation says, "I have to stop cussing, lying, smoking, and fighting children."

The divine motivation says, "I love Jesus for who he is and what he's done," and incidentally, you find yourself moving away from destructive behaviors without having tried very hard at all.

The devil will often make you doubt that "you don't have what it takes" — when really, *you don't ever have it*. God has you. True assurance in our walk is knowing the *object* of our faith, not our degree of it.[3] God keeps working through you: and if at times you feel that your faith is a very tenuous, intermittent, strobe-light walk, then welcome to Authentic Christianity. God is strong; humans are weak. God works; humans fail. We live within this crevice of our fallen-ness.

In that Giant Gap between who you want to be and who you really are, every other religion, including the evangelical church, tells you to "close the gap." That's religion.

Jesus is the only one who said, *"I will meet you where you are. I am running backwards through the gap to you. And we will walk this walk together, one step at a time, me in the lead, and I will be with you whether you feel me or not, always."* Faith is being more and more sure of this reality, and it's *not* being more sure that you're sinning less. It's never just running from sin, but running to Him.

I also believe so many of us are concerned about "overcoming our struggle" that we forget God has a purpose, a mission, a Kingdom of love, goodness, and glory that He wants to expand on earth. **We are not only forgiven for our failures, but empowered for a fruitful, joy-filled future.** And if you can plug into this, into the way He has wired you, you'll find that *the volume of sin decreases and becomes less attractive as you do what you're made for and saved for.* The Christian life cannot be only about scrambling up a pit to the edge, but seeing the light who breaks in to rescue us towards a mission. This is why Galatians 5:16 says, *Walk by the Spirit, and you will not gratify the desires of the flesh.*

And maybe you're doing better than you think. Perhaps you still have more to discover of what Jesus has really done, and God's grace covers even those moments when we don't fully understand His grace.

---

[3] This concept of "degree of faith versus object of faith" is inspired by Timothy Keller.

As you follow Him, you'll look back on the bloated corpse of who you used to be. It happens almost by imperceptible degrees. There's a progress that happens when you quit looking at progress.

You'll find that the less you focus on trying to be better, you'll automatically get better. The less you have a morbid introspection of your failures, the more you can look towards the Only Perfection. *Being a Christian doesn't mean being a good person, but following the Only One who is good.* So stumble after him. Don't think you have to run this marathon in one day. Sooner or later, you'll be moving from trauma to trophies. Celebrate the small victories. Even then, be humble to recognize it's all His work.

> *"Thus if you have really handed yourself over to Him, it must follow that you are trying to obey Him. But trying in a new way, a less worried way. Not doing these things in order to be saved, but because He has begun to save you already. Not hoping to get to Heaven as a reward for your actions, but inevitably wanting to act in a certain way because a first faint gleam of Heaven is already inside you."*[4]
> — C.S. Lewis

---

[4] C.S. Lewis, *Mere Christianity* (New York: HarperCollins, 1952, 1980), p. 148

3. I Need Motivation For Prayer

"I've been struggling these days on how to balance my life altogether and my walk with God is suffering from it. The less I pray, the further I stray from him and the less I want to pray. Any tips on how to pray on a daily basis? How do you develop that fire to reach out to him every single day?"

I wish I could tell you I've developed a Secret Eight-Step Plan to being a Super Prayer Warrior, but I know how hard this is. I'd also be a hypocrite if I told you I'm the best example of prayer. There are all those gloomy surveys about low average prayer times, including pastors, and I bet even those few minutes of prayer are sporadic and sputtery.

Every single Christian I've ever met always says, "I should be praying more." I've never heard someone say, "I'm totally praying more than I need to." It's the same when you ask someone, "How's your spiritual life?" I never hear back, "I got that thing on lockdown."

The opposite problem is that when people do pray, they sometimes think, "I just filled my quota" or "I feel good about myself now" — when they had zero intimacy with God Himself. Prayer is not a video-game energy meter that you fill up by mushrooms and first-aid kits. There's no professor grading your prayer-life. *Praying is your time to get totally honest with God and tell Him everything.*

Let's recognize that prayer is straight up tough. Most of us find it difficult to pray because 1) we have tons of shiny distractions, 2) we're not accustomed to silence, 3) it's human nature to forget aversive disciplined habits, 4) we all wonder if it actually does something, and 5) if spiritual religiosity is one more thing you add to your schedule, it'll be the first thing to go when life gets busy.

What I've found is that at least several times per week, I'm able to pray very intensely after I *prime the engine*. In other words, there are some "failed prayers" that happen first in which my mind wanders down thought-chains into oblivion, but the next day I break through the barrier and it's smoother sailing. Some days I can barely get it started, but it's often the next day that I'm talking with God like He's really there, talking to Him with all joy and passion and repentance. The same is true for reading the Bible or serving your church or fighting against addiction — it will take some false starts and flailing to get it going.

Most of us get stuck in the priming part. We think when we "fail a prayer," that we're just not a praying kind of person. It's uncomfortable and disheartening: so we build an aversion to it, like how some of us don't check our voicemail or call our mothers. But if you can run through that initial greasy discomfort, you'll build a groove. And since we're human, we do fall out of that groove sometimes, but that's when you prime the pump again. God is very patient with us, if you know about that thing called the cross.

It's good to try all the regular advice with prayer, like setting aside a regular time, praying no-matter-how-you-feel, writing down your requests, turning on music, and finding a dark corner — but also please remember that **an accurate picture of God** will go a long way to building intimacy with Him.

If your picture of God is a stern disappointed uncle with a stun-gun, prayer will not be fun at all. I hope it's more like the friend with all authority who you can bring to the schoolyard fights; like the father whose lap is always open, ready to embrace you. Pray like God can change something, because He can and He will.

If prayer by itself is a scheduled ritual, you'll cast it aside when you need more room for your life. But the more you can understand your need for Christ and His fullness and your dependence on His provision, the more you'll actually come to Him when life does get busy. Like we do with our older wiser friends, God will be the one you call when life happens.

Lastly, don't ever, ever, ever think that you've been gone too long to come to Him. God is not some spiritual parole officer waiting for you to fail. If you've strayed from prayer, He is not keeping some score. If you don't feel Him at all, tell Him that: "I don't feel you right now, God." Pray with any amount of faith that you have; believe that prayer works; ask for faith if you have none. If you're mad, tell Him. If you're ashamed, guilty, confused, afraid, doubtful: tell Him. He can handle that. He is understanding, patient, gracious; He loves you. You'll soon find you'll want to talk to Him, because He's actually pretty awesome to talk to.

4. Does Grace Make You Lazy?

"Does Christianity encourage laziness? The whole concept of Grace you often speak about lets people off the hook too easily. The Bible says faith without works is dead and Jesus said all trees that bear no fruit will be chopped down and thrown into fire. The reason people are so lazy and under-motivated is because they are always told they're some special person while no one really is all that special. So how does telling them God loves them help deflate their ego?"

Christianity encourages laziness just as much as atheism provokes genocidal baby-eating evil. Which is to say, you can take an issue and spin it any way you want, and you end up with a simplified straw man that's getting beat up by the other straw men. This is a "deconstructive reductionism," like when movie buffs reduce a movie plot into a Hollywood executives writer's room. It doesn't add to the discussion, *at all*.

At the very least, you might be taking the Grace of God and reducing it to a parody of itself, which I would reject too: because it's not really grace.

Still with me? *Grace is not so much any one action or rule or attitude, but* **grace is more of a story about broken people being loved and healed: and this grace always comes at a price.**

Let me tell you about my first pastor. When I first came to church over ten years ago, I was a stubborn thick-headed horny atheist who was looking for hot Christian girls. I hated the sermons but I kept coming back, because there was something about this pastor.

He endured with me. I asked him *tons* of annoying questions about God and the Bible, but he answered them patiently. I screwed up a lot. I slept with a few girls in the church and confessed them all, but he never flinched. He called me and texted me when I never replied. He bought me lunches, dinners, books, and sent cards to my house. He spent hours praying for me. He never once lost his temper with me.

Over time, I realized how much of a jerk I was to him. I didn't listen; I was late all the time; I got drunk and went to strip clubs on Saturday nights before strolling in hung-over on Sundays; I hardly asked how he was doing. But he was endlessly loving. And the grace of this man completely melted me. Of course there were times when he rebuked me, when he laid down the hard truth, but it was always with a shaking voice, with a gentle hand. I've known him now for fifteen years, and there's no way I could be the person I am today without him.

I remember small moments. When one day I was horribly depressed, and he wrote me a letter right in front of me. When I got out of the hospital from swallowing a bottle of pills, and he listened without judging. When I was sobbing hysterically one day and he gripped both my hands and told me, *It'll be okay. God still loves you and He will never stop.*

Even now, my eyes glisten and my heart swells at his sacrifice. **His grace fundamentally ripped away my selfishness and disturbed my ego.** I deserved nothing and he gave me his all.

Out of gratitude, I came to love my pastor, and I realized I would do anything for him. When you love a person, *nothing* is off the table. And when you realize this person loves you back no matter what, you will be alongside them for eternity. There's an **endless freedom and security** there found in nowhere else.

But why was my pastor this way? Because of Jesus. It all pointed to him, and as much as my pastor loved me, Jesus loves us infinitely more. You see: *For all the ways my pastor endured with me, he was showing me a small glimpse of the outpouring love of the crucifixion, and the more I looked back on his reckless grace for me, the more that such grace punctured my heart and tenderized me.* And the grace of my pastor was fueled by the grace of Jesus.

I began to understand that grace is a love-relationship, a journey, an adventure, a story of a restless human heart who can only find wholeness in Christ, and he died so we might have such rest.

That's why **grace is an enduring narrative that never really ends** — because it will always be about a big picture filled with little moments, instead of a principle or philosophy or theology.

If this bothers you, it should. No one naturally likes grace. It feels too easy, and certainly some people think they can abuse it. But grace in and of itself can't be abused anyway, because it's a gift given freely regardless of how it's received.

When someone unconditionally loves you despite you with no end in sight, it changes you. The only other option is to beat you up with religion and rules, which can't sustain you. **While grace takes longer, it will become *a part of you* in a way that moral conformity never can.**

Without grace, we're just clocking in our daily tasks until we "feel holy" or we're desperately trying to hit an arbitrary standard. With grace, we a have a limitless love that provokes us into the same kind of love. It changes not only what you do, but what you *want* to do. It turns nobodies into somebodies as long as they remember they're nothing who received something.

That's the only truth that could ever motivate someone to anything. We work hard, but grace empowers every effort.

"Cheap grace is the preaching of forgiveness without requiring repentance, baptism without church discipline, Communion without confession, absolution without personal confession. Cheap grace is grace without discipleship, grace without the cross, grace without Jesus Christ, living and incarnate.

"... Such grace is costly because it calls us to follow, and it is grace because it calls us to follow Jesus Christ. It is costly because it costs a man his life, and it is grace because it gives a man the only true life. It is costly because it condemns sin, and grace because it justifies the sinner. Above all, it is costly because it cost God the life of his Son: 'ye were bought at a price,' and what has cost God much cannot be cheap for us. Above all, it is grace because God did not reckon his Son too dear a price to pay for our life, but delivered him up for us. Costly grace is the Incarnation of God."[5]

— Dietrich Bonhoeffer

---

[5] Dietrich Bonhoeffer, *The Cost of Discipleship* (New York: Macmillan, 1963, 1995), pp. 43-45

5. How Do I "Love God"?

"I get so bogged down and depressed when I try to be a 'good' Christian. Things begin to feel so legalistic and joyless that I find myself wondering how I could love anyone that will take over my life at any moment, twist my arm, and whisper things like 'If you loved me you'd ___' or 'If you had faith/believed more I wouldn't ___' like some abusive relationship that won't let you think, feel, or do things for yourself. Is there any way to overcome this feeling?"

Dear friend: It's very possible you could've been sold a pile of lies about God. I've heard some of those conditional statements and they do have good intentions, but they're jumping off a false premise.

I think your question boils down to a very simple one.

How do I actually love God?

Most of us (including preachers like myself) say bizarre things like, "If you know God really loved you, then you would love Him back!" And we're supposed to reply, "So convicting!" — and then feel really bad about our sorry little Christian lives.

But if some random lady on the street yelled "I love you" at me, I'm not going to immediately reciprocate. Not even if she's Salma Hayek or Scarlett Johansson. The most I would say is, "Okay thanks lady," while backing away slowly.

The truth here is: *No one can make you fall in love with God — including yourself.*

So let's ask an easier question.

How do I fall in love with someone?

Now we're getting somewhere. Are you ready?

The more you get to know someone, the more you fall in love with them — and the more you fall in love with someone, the more you get to know them.

I recognize that my "job" as a pastor and as your friend is to *hook you up with God.* By God's grace and His Spirit, I'm trying to get myself out of the way and help you encounter Him. The more I can reveal who He is, the more likely you'll fall in love with God *as He truly is.*

Anyone who really encounters God can't say no to Him. Not because they're coerced by God, but exactly because *God doesn't have to.* He is who He is. He's awesome. His love and glory are undeniable. A simple glimpse of His nature is enough to melt your face off.

The more you understand God as He really is, the more you will automatically begin to trust Him, spend time with Him, and go totally radical for Him.

How do I know this? *Because you do the same thing with the people you most dearly love.* There's no question you'd take a bullet for your friends or your spouse or your kids. You would drive hours to see them, you'd do anything they ask, and you'd sacrifice your blood and sweat to see them happy.

All this without thinking, "Why are they bothering me?" Because love makes you crazy in the best way possible.

But it takes time to get there. No one can force you. You can only have an open mind when you go to church and attend Bible study and go on mission trips and embrace serving opportunities, and perhaps soon, you'll encounter the Living God. All the while, you'll see that the Spirit of God was beckoning you and wooing you and opening doors and drawing you to Himself, without ever intruding upon your will.

I've found that **small moments build into a big love for Jesus**. I attend this homeless ministry on most Mondays, and on this particular night I looked at the line of over a hundred people, their plates extended as I plopped down potato salad and baked beans. I had done this many times before — but this time, I was just so dang excited and happy to see the looks on their faces. I couldn't stop smiling as one after another, I was blessed to serve these men and women and children.

Then I realized: *Is this how God feels about me? Is this how happy He gets to give me His grace when I extend my plate to Him? Is this His heart when He gives me the gift of His Son and His Spirit and His Word?* And I nearly wept right there, thinking about how much God loves me. Even writing this, my heart can hardly stand it.

I could never have created this moment out of thin air. It happened because I was *inside the sunbeam that connects to the sun.* And God, in such a simple way, shared His heart with me. I'm still shaken by that experience. I haven't gotten over it. Even in my worst days, I remember what happened there.

I can tell you without shame that in my prayers, I nearly always end with, *I love you Jesus.* It's not easy. Probably not too many people pray this way. I'm not tooting my horn here, but to say, it takes a vulnerability on our end.

To love someone is a big deal, and God understands our feelings of mistrust and risk. He is totally willing to work with that. But God Himself is perfect, unfailing, and always there — so when you get to know Him, it's actually not so hard to love Him. He's really the awesome dad that we're all longing for, and we can be completely open with Him like we've been trying to be with everyone else: except with Him, you won't be let down. And as weird as it sounds, I actually *like* Him. I get the feeling that He likes us, too.

Read the four gospels. Read Acts and Colossians. Read them as if they're specifically written for *you* (because they are). Get to know Jesus. You might be surprised by his love one day. It's okay if it doesn't happen in a moment. It may take many moments over a lifetime to get there. But when you're there, expect a love that will uppercut your soul. Expect something beyond simple platitudes, formulas, quotes, and catchphrases — and expect the Jesus you always suspected all along.

6. What Is The Definition of Grace?
"What would you say the Christian definition of grace is?"

Hey my friend, the technical Christian definition of grace is "unmerited favor, an undeserved gift that outweighs its own need."

But I've never known grace to simply be boxed inside doctrinal boundaries. The second it becomes abstract, it tends to be enabling and pampering and a sugarcoated excuse to abuse the words "struggling" and "broken." Grace is way too costly to be thrown around like cheap lingerie, and if it does not motivate you, then it's not real grace.

True grace is a love that costs everything. It is sacrificial. For God to show us grace, it cost Him the life of His very son.

Let's consider the implications. You create a race of sentient human beings who you've given paradise, and they give you the middle finger and begin to kill each other for fame and glory and pieces of green paper, and you keep sending other little beings called prophets to tell them about True Life, but they kill all those beings too. So you become one of your toy-creations by limiting your infinite power and taking on all their weaknesses and only asking for them to believe you're real, and they torture you and string you up and stab you with jagged metal spikes in your most tender flesh-covered places (which you willingly took on), and there under a sunless sky you still offer forgiveness and love for everyone because this is the best and only way to love them. And to validate your claims, you come back to life from the grave and show yourself to hundreds of people and remind them of their real purpose, and even after all that, two-thirds of the world abuses your name for the worst of atrocities and the one-third who believes in you still chase after mindless, powerless images or lies or approximations of the real thing. And you *still* love them.

You see, romantic love is easy. It lasts as long as the feelings last. Maybe we have a good temperament so we're patient and laid-back. Maybe your friends are all very cool and stable and rich and they're not needy, so you like being with them. Maybe you were genetically predisposed to being generous and truthful and reliable, so everyone around you likes you, too.

But marriages that last fifty years take sweat, blood, heart. Friendships that encounter flaws take a supernaturally forgiving power that is not inherent to our self-preservation. Raising children requires you to stay home when you'd rather be out clubbing and chugging. Serving the homeless and ex-convicts and orphans and the emotionally unstable will demand all your life. Endorsing justice in the world takes more than a blog post or pink ribbons or an X on your hand. Love is not love unless it costs you something, and grace is the love that costs everything.

True grace is a one-way love that persists beyond your own comfort and safety.

It will certainly require your very soul. But the way of true grace, while costing your life, is the only way that gives you *True Life*, and therefore, it's the only real joy. God did not begrudgingly give over His Son, but Jesus willingly followed His Father's will for the joy set before him.[6]

True grace is less doctrine and more of a story.[7]

It's God loving His creation over and over again, regardless of their same mistakes, rebellion, wretchedness, and disunity. It's welcoming the prodigal, the cheater, the liar, the thief back home — all over again. But the one who understands this costly grace will return home to be melted and tenderized by such love, because it's impossible to both see the story of the Cross and to remain the same.

True grace is our rest *and* our resolve.

---

[6] John 10:17-18, Hebrews 12:2
[7] Inspired by Andy Stanley's *The Grace of God*

It's to know that our desperation for validation, approval, and significance is already found in all that God has done for us. It's work *from* God's approval and not *for*. We can rest. We can quit playing these games of achievement and status and the Olympics and American Idol and Viagra. We can quit squeezing expectations from others which we could only receive from God. We can quit living for ourselves under the weight of a self-absorbed egotistical tyranny. We can quit trying to pay off the gap between who-we-want-to-be and who-we-really-are. Yet — *grace also motivates us into the true versions of ourselves.* It is the motivation of no-motivation, because we are not trying to "get better" for the sake of improvement, but rather we become better by being loved for the sake of our own essence through the cross. We are motivated by beauty rather than practicality or function, because God loves us just-because.

And we can be gracious, not perfectly: but with passion, because God gave us grace first. We can because He did.

7. Christianity Is Making Me Worse

"Is it possible to be a worse person after attending church for so long? I feel like I was more disciplined and had better character and integrity when I wasn't a Christian."

Hey dear friend, thank you so much for bringing up something that we all feel, but don't dare to express.

I think the answer, as unhelpful as it might be, is yes and no. I notice a similar pattern among Christians — most of us experience huge growth spurts in the beginning because it's all so exciting and new, but then it turns into begrudging obligation and critical self-punishment. It seems to happen in about 99% of the Christians that I know.

The irony perhaps is that the stronger you grow in faith, the more you become aware of your own faults and flaws. Christians are sensitive to their own shortcomings because we actually *care,* and when we grow in maturity, we stop making excuses and we quit the rationalizations. A sure sign of an immature person is one who cannot take responsibility for their own actions and won't own up to their part; it was always someone else's fault or an environmental factor. It could be true, but it doesn't make us less sinful.

You're becoming self-aware and seeing how bad our sin really is. When we get a glimpse of God's holiness, we can't help but feel wretched and naked and low. Even in the presence of better people, of skilled musicians or writers or scholars, we tend to feel like our progress was "dirty rags" (Isaiah 64:6).[8] In the presence of God, this is amplified to an unbearable level. Because of Scripture, we suddenly have a very clear view of our issues. We regard them as *sin* instead of mistakes, and so we get very hard on ourselves.

At this point, most Christians stay in morbid introspection and forget to look up to the cross and to the resurrection. This is the only place

---

[8] Inspired by Timothy Keller's sermon, "The Gospel and Your Self."

where true character, integrity, and discipline could come from. When our motivation is no longer to "be good" but instead to look to the only one who *is* good, then our motives change from self-punishment to love-driven effort.

The essential Bible truth is that our works cannot save us, and only Christ can — so every Christian is the most critical of their own sin but the most victorious in a savior.

You'll often feel like you're getting worse before you get better. The funny thing is that Apostle Paul would bash himself all the time; in 1 Timothy 1:15 he tells Timothy, *"Here is a trustworthy saying that deserves full acceptance: Christ Jesus came into the world to save sinners—of whom I am the worst."* That's crazy to consider, that Paul called himself "the worst of sinners." But the first half of the verse rides the tension between his own sin and the reality of Christ. It really is a tough balance.

If in the end you feel that you really have gotten "worse," I hope you still won't be too hard on yourself and that tomorrow is another day, a different day, to be who you're called to be.

Of course, you'll want to strive to have integrity and all those other things: but not to punish yourself, and instead embody the one who has already saved you. You don't have to shackle yourself to your own record. Each day, I hope you'll begin again. God wants that for you. He's okay about yesterday and all that came before. I would know, because I really am the worst of sinners, to be the most pitied: yet I remember, I'm deeply loved. You're loved, my friend. We are profoundly fractured, yet radically treasured in Him.

8. Five Primers on How To Study The Bible
"Tips on how to study the word of God? Thanks!"

Reading the Bible is hard. The Bible wasn't even mass-produced until the last few-hundred years, and suddenly we're all guilt-tripping each other on "read more Bible or bring the lighter fluid for your stake-burning." But the Bible itself is hard. Am I allowed to say that? It's dang hard.

So I want to say first: *It's okay to feel dumb about it.* The quicker we can admit, "This is way over my head," then the safer we'll feel to get help. Here's some help then to read the Bible.

1) Start with a book and stay as long as you like.

It's a good idea to camp out in a book. I once read Ephesians every day for a month. I've also read the story of David (1 & 2 Samuel, 1 & 2 Kings) about seven or eight times before I really understood it. Books I recommend to start: John, Philippians, Colossians, Ephesians, Proverbs, Isaiah. There might be a lot you don't get, but there will be a lot that you do.

2) Ask a lot of annoying questions.

Ask your pastor. Ask your mature Christian friend. Ask me. Get different opinions. If you're stuck, ask.

3) Find what other people have said.

The best Bible commentary I've ever read is Henrietta Mears' *What The Bible Is All About*. There are illustration versions and editions for different Bible translations. She goes over every book of the Bible, with history and character charts and story diagrams.

4) Engage with the text.

Ask the 5 Ws – Who, What, When, Where, and Why?

5) Engage with what God is telling you.

Every time you open the Bible, believe that God has something for you. Believe it. At every moment, good and bad, up or down, in all seasons, the Bible will speak. The Holy Spirit convicts you of all truth.

Be ready for it to push against you, to disagree with you, to challenge what you always thought was true. The Word of God is a sword that will cut you to your soul, exposing all. The message of Jesus is crazy to those without him, but to believers is the saving truth. And of course, all Scripture is breathed out of God, useful for everything we do and who we are.[9]

This doesn't mean you'll "feel something" every time you read Scripture. But meditate on even a tiny scrap of a verse and let it sit. The Bible has the very words of God pouring out His heart for you. He is big, but by His Word, He is so close. Hear it as a friend speaking, as a leader leading. Be encouraged and convicted.

---

[9] John 16:13, Hebrews 4:12, 1 Corinthians 1:17-18, 2 Timothy 3:16-17

Chapter 1.5 —
Interlude: A Letter To The Tenuous Christian Who Has Left Church And Is Hanging On By A Thread

I know there are some of us who are barely hanging onto the "Christian scene" — it was part of your youth, you like Jesus, you like some of the music, you find many of the teachings and verses to be inspirational, you're into grace and humility, and you understand that not every screaming Westboro picketer represents the movement of Christianity.

But mostly, it's not a part of your life. You haven't been to church in a while. You feel largely removed from your former Christian friends. You don't care to go back, and you feel like you'd be judged if you did.

Sometimes you miss going, but you'll see some horrible news headline about another group of crazy church people or you'll see how the drama is destroying your friends who still attend — and you remember why you left. You'll remember the old wounds, the hurtful things the pastor did, the way the church gossiped, and those one or two opinions that really bothered you.

My dear friend: I'm sorry it's gone this way. I'm sorry the church as a whole has been so awful. Speaking as a pastor and your friend, we've done a poor job and there's no excuse for that.

Yet — I know you still think Jesus is pretty awesome. I know you're thoughtful enough to still be attracted to God somehow. And you have some decent Christian friends who don't act all uppity nor pretend they have it all together. You occasionally check out some Christian blogs, and they've even been a big encouragement sometimes.

I know this is a huge leap here but I'm writing this for you to say, *Please don't completely write off the church just yet.*

Please consider that there is still one out there, just for you, that isn't perfect but is still very passionate for the truth and love of Jesus, and one you could possibly call *home*.

I've been to many, many good churches that are still faithful, loving, and kind. There are still many churches that really care, where you are free to be yourself, where it feels like God is actually in the house. They still exist. I'm not saying that drama never happens there, but they're honest about it and they love one another through it all.

Sure, church is always going to be a messy sloppy place. But the most gracious ones are also absolutely beautiful in the mess. It's because they meet each other where they are, like Jesus does. Deep down inside, some part of you wants to be a part of one of those. It probably scares you like it scares me — but it's much like the moment when you take a chance on love again. It's terrifying, but you're right at the edge of adventure, and it could be something incredible.

Please think about just asking a friend to attend a church event, or even this Sunday. If it goes bad, try a few more times. Keep an open mind. It's a lot to ask considering all that has happened — but certainly we've invested far more time into things we had less faith in. I've seen so many people come back to church and find healing again. Maybe you'll find a new safe place where you can reconnect with God and start once more. At the very least, you'll know where *not* to visit again, and perhaps you can try elsewhere one more time.

I'm excited for you. I'll be praying for you. If you're excited, don't hide it. Tell your friend. Get your hopes up a little! Enter with the anticipation of Jesus welcoming you with wide open arms.

God loves you and so do I, my friend.

—J.S.

Chapter 2 —
Everyone's Doing It:
Sex, Dating, the L-Word, and the F-Word

Before we ask about the L-Word, maybe we can ask about the F-Word.

I mean, before we talk about Love, maybe we can talk about *Faith*.

Most advice on dating and relationships is about technique, methods, and good habits, but we're quick to jump into the action without serious reflection. Maybe there are some questions we can ask of ourselves before we ask someone on a date. Because without a direction or purpose, then dating will take us from nowhere to nowhere, with serious hurt and confusion in between.

All of us, whether we're fourteen and single or a college graduate with five exes or on our third marriage with five kids or a pastor giving pre-marriage counsel, have bought into paradigms of romance without always thinking through to the bottom of them. I've probably been misled about relationships just as many times as I've unwittingly misled others.

When we shrink dating into a conservative box of legalistic values, we've killed our God-given sexuality. On the other hand, if we compromise to chick flicks and pop songs, there's bound to be the disaster and enslavement and heartbreak. Neither can work. Both Hollywood and the church community don't have a singular consensus on the L-Word, and either we go backwards into over-hyped romanticism, or we diminish ourselves by mechanical checklists.

We've learned how to dance before understanding the purpose of dance itself.

We jumped ahead to dating instead of examining our identity.

Maybe we can get back to the fundamentals of the F-Word: our Faith and all that we believe about life, before exploring the even more difficult contours of the L-Word.

So we could back this up, way up, and perhaps un-learn and re-learn all our ideas about sex, romance, dating, and this complex thing called love.

1. The Weird Subculture of "Christian Dating"

"How do you feel or have personally experienced the Christian subculture's treatment or approach towards dating/courting/romantic relationships?"

You know, I had really bought into the modern Christianese idea of dating because it appeals to the legalistic Pharisee in all of us. It's not all bad, but it often results in a panicked paranoia about the opposite sex that leads to unhealthy self-slavery.

Basically, the Christian subculture of dating says:

- Don't date.
- If you date, do "courtship," which is dating only for marriage.
- The warning: if you decide to date, you give your heart and soul away.
- If you break up, you're practicing for divorce.
- Sex is bad, filthy, gross, and disgusting. So save it for marriage.

I completely understand this rigid idea of dating. It's a reactionary philosophy to all the messed up Hollywood values perpetuated in romantic comedies. So for the average Christian, it makes sense to "only date for marriage" and to "guard the pieces of your heart."

But the opposite of a bad idea doesn't make a better idea.

So "Christian dating" is essentially saying:

Screw all those people who have a traumatic past of dating because they're obviously evil serial daters and life is black-and-white and there's no hope for people who have given away pieces of their purity. Just line up all your exes in a room and look at how dirty you are. Jesus can restore broken people to a brand new life, except if you dated some loser who played your innocence and stole your childhood when you didn't know any better since Freud says that's subconsciously all your fault. Sorry, Jesus saves — his salvation-juice for only the good people.

I absolutely believe that we should be careful about who we date and to set high standards. You should *never* have to settle for less out of loneliness or desperation. There should definitely be safe physical boundaries, and yes, sex is awesome within the divinely ordained exclusivity of marriage.

But we need to relax a little here.

If you break up, it's not the end of the world.

If you crossed those physical boundaries, you haven't "ruined your purity forever."

If you kissed a few frogs to find the prince, that doesn't make you a "serial dater."

Some of us learn the hard way, and others follow the textbook to the letter. I'm not giving permission to do what you want, but for those who are beat up by consequences, God still gives you a renewed heart as you stumble back towards Him. Your past is the past; it does not define you. There's no such thing as "Once a cheater, always a cheater," so long as you're moving towards Christ.

The Bible doesn't have a lot to say about dating, but it does have a lot to say about friendship and marriage. I would look over those passages carefully to better discern both the Christian subculture and Hollywood hype.

Here are a few things I'll say about dating that you can consider. They're not from the Bible, but are hopefully biblical.

1) If you can be *your entire crazy self* around the person you're dating, they're a keeper. This person will almost always be your best friend.

2) If you're going to talk seriously or discuss the future or break up, try to do it in person. All this technology stuff only prevents us from having normal human interaction.

3) You do *not* have to be friends with your ex. *Forgiveness does not mean friendship.*

4) You're allowed to mourn over a break-up. It doesn't mean you've "idolized" anything. Any preacher who tells you otherwise has no idea how to be human.

5) Pray with the person you're dating. Find time for God together. It's always a little awkward at first, but break through those spiritual hang-ups and share your convictions. Also, praying together does *not* mean you're having "soul-sex."

6) Know when to say no. Dudes: no always means no, even when it's not spoken out loud.

7) Dudes and ladies: you will not be alone forever. Loneliness sucks, I know. But God has handcrafted someone who is imperfectly perfect for you, so what you need to do is grow yourself first.

8) Singleness and celibacy are legitimate choices you can make between you and God. Christianity was the first system of thinking to endorse such a choice. Take a look at Apostle Paul, the Old Testament prophets, and Jesus himself. Marriage is not the end-goal for everyone.

9) If you read any Christian books on dating and marriage, use heavy discernment. By far the best books I've read on the subject are *The Meaning of Marriage* by Tim Keller and *Sacred Marriage* by Gary Thomas.

10) Purity is important, but it's not everything, and no one is really pure anyway. It's something Jesus gives us, not really something we can

fight for. If you fight for it, you will constantly define yourself on this one parameter and either become prideful or devastated.

11) Dating will look different for everyone. There's no "checklist" — because if there were, we instantly become Pharisees who ease our conscience with a mechanical set of rules.

12) Dating shouldn't be the focal point of anything we do anyway. Pursue hard after Jesus; maybe you'll find someone running alongside you.

On friendship - Proverbs 17:17, 17:9, 18:24, 27:5-6, 27:17, Romans 12:15
On marriage - 1 Peter 3:1-7, 1 Corinthians 7, Ephesians 5:22-33

2. So About Soul-Mates and Finding "The One"

"Hello! Do you believe in soul mates? Do we pick and choose who we want or does God have a way of placing a certain someone in our lives?"

I say this with as much grace as possible, but I don't really believe in soul-mates.

I do believe God has a plan and a blueprint and a vision for your life: but I also believe that if we fall off the tracks, God still has something else in mind.

Mathematically, the idea of a "soul-mate" doesn't work out. If you don't end up with your soul-mate, then they don't end up with *their* soul-mate, which means their soul-mate's soul-mate doesn't either, and so it goes for infinity. It's a philosophical regress.

But more than that, this idea can accidentally lead to a passive laziness as if a knight will bust in the tower and rescue you. It can lead to a paralyzing fear if you target-lock on someone and lose them. It can make us stop working on anything, thinking that marriage "completes you," that the chemistry is enough to keep it working, that the person you're looking for "accepts" you and is not interested in pushing you to your higher self in Christ — and I know none of that is your intention, but I've seen it happen so much that I must gently say how it is.

I find that friendship is already extremely difficult work. Certainly there's a comfort and openness and honesty with my close friends that allows me to be totally nutty around them, but friendship, even the kind that feels like fate, requires hard work. It needs nutrition, sustenance, and caretaking, like everything else. Maybe "soul-mate-ness" brought us together, but it doesn't keep thriving from it.

While I don't want to get caught in the crossfire of predestination and free-will, I believe God knows the person we're going to end up with (God would know because He's God) but He also lets us choose this with active determination and participation in His Story (God would allow this because He's God). How these two fit together, I don't know. My three lb. brain is allergic to paradoxes.

On one hand, you are wired for a certain type of person. You can rule out a lot of stuff by knowing your non-negotiables. But on the other hand, if you haven't met "the one," you can hardly imagine what they will be like and it won't be someone you could've guessed. It's like looking back at the last ten years of your life. Most of us couldn't have guessed where we'd be today nor the type of person we are right now.

I can almost guarantee your "one" won't fit your current checklist — though he or she certainly could — not only since God enjoys surprising us, but because every single person is uniquely crafted, wildly complex, and wonderfully flawed. A soul-mate is infinitely more boring than the real whole person we will eventually find.

I must also close here by saying, to "become" the right person for someone else is good, but it's less important than just belonging fully to the Lord. We probably make a very big drama out of dating and romance when it's a little easier (and more thrilling) to pursue Jesus, and along the way, we'll see someone else pursuing Him too, and we can call that a green-light blessing.

3. Why Save Myself For Marriage?

- "Hi there! Can you explain to me what's so great about marriage and saving myself? Won't I be missing out on having sex with other people?"
- "Pastor Park, I am Christian as is my boyfriend. We are older and I have told him from the start that I do not want to engage in sexual intercourse before marriage. He seemed fine with it but every now and then pressures and or guilts me by saying that everyone does it but us. We have friends who are Christian and do it themselves but I cannot bring myself to do it. How can I convince him in a Christian manner that I do not want to because I think it is a sacred act?"

Hey dear friends: So this is a very complicated issue that I know the world increasingly pushes away as old-fashioned moralism. I understand that most people will not see eye-to-eye on anything the Bible has to say about sex, and it's in fact the very reason that most visitors think the church is an out-of-touch institution that polices our behavior.

But I strongly believe the more we look into God's plan for us, the more it will make sense at the logical, emotional, physical, and spiritual level. If we can really think through why God would even give us this vision, I believe it will win as the most sensible option.

Before making objections like "What about ____?" — please at least consider that *fasting from sex until marriage could certainly work out for the mental and emotional health of the couple.* It's easy to just buy into the societal "norm" about sex and shrug off the Bible on this area, but I've seen (and been through) too many miserable sexual disasters to not at least speak up, because I love you even at the cost of sounding archaic and not-cool.

I know many will disagree quickly and say, "Sex and morality are two separate issues." While I do believe sex has a moral dimension, I also believe it's equally an issue of *wisdom*. When the church says the phrase *sexual sin,* it sounds very hokey and eye-rolling, but really it means any kind of sexual expression which goes against God's goodness for us, therefore causing profound harm and relational breakdown. *Sin always goes against God's best,* and it will leech the life and joy right out of us. God would only give us these sort of commands for a broken world if He knew the trouble that sex could cause — and if He also knew the best way to find maximum joy through it.

Sex has the power to be either the most destructive or most joyful thing in the world.[10] However you feel about the modern state of Christianity, I very much hope we can consider hearing (and following) what the Bible has to say about sex. Please consider that most of us already have a predisposed bias to shutting this out as crazy church talk. Whether we admit it or not, we have a vested interest in wanting to have mindless intercourse. So maybe we can drop our biases, even for a moment. God loves you and cares for you in this area, regardless of how the church fumbled the message. The heart of God is *for* you, and for *you.*

So a question upfront: **What else would we expect the God who loves us and knows what's best for us to say about sex?** What would a loving father say to his thirteen year old daughter? What would a loving mother say to her son? In fact: what would a fifteen year old brother tell his twelve year old sister?[11]

---

[10] Inspired by Timothy Keller. Check out his book *The Meaning of Marriage.*
[11] Inspired by Andy Stanley's sermon series, "Love, Sex, and Dating."

A side-note: If you're being pressured into sex that you don't want, please immediately draw safe boundaries and enforce your dignity as loudly as possible. Any unwanted sexual advance that violates your space is classified under sexual assault, and it's a crime. Be willing to remove yourself from that situation, even permanently, and to alert the authorities.

Another side-note: I'm not the most qualified person to write on this because I've struggled with it my whole life. But by God's grace, I've grown very much in this too.

1) Premarital sex causes confused intimacy.

Physical sex was designed to bring a husband and wife closer together, to re-create and renew the exclusive covenant bond, to be absolutely vulnerable and give-all with one another.

When it's done outside marriage, it will make you feel closer to the person than you really are. Several pathologies result. You will bypass the biblical pace of intimacy — discovery, sharing, encouraging, prayer, self-control, honor, respect — and build a false connection on physicality. Any time you bypass God's commands, you'll soon become a half-formed, unrealized, virtual copy of yourself. Because God's commands are *how things work.*

Since premarital sex has no guarantee of long-term commitment (and even if it did), any real intimacy is short-circuited by a pride to protect yourself or a desperation to "win" that person. So people break up like disposing trash or they stay much longer in a relationship than they should for the wrong reason. In church we call that *bondage.*

Objection: "What about trying out a person to see if they're the right fit?"

Please know that this immediately dehumanizes a person into a shoe or a car. People are not shoes and cars. If a man came home with your daughter and said, "I need to test-drive her for a while, see if the sex is what I want" — how would you respond?

For some reason, *women always become abused property when we have no guidelines for sex.* In any nation's history, this has always been true. That should tell us something about "sexual freedom." In a place where people leave sex unchecked, inevitably women always end up objectified, diminished, and tossed around like chattel.

If you think you're "missing out on sex with other people," I can tell you from firsthand experience that this is a baseless thought with zero grounding in reality. Romantic intimacy is best when it's an exclusive promise to be faithful to one another for life. When you have this kind of security and safety, you can fully let yourself go into the kind of relational trust that we've all been looking for.

2) God shapes the vision of your spouse's beauty on *one spouse*.

First Corinthians 7:3-4 touches on this. As one pastor said, Adam only had one spouse and one vision of beauty: "It's either Eve or aardvark." Adam didn't practice physical prowess with anyone else, nor did he have a catalogue to compare. When you have multiple pictures of so-called beauty in your life, it's almost impossible to be satisfied with one wife or a million.

It's quite a tragedy when we can never be satisfied with consistent stability. This is why porn is so destructive to marriages. It destroys a man's desire for his wife when he has a buffet-mentality. The culture still celebrates fifty-year marriages for this very reason: because the husband and wife dedicated themselves to one wonderful vision.

Objection: "What if I don't want to get married and I'm just fine sleeping around the rest of my life?"

I'm just wondering if we're all okay with settling for a cheap imitation of the real thing. I know that sex is hard *not* to do because it's good. Of course it's good, and God knows that.

This is where we must look forward instead of looking back. I could tell you all the reasons why premarital sex is immoral, but let's instead see God's better plan.

When you have the covenant blessing of God, a commitment made in front of all parents and friends and family, a legal union made public to the world, a heart promised to your spouse forever, a bed that will only have one lover for life, a mind that is full of your spouse's body as the standard for your desire, and the loving devotion of your spouse to sanctify and encourage and rebuke and know you as you really are — imagine that sort of sex. *It's the best sex imaginable.* Anything else is a low budget, laughable, poorly assembled knock-off.

I also think celibacy is a great viable option if you're called into God's mission for a specific reason. But it's very rare. Declaring celibate status out of resentment for relationships won't work out. It's really for those commissioned for something unique, like Jesus or Apostle Paul or Mother Teresa.

3) There are psychological ramifications of premarital sex that are impossible to ignore.

I know this will sound like heavy-handed preacher-talk, but if you're having premarital sex, whether with a random person or your fiancé, it exposes a lack of discipline and self-control. In general: *a lack of control now only explodes in marriage and in life.* We bring all our problems forward, including that one. If you're not good at budgeting, don't clean well, raise your voice a lot, punch walls, and don't like children, none of that will get cured by marriage or getting older.

I understand this is ridiculously hard to accept in a world of impulse and access. Today, there's almost no gap between *urge* and *gratification*. If you want tacos at two in the morning, by God, you'll get them. If you get feelings for your opposite-gender friend, we automatically fool ourselves into thinking "I need to be with her" instead of realizing *we don't need to chase our feelings every time they happen to us.* Most of it is just hormones stirring in your pants. If you're one of the 39% of people in the world who have the internet[12], then nothing is stopping you from stealing a movie, cheating on your homework, or watching porn. In our Westernized whip-fast climate, we presume this is how life should work: at my fingertips, at my bidding, whatever I want, whenever I want it.

---

[12] http://www.internetworldstats.com/stats.htm

I hate to sound like an alarmist. And I don't believe that we need to become an ascetic vegan monk who lives in a temple made of homemade hemp (which actually sounds fun). But all this entitlement and privilege and affluence can only distort our desires and drunken us with power. We're an entertained generation of instant delivery. Try to remember the last time you told yourself, *No*. It's probably been longer than you think.

Objection: "I already gave in so I might as well keep doing it."

Here's what so great about the God of the Bible.

He never, ever, ever calls it too late to turn away from unwise decisions and to trust in His goodness for you. *God never says it's too late to turn from your sin and trust in Him.*

Certainly there will be some consequences for choices we have made. But that's true for everyone. No one walks around with a baggage-free life, and God can work with that.

I've talked with too many people (including myself) who regret so many past grievances in their sexuality — and I'll go as far to say that *most peoples' major regrets in life have to do with their bodies and expressions of sexuality.* They feel hopeless, dirty, beyond redemption, used up, with a give-in sort of resignation.

This is where God always meets us with grace and restoration and the gift of a new start. You might have tons of guilt and shame over this, *but Jesus died for that very reason, to offer grace and healing for all the ways you've messed up.* When you believe that, God calls you pure and new when the world says otherwise, when even you say otherwise. God calls you clean when no one else will.

We begin to understand that purity is not something you fight for, but a gift that God gives you so that you'd fight *from* it. God can rewire your old patterns of thinking, and much of that begins by simply knowing *you are now an adopted, re-created, bought-with-a-price child of God in Christ.* It's hard to think with your old patterns when you know the price that was paid on the cross and how much God sincerely wants you to be free from everything that hurts you.

You'll also discover the sanctity of really getting to know a person beyond their physical chemistry.

If you're a dude, I can almost guarantee that your girlfriend would be absolutely thrilled if you told her, "Babe, I want to save ourselves for marriage now. I'm really sorry about before. I respect that you're a God-created human being and not just a body. I want to get you know you for who you really are."

If you're a lady, I can almost guarantee that if your boyfriend told you this, then you found a keeper, and every other dude would look like a scrub.

My friend, I encourage you to please keep seeking the answer on this one for yourself. For those who are committed to wait: I know it's tough and it won't be a perfect process, but please don't let that be an excuse either. God will give you the grace to fight for your dignity. God will restore your purity from the past too. I've barely scratched the surface on this, and I pray you find that *sex within marriage is the best possible sex you could ever have*. Anything else by comparison, is no comparison.

4. But I Already Crossed A Sexual Boundary: Am I Doomed Forever?

"Recently I got involved with a girl that I really liked for a long time. Unfortunately, things are moving a little faster than I would like and it's largely my fault. Today, we even did sexual acts, though we did not go all the way. I am wondering if it is possible to return this relationship to a place where it is glorifying to God. I also feel like crappy because of guilt and regret. How do I deal with the sexual sin? Is it sexual sin if you did not go all the way?"

My dear wonderful friend: Thank you for your honesty here and sharing such a personal story. Again, I don't feel entirely qualified to speak on this because I've had my share of failures in the past, but please allow me to be a lighthouse for you so that you would not crash your boat as I did.

The good news is that it's *never too late* to return a relationship back to centering on God. If you know about David and Bathsheba, then you'll know that despite David's horrible sin — sleeping with a married woman and then killing her husband — they decided to stay together and had a boy named Solomon, the wisest man in all of human history.

I'm not at all condoning what David did. He did suffer some wrenching consequences. But any decision that has a bad start can be reversed toward the glory of God. If God's grace can cover David, then certainly God's got your back too. While your guilt is a natural response, please don't let it crush you into further self-loathing.

The tough news is that by falling to temptation —
1) You have increased your appetite for sin, and
2) You have weakened your resolve to fight against it.

This doesn't mean that the relationship has to be over. It only means that you'll need a more wisdom-filled **Battle Plan** to deal with the issue.

You'll be tempted now to keep going physical, and this will prevent you from really getting to know her for *her*.

This means you'll need accountability with mature Christians. It means *no ninja-dating* — it's unwise to sneak around behind her parents' back or without counseling from your pastor. It means having wisdom about your time, your space, your triggers. In a sense, it will mean fasting from certain physical contact until you're both married.

The best way to know these boundaries is simply hang out with your lady as if she were a male friend. I wish I had a much more profound method here, but that's the simplest rule to follow.

If you absolutely feel like you can't do this: then break up. Wait until you're ready. I'm not trying to be a moralistic old-fashioned preacher here, but I'm saying this to promote your maximum joy. I meet too many couples who think they can handle each other, but they end up in miserable exhausting cycles of defeat because they weren't willing to be wise and disciplined. I don't think breaking up is always a first option, but it's not a last resort either.

If you decide to keep pursuing this, remember that if you only set physical boundaries to run from sin, you'll always fail. You need to run toward something too. The battle against lust can't be just about running from sin, but also about running to God's purposes, plans, His presence, and His people.

There are no magic words to turn off lust. There's nothing I could say that would make you want purity without turning you into a self-whipping flagellator. The only way to beat this is to *circumvent your desires towards a greater desire, so that you are funneling your energy into the perfect will of Christ*. It's a messy process, for sure, but it's one you can start today.

Consider serving together with your girlfriend in some kind of ministry opportunity. Whether it's feeding the homeless or babysitting for families or starting a project to raise funds for orphans or leading a Bible Study or building houses downtown, go discover what God has specifically wired both of you for and then pursue His heart for the world.

As Francis Chan said, all couples are two people with one mission, and following God together will already solve most of your problems.[13] This is definitely not easy and it won't be a perfect journey. But the decision to pursue this relationship and the motivation to keep it going is knowing that this is about getting on God's adventure together with your one life on this earth, to know that nothing is more exciting for a couple than to take God's hand and set sail for His unfolding story.

You will then barely even have to fight lust because you won't need to. Of course it will still be tough, but now you're both fighting *towards* something greater than yourselves. You will have a motivation simply beyond being "good" or "pure" or "Christianese." You might even find out while dating that you're both not meant for each other, but you won't be breaking up because of lust. It will instead be about finding a partner to serve Him.

My friend, I know this sounds like pretty words on a page. It sounds theoretical. None of this is meant to be an instant cure. It will require a daily conscious choice from you to have a God-centered relationship, to repent of lesser things, to be a leader, to protect the sacredness of a woman's dignity. It requires your entire reliance on God in a way that you might never have before. In short, you will become a man. I hope you consider the seriousness of this task, and at the same time enjoy this relationship by serving our God together. I pray you will both cling to Him for not only His wisdom and strength, but also His purposes.

---

[13] "Two People With One Mission," https://www.youtube.com/watch?v=ruPVtcXD2Kw

5. Keeping Physical Boundaries in Relationships

"First off, thank you for being such an encouragement through your posts! I understand that when dating, the physical boundaries are different (to a degree) for each relationship, but what are some ways to figure out what those physical boundaries should be?"

Dear friend, I'm waiting for the day that "Christian celebrities" like John Piper or John MacArthur talk about how tough it was to keep their sweaty sixteen-year-old hands off their wives-to-be — because you know, it would be nice to know we're all human beings. I can guarantee that your favorite Christian heroes and heroines went through the same woes we go through, because they were all sixteen too, and each of them certainly had their failures through it all.

So with that out of the way, please allow me the grace to break down a few things.

1) Physical boundaries cannot be merely to limit something, but to lead to something greater. If you're only concerned about how to avoid things, then your focus is an anti-state of negativity. This will never work. There has to be some kind of direction forward and a bigger picture.

2) There is *way more* to a relationship than your sexuality. I know it's really difficult to keep your hands off each other, but one day your hormones will burn out anyway. If your relationship is wrapped up in either super-purity or hyper-chemistry, then it won't be grounded in anything real.

3) A relationship focused on purity is bound to fail. If you think staying "pure" is tough, you don't know the half of it.

There's also: communication, speaking encouragement, praying with and for each other, sharing Scripture, staying intimate with God, graciously rebuking, spiritually guiding, having date night and enjoying one another, finding a stable church, serving in ministry as a team, getting on the same page, financial unity, aligning visions, aligning convictions, settling disagreements, learning how to fight well, handling extended family members, raising other human life-forms, staying faithful, staying friends, and dying together. Physical boundaries are important before marriage, but they're nowhere near the top priority.

4) Purity is a virtue given by God, not achieved by you. I understand our need to stay "pure" and all the cultural stigma with impurity, but no one is really pure. Yes, we can fight for it, but no, it is not a grade of your human value or identity.

5) You already know your physical boundaries. When most people ask me, "How far can I go?" — they're already asking the wrong question. You and I know the motive behind it. It's like when a kid puts his hand in your face and says, "I'm not touching you!" They're still being an annoying punk.

I think if you search your heart on this, even without consulting God (which you should), then you know what's best for you. I think you have a good idea of what you want for your kids. You know at which point you become a mindless monster. You know what needs to change. You know that if you cross a certain line before marriage, the relationship can change into an impersonal, flesh-dumping receptacle.

I don't mean to be so crude or prude, but nearly everyone who asks "how far" is just playing dumb. I want to give you some credit here and suggest that you are smart enough to know where to draw the line. More than that, I believe we're smart enough to know that drawing a line is only one part of the whole picture. Certainly, we must consider a battle plan to fight off sin, but as I've said before, the entire point is to *run towards Him*.

I must also add: **If you've already crossed the line, God still has grace for you.** You're not "dirty" or "ruined" or "bad news." You are not your past and you are not what's been done to you. God loves you regardless.

I'm friends with those who have been raped who feel like it's their fault; I've talked with sex addicts who think there's no hope; I myself was a porn addict for fifteen years — and God has grace for all of us. He restores all the broken pieces. He heals the wounds and He makes things new. He is the one who *"gives life to the dead and calls things that are not as though they were"* (Romans 4:17). No one is outside the gracious powerful sovereignty of God.

If you're in a relationship now where you've broken a boundary, it's not too late. Make a plan, get accountability, and pray for a vision moving forward. Serve together and get on God's mission and draw to the heart of Jesus. It's okay if you decide to take a break or break up or fast from one another for a while. Whatever you decide, cling to Christ. You'll make it through.

6. Struggling With Porn For The Last Time (Again And Again)

- "What do I do, if as a Christian, I am addicted to pornography and I can't seem to get out of it?"

- "I've been struggling with pornography a lot and I keep failing Him by giving in. I don't know what to do anymore. I need help, please. It's ruining my relationship with Him. I know I can't serve Him with all this continuous sinning and the guilt that comes from it. I do pray for His forgiveness but I'm constantly failing. I was clean for a few months, but this week, I went back to my old ways. I don't want this old life anymore. Please pray for me."

- "Hey Pastor JS Park! I've been addicted to pornography for many years now and have tried to quit countless times. Sometimes for weeks and even months but I feel like I keep going back. God showed me this weekend that He's taken the shame away and I want to run back to him and honor Him so one of the first steps was listening to your 'First Week Off Porn' podcast. Could you please pray for me?"

Dear friends, you're awesome for your courage to share this. I'm no expert on the matter, but by God's grace, I was able to overcome a fifteen year addiction. Here's hoping that some of my story will help yours. As always, please feel free to skip around.

1) You can't just quit porn.

I have said this roughly a million times. The key to quitting anything is not about the quitting. It's about *moving forward towards better.*

The drum I keep beating is: *The Christian life is not about running from sin, but running towards Him.* It's not primarily a propositional set of rules, but a relational thriving dynamic with God.

2) You have to want this for yourself as much as God wants it for you.

In every AA meeting, they tell you that the successful recovering alcoholics are the ones who really want it for themselves. Those in AA who are forced to go or tag along don't really make it. It's not their fault. It just means that until we are serious about our recovery, then serious recovery isn't happening. You have to be willing to say goodbye to porn forever, and it will hurt. This will sound over-dramatic, but it'll really feel like amputating your leg or giving up your baby.

3) Your first week off porn will be crazy difficult.

Since porn is now known to destroy your brain as much as heroin[14], (and worse, expect your private parts to stop working[15]), you'll experience all kinds of classic withdrawal symptoms when you try to quit. Just be prepared. When I quit, my first month was full of sweating, shaking, foggy thinking, relapses, and fixation. It can take up to 60-90 days for your brain to recalibrate and your grey matter to get healed up.

4) It will be a lifelong battle.

Former alcoholics don't walk into bars, former heroin addicts don't call their drug dealers, and former cheating businessmen don't hire cute secretaries for their office. You can be clean for a long time and suddenly relapse. The feelings come back. Memories linger for a long time. It happens. There's nothing wrong with you that isn't wrong with everyone else. What's important is how you react. Stay vigilant. Call a friend. Run out of the house. Go to Starbucks (or support your local café). Go fishing or play ball or build a bookcase. Whether in minutes or days, the urge will pass.

---

[14] http://jsparkblog.com/2011/11/25/porn-addiction-part-two-what-porn-does-to-your-brain-the-science/
[15] "The Great Porn Experiment: Gary Wilson at TEDxGlasgow," http://youtu.be/wSF82AwSDiU

5) Keep it honest.

Often the first step (and entire journey) of quitting porn is to tell a friend and keep an open line. Preferably it's with someone who does not have a porn problem or has overcome one. I know that's hard to find, but even if it's an eighty year old elder in your church, you need a mature person to confess to openly. If you want to hear about the first time I confessed to a friend, it's on my podcast[16]. It was messy, full of slobbery tears, and bursting with rejoicing.

6) Even if you're triggered, you can still choose your way out.

I know we're told to avoid "triggers," but even when your entire body is screaming at you to use porn, you can still say *no*. God always gives you a choice. At any moment, you can close your laptop, pull up your pants, and choose something else.

I understand our culture doesn't make this easy on us. Sixty years ago, a black and white picture of an ankle might have been porn. Imagine guys wearing monocles in the back of a bar saying, *"Unfh, dat ankle."* Now we're bombarded with a deluge of sensuality in even the most innocuous places, so I really do know how difficult this is.

Yet for a culture so obsessed with free will and freedom of choice and self-autonomy, we over-play the act of, "I can't help it." I absolutely believe we should stay away from "triggers," but unless you've been seriously traumatized or abused and you need real therapy, even the idea of triggers sometimes promotes an air of helpless self-pity. There's a generation of young men and women who are living proof that we *can* help it. By God's grace, I'm one of them.

When you open up your browser and start hunting for the perfect video — it's not too late to stop. Even though I have not masturbated to porn for over three years, there were times when I started looking again.

---

[16] http://thewayeverlasting.libsyn.com/cutting-it-off-your-first-week-off-porn

Maybe it began with a picture or two, and then I approached more lurid stuff. *But every single time, I was able to stop myself and walk away.*

I felt guilty, sure, but I also realized this was a victory. It's a long way from where I was. If you can stop in the middle of a downward spiral — which you can — then you've won. God celebrates these small steps forward. So long as you stumble towards Him, however imperfectly, you're doing just fine.

7) The moment after you fail, just keep going.

I want to be careful how I say this. On one hand, God totally has grace for you when you mess it up. He loves you no matter *what*. He wants you to cast off guilt and shame, because it doesn't work and it's not who you are and it's what Jesus came to die for.

On the other hand: God does want you to recover. He wants you not only to experience the cover of grace, but also His grace-empowered Spirit for a fruitful, passionate, purposeful, mission-driven life.

I believe God will restore you every time you fail for the rest of your life, so when you relapse and go down a porn-binge, God is still going to love you afterward, every time. But my question is: *Do you really want to keep living this way?*

I'm not asking this to guilt-trip you. I'm only saying that once the old self is dead, it's not worth it to go back there anymore. I don't think Lazarus missed his tomb and climbed into his coffin sometimes. I don't think the healed blind man Bartimaeus wore a blindfold to reminisce on his days tripping over things.

You'll be forgiven by God every single time, but God wants you to experience the *fully forgiven life* too.

So if you break a "clean streak," please don't wallow in self-pity. When you mess it up, it's okay. But what's even better is getting to the place where going back is *no longer an option,* and you're so in love with God that turning around is unthinkable. I believe we can get there. I believe our God is that powerful. I believe we are not merely works in progress, but we are empowered by *It Is Finished.*

Maybe this is all corny poetic talk to you. But really, I'm excited for your journey, because you're going to be flat-out knocked out by what's ahead. When I finally quit porn and shook off the withdrawal, I couldn't believe the freedom I experienced in Christ. I kept thinking, *Why didn't I just do this sooner?*

To be able to walk into church without this burden on my chest was too good to give up. To finally be free of my old self and to enter the new self was so dang liberating. I hope you take hold of this. I pray you'll discover that this is what you really want. Not just to quit, but to truly be free. I love you and I'm praying for you, dear friends.

7. Women Pursuing Men?

"I have set a standard of not pursuing men whom I am interested in. However, this makes it so difficult as a woman because it's hard to show interest without being the pursuer. In addition, having a crush is difficult for me since I desire a committed relationship that will lead to marriage someday, not just petty relationships that fill loneliness. How do I go about relationships with men whom I'm interested in without pursuing them?"

I'm saying this because I love you, dear sister, but I totally chuckled at your message. Especially this sentence: "How do I go about relationships with men whom I'm interested in without pursuing them?" I'm not trying to be mean here. I also completely understand that a woman can look "desperate" or "man-crazy" if she pursues a guy. And there's a very slim chance that a guy might notice you if you make a duck face at him long enough.

So can we step back a bit? Please allow me the grace to say: *Ladies, it's okay for you to throw a direct message at a guy if you're interested.*

I'll go one further and say that a nice Christian dude usually *needs* a direct signal because they would never know otherwise. Most of my guyfriends, as educated and professional as they are, can be as *dumb as rocks* when it comes to women. I include myself in there.

But I think a lot of this has to do with the strange subculture of Christian dating. We really need to relax *a lot* about dating and romance. Like when an older lady tells you, "Stop thinking about the way that boy brushed your arm!" — well, sorry, but Elisabeth Eliot spent a page talking about the way Jim brushed her arm in *Passion and Purity,* and Elisabeth Eliot is the ultimate mascot for pure Christian ladies. I've read her book twice and she went sort of crazy going after Jim. It was also totally sweet.

Oh, and Timothy Keller's wife Kathy actually pursued him by declaring, "We're either dating or we're not going to be friends anymore." Pastor Tim admitted he had no idea she felt that way until she said so. I don't hear anyone dissing Tim Keller's wife on this — and in fact, I applaud her.[17]

If you need a biblical example, I seem to remember Ruth, the ancestor of Jesus Christ, approaching a certain Boaz by laying under his covers and proposing to him for marriage. That's not very subtle.

I'm being a bit silly here, but this is our human reality: that we're hardwired to be attracted and feel chemistry and get hormonally excited, and when we're chained down by weird subcultural etiquette, you're also diminishing your humanness.

So please, please, please be okay with going into an environment where you can meet many nice cute Christian men. And if you're rejected, it might hurt, but it's not the end of the world. Certainly there must be wisdom for all this. I'm not condoning casual dating nor philandering nor even an emphasis on the dating scene. I'm not saying every woman needs to start pursuing a dude. I'm not saying you shouldn't be careful, because you should, and if you feel some red flags, then bounce.

Yet please do not enslave yourself to a chokehold mentality that is supposed to be "helping" you when it's only throttling your God-created femininity. And pursue God first in all this, because the main focus is not about finding a right partner, but becoming full in Christ, so that no one else may be your savior but Him. In between that space, you might find the guy you're looking for, and he'll be looking for you too.

---

[17] Timothy and Kathy Keller, *The Meaning of Marriage* (New York: Riverhead, 2011), p. 247

8. Stepping Up: I'm Afraid To Ask Out Really Good Women

"Hey man, I've currently been struggling with feeling that I am unworthy of the time and love of Godly girls. I don't feel like I'm good enough to even ask them out. Do you think that's a valid thing to be feeling or is it more of a copout?"

Hey my dear brother, may I first please say that the very fact that you even care about this and cared to ask me shows a huge step of maturity and humility. It's not easy to confess this sort of thing to another brother, so you're already making the right moves.

Please allow me to break down some motives here.

When a dude says they're not good enough for a God-centered woman, they're either saying

1) I really want to step it up in my faith to find a good woman, or

2) I'm not really a leader-type, so I'll allow the woman to lead me in our relationship.

So a question. Are you #1 or #2?

And of course, it's a trick question. Neither options are good, at all.

1) If you only focus on trying to be a good Christian man for a woman — you already know where this will go. You'll be enslaved to making your life about a woman. You'll try to squeeze the benefits of "better behavior" from God rather than just getting God for God. You'll also be pretty dang neurotic and twitchy every time a girl walks in the room.

2) If you think that some dudes are meant to be "led" by a woman in the relationship — what you're saying is that you want *less responsibility* in a relationship, which is a loophole to keep yourself stagnant and lazy. It means you don't want to work or grow or lead or be responsible. I hear so many Christian dudes use this particular excuse that it's *no wonder* the

Christian women are finding it impossible to meet a good man. Please know that I'm not saying anything about gender roles. I'm saying that anyone, man or woman, who doesn't want to take up responsibility for their life and their relationships, is really just opting for laziness and self-entertainment.

But I don't think you're operating out of these motives. You're probably being really hard on yourself, or maybe there's an insecurity or inadequacy you haven't confronted, or there's some kind of history or baggage or secret double life that you're still struggling with. And maybe no one has told you how to handle *you* before you try to handle a relationship.

Somewhere along the way of our faith, most men hear two very different messages. The first is, "God says you're good enough!" But the second is, "Most men are deadbeat dads and jobless losers and feminine nobodies, so don't become like them!" And neither message actually helps anything. The emphasis on both sides just disorients us into confusion.

The truth is that *no one is good enough on their own*. That's why we need God's grace. And even with God's grace, it's hard to be a dad and find a job and to "be a man." So we need the humility to know "I'm not good enough," but also the confidence to say, *"My God is good enough."* It's within this balance that you'll find the confidence to do everything else, with a reduced anxiety and less fear of rejection and a more teachable spirit.

A woman isn't looking for a guy who thinks he's perfect. She's looking for an honest dude who's aware of his limitations but who's also aware of God's limitless goodness. I can lead when I'm led by God, because on my own, I can't lead anything. Any man who claims to lead on his own is not even qualified to be the boss of himself.

If you really think you're not "good enough" to find a good woman, you're right. Just back that way up and start from scratch. Navigate the depth of your own shortcomings in the light of God's grace found in Jesus, and you'll become better without even hardly knowing it. No Christian ever needs to "try" to become a Christian. You're His the second you believe. The sooner you embrace your adoption in Him, the more you will embrace both equal humility and confidence, because Christ died for your very real sin, but he died out of his very real love for you. Don't waste another second on self-pity or shame. Jump into what Jesus did for you.

A last word. Any time someone pursues God with the secondary intent of finding a date, they get really bitter when no one comes along. I can understand that, because loneliness can certainly be painful. But if we turn to God even with the good intent of trying to "upgrade" ourselves, then God becomes a bank. Then our faith is just a transaction, and we'll either push God in our debt or we'll wallow in our own. So please focus on *you and God* before you throw a second person into the equation. Discover God on your own. Any secondary motives will have to be set aside for now. *Pursue Christ first and you will grow in confidence and character.* Or as Jesus said,

But seek first his kingdom and his righteousness, and all these things will be given to you as well.

Find Jesus, you find yourself, and maybe you'll find someone else. And if you don't, just keep running.

9. The Impossible Search For Someone Who Cares

"As a Christian woman who deeply cares about social justice issues, I find myself really despairing of finding a Christian guy who genuinely and actively cares about women's rights, black rights, POC rights, etc. And all the while, my church culture pushes marriage and dating in my face pretty much every Sunday. I honestly sometimes feel like I won't ever find the right, God-loving, guy and I've also been very fixated over my singleness. Any advice?"

Hey dear friend, I think it's tough to find *anyone* who cares deeply about social issues, or even worse, much of anything. Most people who appear to "care" are either antagonistic and will constantly demonize the other side, or it's very shallow and only for hogging attention. So when it comes to finding a friend with depth, it's a long, difficult search that can take a lifetime.

As far as your church culture goes, you can consider talking with your leaders about the over-emphasis on marriage — but regardless, please don't let this shame you about yourself. Don't trust me or your church or a blog or a romantic comedy to say anything about who you are or your decisions. And yes, singleness can be wonderful.

I want to gently encourage you to consider one thing. It's possible you have a "Wishlist" for a guy that would be an impossible unrealistic standard, and you might inadvertently pressure a date to fit your mold. When he doesn't, you'll be constantly disappointed or you'll belittle him. The "Wishlist" type of thinking is cute but dangerous. It revokes the capacity to accept that your partner could change, hence removing the humanity of that person. I'm not saying you're doing any of this, but it's a crushing temptation we must examine.

The thing is, everyone is uniquely wired unto themselves. No one, and I mean *no one*, will fit your dream-guy, and even if he did, then life will change him into someone else over the course of time. You might even meet a guy who cares very deeply about social causes, but then every other area of his life is downright terrible.

The other issue here is that if I bank all my chips on this dream-person fitting my interests, then I'll begin to idolize or even demonize the interests we share. In other words, if you actually do find a guy who's really into your passions, like social justice, then you'll be shaken if he changes his mind. You'll be angry when he disagrees with particular things about justice. You'll be pressured into maintaining a certain level of passion. You'll be upset on days when he's not "at your level." You might ignore his other interests, or you'll over-emphasize this one so much that you won't be well-rounded enough to discover new areas of your own. Building on any one particular foundation outside the actual person is going to make you fluctuate all over the place, because you'll be too anchored to the trait you wanted.

I had to let go of my idea for who fit my physical and moral preferences. The person you'll be attracted to will be a million times more interesting than your "soul-mate" could ever be, because they'll be a real whole person with their own thoughts and choices. While I do believe we should look for someone who's compatible, I also think it's enough if the guy you're attracted to *at least* respects your passions even if he doesn't fully understand them. And if you do both fall in love, he will come around to sharing the deepest parts of you, but only if you do not crush him with an unfair expectation of how he must meet them.

Here's my wager. If you're running after Christ and the way He has made you, that means you'll be running in the sphere of what God has called you to do. You'll be a part of what God is doing on the earth. And perhaps in that mix, you'll find someone running alongside you. You'll find that while his specific ideas about social justice might be quite different than yours, that he still cares just as deeply, and it's actually his little differences that will make you more well-rounded and whole as you chase God's heart. Maybe this guy will turn out to be more than a friend, or maybe not. But our priority is that we're going after God and His mission first, and everything else will flow from that fountain.

10. I Got Marriage Fever: Hunting For A Spouse

"Hey pastor. I've recent realized that I have a habit of going to church and looking at all the ring fingers on the beautiful godly women around me. It's not that it's a common thing in my lifestyle. I try very hard to stay pure and prepare myself accordingly for my bride. But it seems like when I go to church, a pretty specific time when I should be focused on other things. I seem to instantly become desperate to find my bride. Are you familiar with this struggle?"

Hey dear friend, I'm with you on this.

There was a time in my own life when I just couldn't stand to be single. I would go after every new girl in the room. It doesn't mean I got them; it's just that I desperately wanted to be in a relationship all the time. Of course, when I got in one, I wanted out. It was a selfish, vicious, stupid cycle that I confess to my own shame.

I'm not saying this is where you're at. But in psychology, there's an informal phenomenon called an *aspirational crush*. It's sometimes a *paranormal relationship*. It's not exactly sexual or even relational, but it's that thing when you have a crush on every person who makes your stomach flutter. You could call it "girl-crazy."

There are all sorts of reasons this happens, especially because we're bombarded by overly sexualized media. The church is just as guilty. There's a church in New York that has an entire wall of pictures of married couples who met at the church, and while I understand they want to celebrate this, apparently the church is huge on hooking up singles. I can't imagine what this does to the "less socially acceptable" single people. Overall, I find it a bit tacky and demoralizing.

But ultimately, this comes down to reflecting on what you're really about. The two best things I can say are:

1) Relationships are hard. They're not fun-filled little fantasies that will satisfy your emptiness. They're *hard work*. Don't be in a rush to get in one. Work on yourself. Run after Christ. If you do this first, you'll already be in shape for the marathon of relationships.

2) Marriage is not a trophy. Women are not prizes. As long as you see single women as a prop in your own story, then you'll suffer from Main Character Syndrome. You'll assume you're the hero of your narrative, and women will be a catharsis in your self-completion. You'll be devastated if you break up and you'll be disproportionately angry if she disagrees with you or tries to live her own life.

Men do this all the time, including me. I couldn't get married until I respected my wife as a human being with her own thoughts, her own life, and her own dreams and insecurities.

I had to stop being some lone ranger who needed an accessory on my arm. I had to stop being that guy in the back of parties who thought I was "above" everyone in the room and that I deserved special treatment. Life isn't about *me,* it's not about my solo epiphanies and my own agenda. It's a partnership with other people. Marriage is a unique exclusive partnership in which you promote each other to your best, towards God, by God.

Until you can let go of self-idolatry, you're not ready. It's okay to feel what you feel and to desire a relationship, but let's think through to the bottom of why you want to get there.

11. The Painful Non-Romantic Endeavor of Getting Back Together

"What did God's grace look like when He brought you and your now wife back together after you parted ways? Your story is beautiful, and I have been so very encouraged by the parts you have shared with us. God bless you!"

Hey dear friend, for some back-story: My wife and I dated for six years before we got married, and at the three year mark, she broke up with me. It was for perfectly legitimate reasons. I was addicted to porn, I had an anger problem, and I was a control freak. It was over. I didn't think we would get back together.

Though I couldn't possibly give you all that I learned from the six month break-up, I can tell you two things.

1) I had to learn not to accuse my partner over her issues, but to focus on my own wrong first. Whenever we argued before, I would always blame-shift. Eventually, I made it a habit to call myself out even when I was right, and we would meet in the middle about our differences.

2) This will sound obvious, but I needed to learn to "draw from God" more than my partner. My wife cannot be everything I need her to be all the time. It's such a dangerous, unfair, toxic, soul-killing concept to make her my entire source of happiness. We don't consciously want to do this, but it happens most frequently in marriages. When I can be led by Christ and draw my primary love from Him and even love Him more than my wife, than I can rightly love my wife with all that Christ has given me. This takes practice and deliberate choice. It takes a constant saturation in Christians who are smarter than me and in Scripture taught by wiser people.

When we did get back together, the hardest part was trying not to "win" her. I was afraid she would break up with me again if I made the smallest mistake. It was a fearful paranoia. I spent a while trying to prove that I was changed and different and better. And in fact, I *had* changed — I had sought counseling and accountability and rebuke and had quit porn. But I wasn't resting in grace. I forgot that I didn't need to prove myself, not to her, not to me, not to anyone. God had already done that part through His Son. I only needed to receive it and to continue growing.

I'm extremely thankful to my wife because for all my frantic attempts to keep her the second time around, she never actually pressured me. I was putting pressure on myself. She gave the relationship a second chance, and that was that. I was through the door. She never held anything against me from before. I was slowly able to unclench, to rest. This is what the grace of God does, both through Him and through others who understand. Fortunately, my wife understood.

Grace is not merely unconditional, but counter-conditional. If it wasn't for grace, I would still be jumping through hoops. But because of grace, we were able to start over, towards a real relationship that wasn't found on conditions, but truly on each other.

Chapter 2.5 —
Interlude: Three Lessons I Learned Instantly in My First Week of Marriage (That I'll Need For Life)

They say everyone gets a honeymoon period at the start of your marriage, but whoever brandished that idea: I want a refund.

Marriage is hard work right out of the gate. Our sentimental ideas about romance get tossed out very, very quickly — and I want you to be ready. Everyone told me what to expect, but no matter how much you prepare, it's still a jump in the deep end. The more you know about what's coming, the quicker you can stand on your two feet.

I know that marriage isn't for everyone (contrary to our culture, singleness is not an illness), but whether you're not in the dating scene or you've been married for years, here are three things I learned instantly in the first week of marriage. These lessons could be valuable and necessary for our entire journey.

1) Marriage pulls down the hologram and brings about the gritty reality of your spouse (and yourself too).

My wife and I dated for six years before we were married, and in those six years, I have never heard her pass gas *once*. I would constantly tell her that it was okay, but my wife was dead-set on maintaining an air of elegance. No pun intended.

About four days into the marriage, on a wonderful crisp morning in Florida, I asked my wife, "Are you boiling eggs?"

She said, "No. I'm not boiling eggs."

"Are the sprinklers on outside?"

"No. The sprinklers are not on."

"But then what's that sm—"

And it hit me. Pun intended.

[By the way, I have my wife's permission to share this story. I'm proud to say that she now regularly passes gas around me with the most exuberant freedom.]

In dating, we're often on our best behavior. It's like a job interview, where both sides show off their impressive benefits and credentials. In marriage, you see the rough, raw edges of the entire person. Marriage creates perhaps the closest proximity you will ever have with another human being. You'll see every insecurity and neurotic tendency. There will be friction.

This is more than just about keeping up a pretty image.

It's also a way of learning how to love an entire person and not just the parts that you like.

In Timothy Keller's *The Meaning of Marriage,* he discusses how we each have fault lines in our hearts, like the cracks of a great bridge. These fault lines get exposed when we collide with another person, so that we spill anger or jealousy or anxiety. A married couple, because they're so close in space, will inevitably drive a truck through each other's hearts: which exposes *all* the fault lines. Deep-seated flaws will shake out of us like shaking a tree in the autumn. It's in this exposure that we can choose to face our flaws, so that they would be re-shaped by the love we share. The sooner, the better.

You'll also see every dream, hope, talent, passion, and ambition in your spouse. You'll see what lights them up and gets them excited.

This means that marriage is often about showing grace for your spouse's worst and promoting their very best. **Love has a wider vision for someone than they could possibly envision on their own.** And if marriage is one of the most intimate unions in the universe, then it has the power to encourage a person beyond their self-imposed limits. Though this can happen in many types of relationships, marriage offers a profound intensity to spiritual growth. Finally, we can pull down our holograms of who we pretend to be, and actually become the people we were meant to be.

2) Marriage means your stuff isn't your stuff anymore.

In our first week, we didn't fly off to the honeymoon, which was another two weeks away. We spent time unpacking, opening wedding gifts, frolicking in our new home, and merging our lives together. About five days in, I wanted to meet up a friend to hang out, one of the groomsmen in the wedding.

I neglected to tell this to my wife. This is one of those very obvious things that I should've known from the get-go: but in my defense, I'm an idiot.

Marriage is about *Two-As-One,* as We instead of Me. My time was no longer my own. It was *our* time. Our things. Our bank account. Our bed. Again, this sounds obvious, but I've spoken with so many singles and unmarried couples who were dismayed at the idea of splitting a life in half. No one is quite prepared to completely surrender unilateral decisions. We quickly learn why Apostle Paul compared our relationship with God to the marriage union — because we are entrusting our will to another.

The wonderful advantage is that rather than "splitting in half," it actually feels more like a merging of strength. Our individual abilities can make up for each other's weaknesses. Our knowledge and our view on life is suddenly augmented with an entirely new angle. By the end of the week, I was figuring out what she would want and why, which helped my tiny brain to open to new avenues I had never considered.

While both dating and engagement can offer the benefit of unified minds, the promise of marriage solidifies an active undercurrent of cooperation. There's now a lifelong goal: for the health of the couple, and not what works for "me," but for We. What works for you as an individual might be good, but what works for the couple turns out to be *great.* It's not half plus half, nor is it one plus one, but with grace and synergy equates to an exponential growth of each other's hearts.

3) Marriage means there's nowhere to run: except towards each other.

Our first argument in the first week was different than any argument we ever had.

When we were dating, our conflicts were always able to be delayed. A few days of separation could cool us off. The problems might come back, but a little bit of distance smoothed things over. We could just bury it and move on.

Now we had no such apparatus.

No buffer, no denial, no escape.

We could either go to bed angry, or we would have to wrestle with our exposed demons all the way to resolution.

For those who are more likely to avoid confrontation, this proves extremely troubling. If you're like me and you absolutely *need* to resolve things on the spot, it can still prove difficult, because you'll end up defending yourself in the most tone-deaf ways possible. It's all rather very embarrassing when we realize how bad we are at the Rules of Engagement.

We had to figure out a system. We had to know what words we would never, ever use. If we were going to fight, we would have to fight fair, with no low blows and no dragging up the past against each other. None of this is a perfect process. The initial start of a conflict will never be smooth; our first reactions are always emotional because it feels like your own value is at stake.

It's in these moments that my wife and I had to learn to seek an endpoint to our arguments. The beginning would always be rough, but with enough humility and self-awareness, we could run towards intimacy instead of towards an exit. This kind of spousal love is not only a means to an end, but the end itself.

We've discovered that when confrontation has a direction, it's always an opportunity to grow.

And if a guy like me can learn these things:

I guarantee you, we all can.

— J.S.

Chapter 3 —
Confrontation and Conflict: Dealing With *People*

We all need rebuke once in a while.

We need to hear the hard truth about ourselves because no one gets it right all the time, and that's really okay. It's not the end of the world to say you're wrong. We can quit pressuring ourselves into putting off a better holographic image than we really are. I can't sustain that sort of tyranny over myself for very long.

"I'm wrong, and I'm sorry." It's not so hard. It's the first step to healing. It cuts our illusion of perfection. It says that weakness doesn't mean we're weak.

It's *not* okay to cry our way out of this. It's not okay to put up a mirror-defense by yelling "What-about-you." If we get offended or take it personally or defend ourselves, that's fine: but it doesn't absolve the truth we heard. If your friend is really your friend, it hurts them more to tell the truth than it hurts you. They get no benefit from this; they're risking your friendship to be real.

Friendships are not all fun little fantasies that pamper our childish impulse for entertainment. Sometimes they are forged in the fire of love and vision. At times we require the gracious force of undressed honesty, and that means trusting the pain of the uncomfortable truth from the mouth of your loved one.

It doesn't mean we get to be the truth-police. We don't wield rebuke as a weapon to win. It just means that love between friends isn't all games and giggles. It means I want to see the best in you, and I hope you have the outspoken audacity to see the best in me. Real friends speak with tears in their eyes, voice shaking, heart breaking, a quiet courage to say, "You're better than this." Friends do not multiply kisses, but move in for surgery.

I thank God for friends who do this for me, without fear, in full grace and humility.

We can own our part of the problem and be liberated from our blinding pride. Without that sort of self-confrontation, you'll get deluded into thoughtless decisions. We'll be imprisoned into unwise patterns of thinking, circling the same drain, anchored to twisted coiled roots of outdated judgments. When you don't confront sin in your own life, it controls you for the rest of your life.

I hope we have ears to hear each other in that awful, awkward, dizzying gut-shot of reality. I hope we can earnestly seek a wake-up call. I hope we do not shelter ourselves between yes-men and groupies and pushovers. I hope you can take it as much as you dish it. I hope we consider our own flaws before jumping at someone else.

I hope you know that God sends people your way, always, to deliver what's real. And even when most of it is outrageous and unfair, there's *always* a kernel to discern your own heart, to see where you might have gone wrong. You can own that tiny seed of truth. Grow, together.

1. Praying For Jerks and Worse

"I find it difficult to pray for my enemies. I mean, it's obvious that it wasn't meant to be easy, but, Jesus instructed us to. What I find most difficult about that instruction is, where do I draw the line with praying whether or not God gives unto my enemies 10x what they did to me (if that's even biblical at all?) Most importantly, *how* do I pray for them?"

When God says, "Love your enemies," every single person in the world has a story of why that can't happen.

If you and I were to sit face to face across a table over coffee, and you were to explain your story, I would be tempted to agree. Most times I'm tempted to peel out and go MMA all over that guy who hurt you.

Here's the thing. When we use the word *enemy*, we're suddenly describing a one-dimensional horrible evil monster that twirls his mustache at night and dreams of ways to torture you. But besides the rare historical exception, that person almost never really exists.

Most of us are multi-layered, struggling, conflicted, confused people, and when humans collide, our natural tendency is to 1) protect our own interests, and 2) let our sinful tendencies react first. Hence, we get enemies.

When Jesus said, "Love your enemies," he had a very different picture in mind. He is saying, *"You know, before you had a love for me and for the things of God, you were pretty much an enemy of the cross. You did what you wanted apart from me even though this was hurting you. But I loved you anyway. I knew about all the stuff that you did before and I still loved you. I know what's coming and I will love you always."*

Jesus, who knows your motives, methods, secret thoughts, and the actions you've forgotten, still has a crazy love for you. He has a holistic vision of who you are *and* who you could be. Jesus found that the best way to destroy his enemies was to love them, regardless of their response.

God wants us to see each other with a **God-Sized Vision** because there's hope for every one of us. He wants us to see not just for the next few weeks or months, but with a *heavenly perspective*. I know how difficult this is, but to go the other way is to become hostile, hateful, and harmful, and God has better for you than to diminish yourself that way.

I understand this is hard in practice. No one expects perfection. You're allowed to feel what you feel. But you know, I've heard tons of stories about divorce, lawsuits, street fights, gang fights, wrongful job termination, and competing businesses: and in all these things, I recognized a simple truth.

*How could we **not** pray for our enemies? How could I **not** love them?*

Because assuming this other person never changes, you still need wisdom in how to handle them. You still need strength, resilience, patience, and compassion going forward. You still need a loving heart greater than your flesh so you don't choke on contempt. Even a "casual hate" is going to kill you from the inside.

I've been going through a situation only recently where I've had to love the "enemy" in full force. And so far, besides yelling all the things I would like to say (in my car in the driveway), I've been able to act loving. No, I don't feel like it. But by simple obedience to the Spirit, I'm praying for them. And it's been keeping me out of a dark place that would only make things worse. God is being glorified, even amidst the worst of humanity, and as hard as it is, I love them. I do.

People can change too. Prayer can change them, because God can change them.

If we start dismissing people as incapable of change, we're also undermining the sovereign grace of God. There are some really difficult people in this life, but in God's unfolding story, you and I were just as selfish, stubborn, prideful, and hurtful until His love knocked us out of our self-glorifying orbits into His Glory. I'm eternally grateful for that, and if God could love a dude like me, then surely I want that for these other dudes too.

Forgiveness, by the way, doesn't mean you're letting them off the hook. It's a divine gift of releasing the pain and anger so that you're not keeping the knife in your wound. Don't let someone who hurt you keep hurting you. And sometimes, you'll need to forgive daily, everyday, for as long as it takes.

I'm not at all condoning the things that have been done to you. I'm not diminishing your pain or downplaying human evil. There must be justice, whether by law or by God, and some people will realize they are wrong — for eternity. But in the mean time, we want to pray for that glorious moment when someone's eyes are opened in the middle of their darkness, that they would repent and be restored.

It might never happen, but please don't let what someone did to you also define you. Don't let the poison of hatred and bitterness drown you. Keep loving on these people because that's who you are now. You no longer wield worldly weapons. Your new weapon is love.

"To forgive is to set a prisoner free and discover that the prisoner was you."[18]
— Lewis B. Smedes

---

[18] Lewis B. Smedes, "Forgiveness, The Power To Change The Past," *Christianity Today,* January 7, 1983, p.26

2. The Dilemma of Loving Jesus But Hating Religion

"Hi! I believe in Christ and I'm experiencing His love and grace on me. I love Him but I'm so annoyed and I hate religion. I hate when people criticize others. I hate how religion divides people. I hate how they always debate who is right and wrong, true and not. I believe that His love is for everyone, that He gives us rest and in Him there is no condemnation. I've been in to other churches but sometimes I just don't agree to what they say. Is it okay this is how I feel?"

Hey my lovely friend: It's definitely okay to feel this way about "organized religion" and the disunity you see in the mainstream church. It's right to get angry at condemnation, legalism, bigotry, and oversized doctrine-heads.

But please allow me the grace to gently challenge you on one simple thing.

It's easy for me to express discontent with the church because there's definitely *so much wrong* with the flesh-driven, man-made, bully-infested hierarchy of smugness in our Christian subculture. It's easy for me to say, "Look at those Pharisees, those uptight religious bigots. Thank God I'm totally not like them." And you would be right to say that, because you have enough clarity to see how moralism kills us.

Yet the criticism we throw at the religious tends to turn into its very own sort of legalism, until we're in a perpetual loop of grudges and animosity and division. Making a distinction against what is wrong always begins with the noble intention of loving people, but we easily boost our own egos when we think "I'm one of the good ones." We're all prone to an elevated platform, because you know, we're all sinners. The devil is laughing his butt off over this.

I would say that 98% of Christian blogs I read are just reactionary finger-pointing separatists that always reeks of an attitude that says, "I'm not like *those other* Christians." We tend to eat our own and shoot the wounded. I'm well aware that even by me saying this, I'm totally defeating my own point too. But my heart really does grieve for unity, with hope and grace even for the overbearing legalists.

You see, the nuanced love of Jesus included even the worst offenders of love. Jesus had grace for those who abused grace. He not only befriended Peter, Martha, Paul, Thomas, and the Samaritan woman at the well, but he also loved Nicodemus and Joseph of Arimathea and Jairus the synagogue leader. Jesus's love was *so off the map* that he loved people we could never imagine approaching, because he smashed all those dichotomous binary categories.

It's probably cool to point at Pharisees and legalists and the religious. You can have a really popular blog by making fun of uptight church culture and satirizing poppy praise songs and even mocking traditional liturgy. I've done this too, and I guess it's funny sometimes. But it lacks thoughtfulness. It lacks consideration. It lacks the grace to see the whole story, to understand *how* it got so bad, to truly sympathize with how a hateful person became so wounded and mad.

Of course, if there's obvious hatred and prejudice in the room, please feel free to find the door. Please speak truth when you see that love is not the goal. I would never make excuses for some of the atrocious misguided hate we see today.

But I really believe the true Christian can eventually weave through party lines, *not* for the sake of looking flexible, but because the line is hardly visible. What Jesus did on the cross was shrunk us to our true size by equalizing both our sin and our need for grace. Jesus wants the heart of the worst rebellious porn addict to those picketers at Westboro to the greediest politician to the most destitute homeless child. Only grace offers the sort of hope to see a person beyond their category into God's very own creation.

Without that sort of hope, even if it's just a tiny grain of mercy, then we'll remain stuck in superiority disguised as higher knowledge. We'll remain snobby while thinking we are "more balanced" than the "other." To hate a legalist is still legalism. Only with the humility that the Gospel offers, can we begin to dismantle all the fallen-ness of our cultures and reconstruct them with the life that Jesus poured out for us from his broken tomb.

3. Betrayal, Forgiveness, Victory

"Tell me of the hardest betrayal you forgave and overcame, please."

If you're going through something now, please allow me to say that I know that it sucks and I completely feel your hurt. I also know there's no easy way through it, and I have no quick formulas.

Here are two quick stories of betrayal with very different results.

In my junior year of high school, my girlfriend at the time broke up with me and immediately dated my stepbrother. The next thing I hear, she does something gross with him that nearly made me throw up in my mouth. Today, my stepbrother and I are friends and we still occasionally keep in touch. He's married with kids and I have absolutely zero hard feelings. I love him to death.

In middle school after my parents divorced, my dad remarried and he and his new wife were both just terrible for each other. He also constantly took her side in arguments and backed her up if I had any complaints. Today, my dad and I talk, but it's quite a strained relationship. I still love him and I do forgive him, but it can be difficult to be his friend.

As far as betrayals go, these could just be First World problems, and I'm sure many of us have been through so much more. The truth I've glimpsed here is that **forgiveness does not always mean friendship**. There's some Christian myth which demands that we must all get along and be buddy-buddy and pretend like traumatic betrayals never happened, but the major problem with this is the Bible. The Book of Proverbs constantly tells us to be wary of fools, thieves, and unrepentant scoundrels.

We can certainly love everyone including our enemies, like Jesus does, but it's harmful to try to be in close fellowship with everyone on an equal playing field. There's no sense in re-drinking the poison of bitterness and anger just to "refine" yourself like it's so very spiritual.

It might sound like the "Christian thing" to just overlook everything that's ever happened to you, but if that abusive ex-boyfriend or cheating ex-wife shows up in church while you're bringing your kids and the church is your only safe refuge, there's nothing in the playbook that says you need to be near them.

The church must be aware of these things and have safety measures to protect you from physically or psychologically dangerous situations. You're always allowed to have healthy boundaries, and that does *not* mean you're somehow an unloving person or less of a Christian.

On the other hand, some people can change. We all have moments we wish we could take back, and we can always consider giving that second chance to someone who is truly, consistently repentant. I've seen this happen in church and in my own life dozens of times — there's always that huge unclenching exhalation of relief when two broken people are reconciled, and **what a grand day of celebration to see two sinners move forward past the pain**. Forgiveness, given and received, is one of the best gifts that Jesus ever gave his people, and it's a matchless joy to see it in motion. If we have to fight, I hope it's for that.

Again, it doesn't mean they need to be best friends, but that at the very least, they can love Jesus together and serve in the same body, both as an example of what Jesus has done and how powerful He really is.

Even if the other person is never repentant or doesn't see a need to be forgiven, that gift of forgiveness is *for you*. It's to remove the knife from your wound so you can live freely without that thing sticking out everywhere, hurting you and everyone around you. It's not simply a one-time thing. Forgive every day, multiple times per day, and don't deny the pain. It happened, it's part of your story, but it does not get the final word. Jesus does, and he says you're more than what has happened to you.

4. When To Give Up On Someone

"You are ministering. Their heart is not swayed. How do you know it is time to let go and stop 'casting pearls'?"

There was a down-on-his-luck guy in my church who asked everyone for money, rides, food, job references, and a place to stay. The guy was obnoxious but we thought the "Christian duty" was to help him out. My former pastor and I poured tons of our time and money into him, hoping he would better his own life.

Soon we find out the guy was using money on shiny things he couldn't afford, unable to hold a job because he didn't like being told what to do, and he was trying to date the teen girls in the youth group.

Eventually we all rallied to stop helping him. As bad as we felt, we refused to give him anything else. In the long run, the only way to help him was to cut him off.

As for you, this is really a case-by-case scenario that will require very clear wisdom and discernment. But Jesus doesn't leave us blind on this one.

Let's examine the verse you're talking about. Jesus only says this line once in his famous Sermon on the Mount in Matthew 7:6 —

Do not give dogs what is sacred; do not throw your pearls to pigs. If you do, they may trample them under their feet, and then turn and tear you to pieces.

Jesus is actually drawing some boundaries. Earlier he says to not judge your brother but instead to first examine the plank in your own eye, and then you can take the speck out of theirs. It was a way of humbly restoring your stumbling brother. Just imagine trying to *remove a speck from someone's eyeball*. We can't rush that one.

But in verse six, about the dogs and pearls and pigs, Jesus is talking about the other extreme. If there's someone who is using or abusing you, feel free to walk out or call the police.

The problem though is that **we run to verses like this a little too soon**. If there's one thing I know, Jesus calls us to *love no matter what*. And love will cost you. It's a sacrifice. It hurts.

If you find yourself walking out the instant that things get a little uncomfortable, then it's possible you're falsely using the whole "don't cast pearls to dogs" as a loophole for avoidance. If you ever decide to let go of ministering to someone, it should make you sick to your stomach. The follower of Christ should hate it. I know I did. It's because love is the primary foundation, and Christians should be reluctant to avoid the opportunity to love.

Yet I also know love doesn't mean pampering, spoiling, or coddling. If you feel your every effort is only enabling someone to be dependent and abusive, then ask God for wisdom on how to approach this (or to back away) with a firm hand. Your motive still has to be love, and sometimes that means taking off the gloves and saying it how it is. Please don't dance around and sugarcoat and water it down. If it's getting bad, then sit them down and have the conversation. That's grown-up time. You'll be doing them a favor. And if they just don't hear you again and again, you have a decision to make.

I also meet some people who are not exactly "bad people," but they can be so very draining. I think it's okay to avoid those people sometimes.

I don't think we're all meant to be friends with just anybody. It doesn't mean we look for this and grade with an unfair scale; it doesn't mean we get to be rude or uppity with them. But if someone continually makes you queasy with their casual racism or flippant instability, I think it's okay to wait things out and keep a distance from their shrapnel. A person might not be immediately toxic or harmful, but an accumulation of their low-grade negativity can lead to a lot of damage. It's okay to be wise in how we step here. And be gracious, pray for them, love them anyway, because we're all at one time the same kind of person for someone else, and we only discovered that by being shown the same patience and grace.

I know this is never easy. It sucks to have to confront people and to make the decision of cutting someone off. But there's a time for these things, and you're doing it because you love them. Just make sure that's really why, and leave the door open.

5. Forgiving Your Parents

- "How do you forgive a parent? I know it's Gods command to honor them but my mom has hurt me so much, I went a college in another state just to heal. She wants me to come home for the summer but I don't want to. I know I have I forgive but it's hard."

- "My dad cheated on my mom, and I have not kept a close relationship with him since. He claims to be the dad of his girlfriend's nine year old daughter, though DNA tests support that he's not. And now, his girlfriend is keeping him from fixing his relationship with me. Every time I get the courage to forgive her for what she did, she does/says something to change my mind. I want to forgive her, but I can't."

I know that forgiving parents can be a tricky thing because of the emotional ties and long history, but God gives you the gift of forgiveness to *help you* and not to endanger you. Forgiveness does not equate to "overlook all hurts and act like it never happened."

My dad and I still have tons of issues that we haven't exactly resolved, but I've learned long ago to know when to have distance or when to move closer. This doesn't make me or you less of a Christian somehow, so long as bitterness has not grown its hairy roots in us. In fact, distance has been healthier for the relationship, and necessary.

I don't want to tell you what to do in your respective situations, but please allow me to share some guidelines that are worth considering.

1) Once again: *Forgiveness does not need to mean friendship.*

If your ex-boyfriend or ex-husband or parents have physically abused you, you don't ever have to go near them again. If your parents have verbally or psychologically hurt you, you're allowed some time for healing before you can safely pursue a close relationship again. Forgiveness does not mean it's suddenly all smiles, winks, nods, and let's be buddy-buddy. More than that, forgiveness actually *acknowledges what happened, calls it a sin, and removes the knife from the wound.*

God doesn't want the idea of forgiving someone to be either über-romantic or a forced obligation. It's a spiritual gift that works *for* you so you can be free of what has happened to you. It should never be a magnetic chain back to a bad place: it's always a way forward. Yes, it's certainly for God's glory that there's reconciliation. But we must balance that with your peace, joy, and growth, which glorifies Him too.

2) Parents are just people too.

A - *They are just one opinion.* I know we give extra weight to what our parents say and do; we are biologically wired to respond to them more. But in the grand scheme of things, they are not our main source of encouragement nor is everything they say always true. There's only one encourager, one truth.

B - *Boundaries with family are okay.* Family has a way of driving you crazy. Just as with anyone else, you can draw a line for yourself and disallow anyone from crossing it. Assuming you are not in their house anymore, it's okay to say something like: "Hey, thanks for inviting me and don't take it personally, but I don't need this right now. Let's hit pause on that and talk later. Please respect my time and my space."

You don't ever have to put yourself in a compromising situation. If your mom or dad re-marry and the new person treats you like crap, who are they to do that? The old adage is true: people need to earn respect. A title means nothing and no one owes anyone anything. Sure, forgive the hurts and don't let it grab a foothold, but that doesn't mean you need to force a plastic-smile and have a pow-wow every Tuesday.

Also, if you've left the house and if you're more or less self-sustained, you are now building your *own* house with the Lord. You can control what goes in and out. You're allowed to say a big fat no to your parents if they steer you off course. Yes, we must honor them, but the Bible has a lot of things to say to both children *and* parents, and if you're caught between compromise or Christ, don't let fear push you into compromise.

C - *They have the same hopes and hurts and history as everyone else.*

Please understand that your parents act the way they do because of an entire lifetime behind them. I remember one of my friend's moms was extremely overbearing, but my friend was superhumanly patient with her. When I asked my friend about his patience, he said, "When my mom was a kid, she was kidnapped during the Khmer Rouge regime along with her brothers. She saw all her brothers shot in the head, one by one, right in front of her. You don't know what that does to a person."

Our parents have been through more than you will ever know, in a uniquely strange era before us, with challenges you couldn't understand. And if they raised you since diapers, they have sacrificed far more for you than you could bear to hear. Have grace for them, like you would any struggling person. I'm not absolving them of responsibility, but please try to see the obstacles they are facing and the upbringing that has wired them to be how they are today. You'll be able to better maneuver around them and with them and for them.

3) You can find a way to help.

There comes an awkward time when many young Christians spiritually outgrow their parents, and while that doesn't make you "better" than them or anyone else, it does mean you are in the position of helping them forward. You can start to see their blind spots, and in a bit of a delicious twist of irony, you can serve your parents as the mature Christian.

At some point you'll establish some credibility with your life. Whether your parents believe that or not, you'll have a right to call them out on some things. You do that with respect, of course, without accusation and with all grace and understanding, but if you feel something is off about their life, you can raise the question. Just like with any other person, they might reject you or condescend or storm off or yell at you, and that's kind of their loss. But there's a chance they'll be humble enough to see you are trying to help.

4) Ultimately, serve your parents like you would anyone else.

One day, time will grow short. Maybe you can't make up for lost time or old hurts, but you can still make peace in the end. If anything, Jesus knows it's better for your soul.

It's the Christian thing to serve them, even if you feel like they don't deserve it. Because Jesus served us, and none of us deserved that either. When conviction calls and the time is right, bring a peace offering like cookies or bagels and just hang out with your parents. Ask if they need a car wash or the kitchen cleaned. You'll be surprised how both you and your parents feel about that.

Please don't be so stubborn to think that this won't "work" somehow, as if we always need to work an angle. Sometimes it's best to wipe the slate clean for the day, head to your parents' place, serve them, and hope for the best. Not every mission trip or church service or outreach goes perfectly, and this one won't either. But we still serve, because Jesus served us. Try to have that long-term endgame in mind. Try to understand them as you would any other human being.

6. Dealing With Family

"I'm suicidal and I need help, I realize that. But my mom verbally abuses me and my dad just ignores what's happening. Also, I don't have any friends I can trust. Anyway, my family can't afford counseling, so how do I tell my parents, respectfully, that they are kind of ruining me and to please stop? I've prayed that God fixes my family and to give me strength to stand up to them, but nothing has happened yet."

Disclaimer: Verbal abuse is just as harmful as any other kind, and while I'm all for reconciliation, this subject requires a wisdom that far surpasses what I may offer here. In some situations, it may not be enough to simply "talk it out" or to engage in a rational dialogue. I offer these following thoughts with the utmost care and respect for those who may yet have hope for their families and loved ones, while knowing that in some cases, it might be best to consult an authority or to seek counsel or, if necessary, to keep a safe distance.

Thanks for being honest here and I'm really sorry about what's happening. I'm glad you recognize your need for help; most people don't. The hard part is that you eventually must have the huge direct conversation with your parents about how you feel. It's going to take some messy dramatic arguments to move forward, and there's really no way around it. The longer you delay, the more you'll bottle up resentment, which will keep hurting you.

I'm often asked "what it looks like" to have this conversation with family, as if there's some clean ideal method with a neat bow-tie resolution. That only happens on sitcoms. It's actually going to look like snot, tears, slammed doors, ugly cry-face, and horrible hurting words.

While it's possible that you could have a very nice chat with no meltdowns, it will most likely be the opposite. I wouldn't expect this is going to look pretty or structured. Anyone looking through your window on a family argument will likely think you're all insane. It doesn't matter how mature you've become — family has a way of turning you into a crazy banshee.

Please let me tell you what *not* to do. When I look back, I did tons of stupid things to show my parents how I really felt. When I was sixteen, I literally ran away from home: I packed a backpack in the middle of the night and walked ten hours on the interstate to a friend's house. I specifically did it to hurt my parents.

What I didn't realize until later is that *I was being a coward.* I was "acting out" in spontaneous rebellion instead of having a real conversation with them. I really should've just twisted my parents' arms to sit down with me and listen. Even after I made all these dramatic gestures, I *still* had to talk with my parents anyway.

In the end, you'll have to ***initiate conversation*** with persistence.

To talk with them, even if it will turn your house upside-down.

You already know that you're supposed to speak in a "loving tone" and to be gracious and humble and respectful. You're smart enough to know not to raise your voice or call names or interrupt. But sometimes being the nice-guy doesn't always cut it. You might be ridiculed for it, or they'll try to "see through" your game, or it'll come off phony. In the end, even a discussion that begins so rationally can always explode in an instant on either side.

Your parents do recognize a mature loving attitude, but they will ultimately respond to **conviction** and **courage** over a long period of time.

It takes courage to tell your parents that they could be doing a better job for you. It takes courage to say, "This is not okay." Eventually they'll have to hear you out and find a better way to do things. Even if not, then at least you tried: and you still need to be able to speak up for yourself for the rest of your life.

You might not be the most straightforward person and I understand the fear of speaking up, but with family, you can't really hold back on the truth. You can't leave words unsaid. Show them you mean business and you refuse to move on until they listen.

The fear says they might not listen or you'll be humiliated or rejected — and maybe this is true for today. But day after day, this is why you must keep trying. Push through the fear. Even halfway good parents will recognize persistence.

You might be with them at dinner or on a weekend or on a car ride. When you do talk with them, they might push you away. That's part of the process. Keep trying.

They might cry in self-pity and blame themselves and go into victim-mode, but that's part of the process. Keep trying.

They might blow up and throw things or say you're wrong and call you ungrateful, but that's part of the process. *Keep trying.*

God and time itself will do their work. There might be weeks where you feel terrible — but keep trying. It's better than holding it in.

I'm not sure if your family is Christian or not, but I've found that having a Christian family is no guarantee of good communication, and vice versa. I didn't grow up in a Christian home, so when it came time to announce I was going to be a pastor, it was another painful conversation. But unless they're always physically abusing you or actively opposed to your faith, then they will hear you out. *You still need to just talk to them.*

I know plenty of Christians who have to "disobey" their parents in a godly way, and I completely understand that — but there will be *tons* of things that your parents agree with or disagree with, whether they are Christian or not. *You still need to just talk to them.*

That's what it takes. Slobbery, snot-filled, red-eyed, ugly-faced conversation.

7. I Want People To Like Me Or I'll Die Probably

"How does one get over the sin of being liked or accepted by the people around them? I struggle so hard by not caring and reminding me that Christ's love is enough, but sometimes it's just so hard not to care and to not forget that Christ's love is enough. I want to change, but it seems like every time I try I keep stumbling and failing. What should I do?"

Along with anger, lust, and pride, this is one of the most besetting sins I've ever had the non-pleasure of battling. The main problem goes by a lot of names: *People-Pleasing, Attention-Seeking, Co-Dependency, Peer Pressure, Daddy Issues, Attention-Whore, Class-Clown, Yes-Man.* It's all from the same motives.

There are some fundamental issues to explore with wanting to be liked by people. As with any affliction, once you can expose the lies, you can begin to see your way to the truth.

1) Trying to get everyone's approval is logistically impossible.

Since everyone has a different opinion about your life and what you should do with it, it's downright impossible to meet everyone's acceptance of you. Whether you're addicted to making people happy or getting people to approve of you (both which come from the same motives), it's a fruitless exhausting endeavor.

A lot of people will also have the wrong facts on you, so you can discard that right out of hand. People will *always* think they have the best for you when they don't.

2) Need people less but *love them more*.[19]

Maybe this will sound a bit harsh, but the biggest reason we look to peoples' acceptance is because we are treating them like "commodity-resources," in which each person is a vending machine that dispenses the drug called approval. Trying to please people is really about serving yourself.

If you can begin to view people as *actual people* with other functions besides getting you "high," you can quit needing them and start to love them. When you really get to know people and love them, you'll already begin to think of yourself less. That's true humility. And that's half the battle.

3) Don't care what people think about you, but do care what they *think*.

It's impossible not to care about people's thoughts. So it's not enough to flip a table and yell, "I don't care what you think!" The second you say you don't care about something, you care enough to say you don't care.

If you don't care *at all* what people think, you have to hide in a tower with a dead heart and a stone cold soul, which is making yourself less human and not more. We must care at least a little if just for the sake of hearing rebuke and the hard truth.

So instead there must be a re-channeling. I care less and less about what people think of me, but I do care *what they think at all*. I might not care that people think I'm a buffoon, but I do care if they love Jesus and are not condemning themselves. I don't care if someone thinks I'm a moron, but I do care if they think *they're* a moron. I don't care if someone hates on me, but I care if they want to kill themselves. Huge difference.

---

[19] The thesis of *When People Are Big And God Is Small,* by Edward T. Welch.

Again, this is about loving people more and reducing our need for them. It takes a disciplined practice to even begin down this road, but that uphill climb is totally worth the freedom. To be free to love people instead of needing them so bad.

My first pastor was one of those people. I always sensed he loved me, but he never really needed me for anything. He didn't feed off my attention or approval or laughter or anything else. He was a free soul because *he just loved me*. That's a good place to be.

4) What exactly can people do?

I totally understand the heartache and fear of someone not liking you. Whenever I find out someone doesn't like me, my soul stretches out to them and I want to shake them by the shoulders and find out *why*. But then what?

Hebrews 13:6 says, *So we say with confidence, "The Lord is my helper; I will not be afraid. What can man do to me?"*

So let's break that down. **Fear is when you exaggerate a perfectly normal response to an abnormal level.** It's like looking at a cat and thinking it's Godzilla. Fear predicts a false future, but you already know your future is secure through the cross and resurrection of Christ. So you (and the devil) can't use that one now.

The Lord is my helper. Say that with *confidence*. It's already enough that God is with us. That verse is mind-blowing in itself: that the God of the universe loves me. But that second part —*What can man do to me?*—is like a wake-up call.

I used to be totally mortified when someone didn't like me. There was fear. But what exactly can this person do to me? If they don't like me, then will I spontaneously explode? Will a train fall out of the sky? Should I suddenly become a desperate sniveling butt-kissing weirdo to get their approval? Make them like me or else? And what does their approval actually do for me? Somehow feed my soul until I'm spiritually full? Make me high-five myself?

If you can dig to the inevitable bottom of this lie — that if people don't like me then I'll somehow die a horrible death — then it begins to look like the ridiculous lie it really is.

If you can dismantle Satan's strategy here, you can see right through it and keep moving. Satan hates that. God wants that. We want that.

8. People In My Church Are Hypocrites

"There are some people within my church that started hanging out recently, drinking together, partying etc. I would like to confront or talk to them somehow, but I don't want to be judgmental or anything. Some of them are close friends of mine. How should I approach the situation without hurting anyone? I want to be loving, but I don't think I can just agree with everything they are doing. It's discouraging somewhat to me and others. I wouldn't want anyone else to be affected negatively."

You have a great heart in you and likewise a good head on your shoulders, and now the two are at war. You want to love your people, but then you know it's better to put them on blast. Your head and heart feel diametrically opposed. So what now?

On one hand it would be justified and honest to call them out on their foolishness. On the other hand, simply calling them out could come off shrill and unloving, and overall unhelpful to the situation itself. It can also make you bitter, critical, and self-righteous.

At this point, I could tell you, "Of course you tell them!" Or I could say, "Bite your tongue and be patient and let it play out." But somehow, neither feels totally right. Logically, it makes no sense to say *everything* (or else you're the annoying nanny) but it makes no sense to do *nothing* (or you're the incompetent sheriff).

Let's look at some possibilities before you become Religious Vigilante or Nanny Of Justice.

1) Pray about it. That's not an option.

Everyone will tell you some form of this, but if you *don't* pray for them, then don't even bother talking to them. I know your heart is hurting for them, but without consulting God on it, you're just a rogue agent answering your own flesh.

Rebuking without prayer is an unsustainable practice that will turn you into a religious tyrant. You won't have the wisdom to speak wisely, which won't earn your neighbor's ear, and then you're not worth listening to, and then the gig is up.

Pray for what to say. Pray to elevate God, not yourself. Pray to love on those people. Pray to rebuke them earnestly (if it comes to that). Pray for God to show them (and you) mercy. Pray you can still love them no matter how they respond.

You also need to sort out for yourself whether it's worth getting involved. Because the second you open your mouth to them, you've entered their world. You'll successfully have implanted yourself into their entangled drama, no matter how much you think you can just "lob words and run."

2) Maybe it's not your job.

Here's a question to ask yourself. *Am I the only one who can get this job done?* Do you also think it's your job to save them? What about talking to the pastor or leaders? What about talking to just one of those friends first? While I'm sure you've thought of all that, it's still wise to consider your motives.

Rebuke usually works best between friendships in which *that sort of relationship is already established.* If you haven't been comfortable enough to rebuke them already, it's most likely not your place now either. That doesn't mean you sit idly by while people hurt each other, but unless they're punching children and beating up pedestrians, it could be better to maneuver laterally.

Some of them are your close friends, so consider going at them first. If that fails, you could talk to one of their friends, or a leader who is in tune with them, or an older brother or sister who is in that circle. Express your concern. Please don't flip the gossip-switch, and if you feel that on either side, cut the conversation and get ghost.

3) Be humble. Or you'll get humbled.

Don't expect to receive a red carpet when you roll up on them. If you decide to rebuke, be prepared for a total non-response and to humbly accept that *you might not be the guy who is part of their change.* It's possible that the Heavens will open and they'll all have an epiphany and breaking into song. If you're lucky, you might be one step in that process of conviction, and even then, not all of them may turn out okay in the end.

I'm not presuming this is true of you, but if your whole thing is to see results when you talk to them instead of letting God empower your words, then you'll be hanging on their every action in total frustration or disappointment. Please make sure it's not about you or a misguided sense of righteous-rectifying. This moment can't be about getting things off your chest. I believe it must be *for* them, *for* God.

4) When the opportunity comes, ask questions.

People work much better with questions rather than accusations. Accusing someone puts them on the defensive and it will suddenly become a semantics nightmare. Asking questions gets someone to examine their own contradictions, and ideally, instead of defending they will confess.

You don't need to get ultra-philosophical or blow smoke up their butt-hole, but with enough sensitivity you could at least get them to see outside of themselves. It's simply dragging the lie into the light. Eventually, it's getting them to see the logical end of their situation. *"What do you expect to gain from all this at the end? Where do you think this will take you? How does this play out for you?"*

Maybe only one or two of them will ask the hard questions of themselves. Maybe that's enough. Even then, you're only a beacon of change and not the change-agent itself. Leave the latter to God. Make sure they know you love them. Then love them.

9. Why Is Evangelizing So Awkward?

"I have trouble sharing the gospel. When I want to share it (either to a believer or a non-believer), most of the time I end up saying nothing and feeling guilty. I know my lack of confidence (is it gonna come out right?) and fear what others may think of me (which I know is sinful) have something to do with it. If I do say something, I get uncomfortable and it doesn't come out the way I wanted it to, even after asking the Holy Spirit to help me. Why does sharing the gospel feel unnatural to me?"

You know, I was nodding my head the entire time I was reading this question, because *every Christian ever has felt the same exact way.* I'll dare to say that as a "professional Christian," I still feel this way sometimes. So I'm totally with you on this and I'm throwing much love for you for confessing the whole truth.

I don't think I've ever heard a level-headed sermon on evangelism. It's always a verbal beat-down of our spiritual incompetence and it's more shrill than cat claws on a metal chalkboard. It also gives birth to weird evangelism techniques like the Cube and the Colors and Closing-The-Sale. The pastor doesn't do these either.

For once I'd like to hear, *"I know how hard it is to talk about Jesus. It's the most awkward conversation you'll ever have. If you even say the whole Gospel out loud right now, it sounds like the craziest thing you've ever heard. But the Gospel isn't some 'speech' you unload on people and then 'leave it in God's hands.' Blasting people with theology is like serving icing for dessert. Evangelism is your whole life, it's sharing your home, it's enduring patiently, it's being a human being, it's availability, it's sharing Jesus through who you are; not perfectly, but passionately. Yes, invite them to church and to that revival and talk about your faith and your testimony, but once you dare to go there, just know you might be rejected immediately, a lot, and aggressively. Except secretly they can't deny there must be something to it, because you're not just a billboard. You're an overflow of a barely containable supernatural miracle."*

If anyone is really all that confident in evangelizing, it could be false confidence derived from "good technique" or polished apologetics, neither which actually care about living breathing people. Please allow me to suggest some things about evangelism to set the record straight.

1) Almost every single sermon I've heard on evangelism uses guilt and shame to motivate you, and this will never work.

Sunday morning, you get your Bible and notepad and you're ready for that hot bread of the Word. Then the first thing out of the pulpit's mouth: *All of you suck at evangelism, and here's nineteen reasons why.* Suddenly you're scrambling to get all nineteen points, analyzing how much you suck at this, and then you determine not to suck by gritting your teeth and unfolding the Evangelism-Cube-Pamphlet available at the He-Brews coffee bar in the lobby selling the pastor's latest book.

I don't mean to sound so critical. But when you actually go to evangelize and your only motivation is, *I have to do this*, then you'll always fall short of some arbitrary standard. You'll beat yourself up over words missed, words twisted, or arguments lost. Then *of course* you'd feel terrible about evangelism. The bar has been raised so high, it's suffocating you.

We need to hear *how* to evangelize and understand *why* we would actually share our faith. If this is coming out of a manic panic to do our religious duty, we will face-plant every time. So brush off the guilt. It won't help, so we're done with that.

2) When we evangelize, we are communicating a crazy message that requires God's power.

Please know that the Gospel is straight-up crazy. Nothing less than the miraculous eye-opening power of God will compel someone to consider it.

Think of it: *So this Jewish, homeless, virgin carpenter was crucified and got up out of the grave like a zombie to forgive your sins and flew to Heaven but he's coming back to earth one day with his head on fire and a sword out of his mouth to judge the human race.*

At first glance, you yourself would never have believed such a thing, much less devoted your life to it. So you might want to breathe out a bit and understand that this is a difficult message, you might not say it right every time, and you'll be rejected right out of the box.

We hate rejection, which is why we sort of hate evangelism, and I want you to be ready for it. I *always* feel awkward when I share the Gospel. But that's okay, because it means you're probably doing it right.

3) Which brings us to: *God saves; not us.*

We can only love people. It's okay if someone does not have ears to hear the Gospel the first time, or the tenth time, or the hundredth. Share it with the knowledge that you're communicating a wildly scandalous truth that only the Holy Spirit can bring to life. Say it and leave it. Your life then will be the proof that this message actually saves people.

4) Lastly, tell your story.

If you're only thinking, *It's evangelism time!* —you might become one of those insensitive doctrine-nerds that overcomplicates things while firing off apologetics to "win" people.

But you're a real human being with a story, dealing with other real human beings who have stories. So, what's *your* story? How did God save you? Maybe you went to church your whole life, and then suddenly God knocked you out of the pew into His total grace and you started feeding the homeless and reading to blind kids. Or maybe you were doing black tar heroin, punching cops in the face while throwing puppies out of a moving vehicle, and Jesus uppercut you in your soul. Either way, you were *saved*. You have a testimony.

If your motivation is how God's grace saved you, then evangelism will become a much more natural part of you. You're simply just sharing your life. You'll also be able to listen to other peoples' stories instead of jumping right to doctrinal orthodoxy, because you care about them, just like God cared about you. Then you're inviting other people into God's incredible narrative.

The truth is, everyone is looking for this Heavenly Father. We really do want a God who has our eternal purpose and who constantly loves us. Most people aren't looking for a rehearsal of the Romans Road or the Four Spiritual Laws. If you can get really get a grip of *what God saved you from and what He saved you to*, you yourself will be excited about what God is doing, and others will know. That's true evangelism. You're allowed to milk your testimony for all it is worth. And even if you "mess that up," you'll still be a real human being with flaws like everyone else. No one is looking for perfection. They're looking for passion.

10. Ten Thoughts About Loving The Unlovable

- "How do you love people who are difficult to love? Some people will accept your love and help with open arms, but some people hurt you the more you try to love them and reach out to them. I know it is God who works through us, and God who gives us His perfect, unconditional love, but sometimes it is discouraging in ministry when members place unrealistic expectations on us, and simultaneously expect us to care more ..."

- "What is the Biblical way to love a self-righteous person when I am asking God and trying really hard not to be self-righteous, myself? To what extent is it okay that self-righteousness bothers me? What are indications that it's bothering me too much?"

Dear friends: This is a broadly complicated issue where I can only hope to encourage you for one more day. Love is such a messy organic creature that I couldn't possibly cover all its nuances. So please allow me the grace to offer some simple thoughts. Each thought is meant to balance each other out for a rounded view on Christ-like biblical love.

1) Love doesn't really count the response. I know it's tough when people reject you or imprison you with expectations, but the more you can be free of other peoples' responses, the more you can love them. If you love on someone and they honor you, then praise God for the opportunity. If you love on someone and they reject you, then praise God for the opportunity.

2) True love only loves the truly unlovable. It's easy to love people whom you like. It's easy to love people when they're doing what you want. The test here is how you treat someone who is messing it up and can't do anything for you. As Jesus said in Luke 6, *"If you love those who love you, what credit is that to you? Even sinners love those who love them."* In Matthew 25, Jesus calls us to love the "least of these." And Paul basically says in the opening verses of 1 Corinthians 13 that without love, nothing we do matters anyway.

3) Please do not set an impossibly high standard for yourself. Loving others doesn't always mean "emotional affection" or "unceasing prayer" or "my front door is always open." Sometimes it's the steady endurance of cleaning up someone else's mess, not judging when others totally mess it up, or not flinching when someone confesses a horrible wrong. Show yourself some grace when you fail at loving others. You'll grow in this over a lifetime.

4) You might be doing better than you think. I once got an email saying, "I don't really love this person — all I've done is listen to her problems and visit her house each week and pray for her and let her cry with me." I could only reply, *Dude, that's actually a lot.* If you're praying for this person, not cussing them out, and keeping a mostly cool head about it, then you're doing okay. Our natural disposition is to totally hate on others and it's not something you can just pray away overnight.

5) Friendship is different than loving on people. This is where many of us get messed up. There's a heck of a difference between loving close friends and loving a stranger on the street or even a fellow church member. Only your *close beloved* get complete access, get to see you vulnerable, and get to know the ugly side of you. You get to choose who they are. Be wise and discerning. Even Jesus had an inner circle. We don't exclude anyone, but we simply can't let everyone totally inside. Please do not force yourself into a sugary-soft New Age we-are-one type of "love" to open up to others equally.

6) However bad this person is, you are probably just as bad, if not worse. You might think this unlovable person is giving you a headache, but you also give the *exact* same kind of headache to others. I'm not trying to be a jerk here, but let's keep this on a level playing field. Maybe they're self-righteous or petty or smug, but we're just as capable of selfishness, envy, and bitterness. They might be a lot to put up with, but so are you. So am I. So don't ever think someone's issues are particularly annoying, because we're *all* annoying. Don't ever think the Sunday sermon is for that other guy, because it's for you too.

7) No one is really unlovable. For a moment, get inside Jesus' head. Jesus saw into the heart of Nathaniel, a racist, and found great faith. Jesus looked into the heart of the greedy rich young ruler and offered eternal life. Jesus saw into the hearts of Zacchaeus and Matthew Levi, two hard-partying tax collectors, and invited them into the Trinity. Somehow, Jesus scoured the inner-landscape of some very awful people and still found something to love. And even if Jesus had found nothing, I bet he would've loved them anyway. He went to the cross for that very reason.

8) Love is balanced with truth. We can't just pamper others. Love does not enable or spoil or let others off the hook. Jesus came with both grace *and* truth. John MacArthur once said, "Truth without love is brutality; love without truth is hypocrisy." We're called to be tough and tender. Without truth we will abandon others to destruction; without grace we will crush them with our truth.

9) There can be no love without forgiveness. I know this is hard. Every time I preach, "Love people," everyone has a story of why that can't happen. I'm so tempted to agree with them: some of these stories of hurt and betrayal are downright maddening. Yet — without the forgiving power of love, we are locked into a cycle of retaliation and inner-rotting that will only perpetuate the exact reason you were hurt in the first place. Forgiveness cuts through sin by absorbing the pain and piercing through our human nature. It's what Jesus did for us and also calls us to do. Forgive, even if it means you must do it a hundred times a day. It won't be a little easy prayer. Forgiveness will often be a way of life: and it is *so much better* than the alternative.

10) Love is defined as *the self-sacrificial effort of pouring out your life for another*. I've always defined love this way. Sure, it can be emotional, but it's not based in emotionalism. It takes work, sweat, tears, blood, and your whole life. It requires the overabundance of God's love flowing so freely through you that others are catching the overflow. If you can peer into the heart of Jesus on the cross, you'll know just a glimpse of what it means to truly pour out your life: and this is your true life. It's tough, but there's nothing greater than pursuing this.

"Love says: I've seen the ugly parts of you, and I'm staying."
— Matt Chandler

"Love is not affectionate feeling, but a steady wish for the loved person's ultimate good as far as it can be obtained."[20]
— C.S. Lewis

"I will love you like God, because of God, mighted by the power of God. I will stop expecting your love, demanding your love, trading for your love, gaming for your love. I will simply love. I am giving myself to you, and tomorrow I will do it again. I suppose the clock itself will wear thin its time before I am ended at this altar of dying and dying again. God risked Himself on me. I will risk myself on you. And together, we will learn to love, and perhaps then, and only then, understand this gravity that drew Him, unto us."[21]
— Donald Miller

---

[20] C.S. Lewis, *God in the Dock* (Michigan: William B. Eerdmans, 1970) p. 37
[21] Donald Miller, *Blue Like Jazz* (Colorado: Thomas Nelson, 2003) p.150

11. The Impossibility of Friendship

"Is friendship supposed to be super hard? Or am I, are we, doing something wrong?"

Hey dear friend — yes, friendship can be remarkably difficult. In fact, most of the time, it's impossible. I guess you were hoping for good news, which there is, but it's front-loaded by a whole bunch of bad news.

We're each naturally going to be selfish and sinful. We're all about self-preservation and protecting our egos. At the same time, we want company and community and we know that life is usually better together. In our friendships, we all tend to collide in those selfish areas, and our flaws and traumas and dysfunctions come spilling out in dramatic fashion. It's unavoidable. You will eventually run up against someone else's fault lines, just as you'll have your own exposed too.

I used to think, "Well the good is worth the bad." But that makes friendship sound transactional, as if I'm weighing how "good" it can be like an opportunistic salesman. Certainly there are some standards for friendship, and if it gets too toxic, we should consider walking away. Yet friendship is about *accepting all the good we have yet to discover and all the bad we have yet to see.* The deepest friend who exemplifies this, of course, is Jesus himself. He knows us as we are, yet loves us as we are.

The hard part is that we often confuse someone's flaws with "morality." We easily devalue people just because they think differently than us.

If I get offended every time my friend disagrees with me, this only shows that I'm deluded by my own isolated perspective — which means I only want a robot for a friend. Some of us probably want this. Some of us live in a bizarro-world where everyone worships our opinion and dances on thin ice for *me*. But this is simply fear of damaging the ego, and friendship is a trust that kicks down that doorway.

God forgive me, I've been that egotistical person, and I'm sure I still am some days. I have to constantly be aware of entering my friend's point of view, to consider their interests better than my own (Philippians 2), to carry their burdens when they cannot carry themselves (Galatians 6). It will require that I care less about being right and more about being true.

These things require a deep humility that will deny ourselves, and we must expect that we'll hate this process since we're self-preservers. When I see it coming, I can be ready for the surgery of repentance. When I confront my own sin, I'm no longer surprised by the sin of others, and can even be friends with them.

The good news is when we un-clutch our claws from our high-up walls and get into the sloppy work of trust, there's a good kind of hurt there that comes from miles of spiritual travel and a lifetime of carving stories and laughter. When we let someone in past the defenses, there's a joy that builds from all that came before, which cannot be had any other way except in through the gates. Such investment is scary and it's self-sacrificial effort, but either way, we are investing our heart to keeping things out or letting things in: and I will choose to invest in intimacy. I pray you will, too.

12. Watching a Friend Walk Away From Faith

"As someone in ministry, have you seen many people fall from faith? If you have, how do you handle it?"

I've been through this too many times to count. It's happening now, too. It's always heartbreaking and always a punch in the stomach. To be truthful, I still grieve for so many friends who went their own way and chose self-destruction. I still lose sleep over it. It's something you don't really get over, and something I pray about every day.

I've blamed myself; I've blamed God; I've blamed bad influences; I've blamed the church. In the end, I know I can't persuade anyone to stay faithful. It's their choice and their autonomy. I must respect that. As God respects our free will, so must we.

The only thing I can do is stay in touch. I text or call or email, at least a couple times per week. It's difficult, you know. I feel like I'm being annoying or that I'm wasting my time (and theirs). I feel bitterness and disappointment and helplessness. But I want them to know: *I'm still here for you. I'm staying. I don't care if I look like an idiot. If it means my life, I'll keep loving on you.*

One thing I had to let go was a Savior Complex. I'm not the hero of anyone's story. It's not that I'm "better" or "further ahead" than anyone else. I would be pretentious to think that the right combination of words will "win" anyone. I would be presumptuous to think I'm the stable voice of reason while they're "trapped in licentious prodigal living."

Everyone must discover for themselves what is truly life. Some (like me) take the long road to get there. If I convinced someone back into faith, then they can be convinced right out of it. My argument would only be an external apparatus that imprisons them out of behavioral obligation or maybe because they don't want to let me down: but it wouldn't be real internal change. I've tried that and it never works; it ends up more disastrous than their current choices. Unless this person is hurting themselves at an unbearably dangerous level, I have to let the whole thing play out or else their change will never become a true part of them.

I believe grace is the only way to rescue a wayward life. Grace is what melted my heart and tenderized my pride. It revoked my selfishness and killed the taste for my old life. When I look back over the years on my dearest friends, who never lectured me nor harangued me, I think of their patience and persistence and I can hardly believe they stayed.

It's only this unbelievable, endless second-chance that could ever break the stubborn, self-centered person towards the greatest love of the universe. And I was shown such grace because the friends who stayed had a God who stayed, too. And so I stay, relentlessly and recklessly, and I embarrass myself to destitution so they may see the riches of Christ. Not perfectly, but passionately: we can.

13. The Church Is Messed Up (But I Still Love Her)

- "Why do people try to make being a Christian harder than it already is? That is daunting in itself if you're prone to doubt and self-loathing. On top of that, we're expected to be smiling faces, loud singers, waving our bibles and screaming the Word from the mountain tops."

- "I do not attend church due to unhealthy amount of judgment and alienation. I am constantly made to feel I'm an abomination because I do not want to be a housewife or a mother. I am a writer, an illustrator, introverted. I've also fallen into depression and this feeling of alienation, even damnation, has gotten worse."

- "I've left church for about a year now because of a friendship which developed many complications. I felt that somehow God would want me to go back to church but pride (or whatever it is) is stopping me. Any thoughts on this?"

- "I've been feeling lost and alone for a while now. Although I attempt to join a church, I seem to not have a connection with them. I would love to connect with the people around me, but they seem so distant. I have been praying to God that I would be able to find a community where I comfortable praise/worship him."

I'm really sorry each of you have been made to feel this way.

As St. Augustine supposedly said, "The church is a whore, but she is my mother." He probably didn't say that, but I can agree.

Please know: I feel exactly what you're feeling on both sides of the pulpit. I've been in backroom meetings with church leaders and I know all the horrible language they use to talk about the congregation. I've visited at least fifty or sixty churches in my lifetime, which is probably not a lot, but enough to know how little they preach on grace or Jesus. I have enough dirt on at least three ministries to ensure they never receive support again (let's just say I know how to press "record" when the drama starts). I've been in places where you are ridiculed for not following "their rules" and it's just an inch away from being a cult.

There are preachers who preach grace like crazy, but act like complete jerks behind the scenes. My mother visited a church where the pastor offered to sleep with her. However bad you think it is, it's even worse.

Yet ...

Yet I still love her. I still love the church. I'm not mad about these things as much as I'm grieved and heartbroken.

As difficult as she can be, the *church is still God's idea.* Jesus said "I will build my church" (Matthew 16:18).

When I get questions like, "Do I have to attend church since ___? Why do so many Christians suck? Can I just pray and read Scripture by myself?" — my answer is always the same. *God created us to be in community together* (Hebrews 10:19-25). There's no avoiding it. It won't be easy, but without it, we will never be the fully formed individuals we were called to be, nor can we become the collective countercultural force for good in the universe.

There are certainly guidelines to consider before committing to a home-church or leaving one — but please, I beg of you to find a church and build your roots. As crazy as she is, we're called to be part of God's body for His glory.

While I can't hope to answer all your specific concerns, here are a few things to consider. Please feel free to skip around.

1) Those hypocrites and critical Pharisees might just be baby-Christians on their first lap of faith.

No church is ever fully represented by mature Christians, and certainly no church can fully reflect God. Some churchgoers are growing, some backsliding, and there are few who actually get it — and they're not perfect either. Even the pastor or church staff could be grossly immature in their spiritual walk. But we can't be too hard on the church as a whole because of a few bad fruits. Seeing a five minute fraction of a person's spiritual walk says nothing about what God is doing through them.

2) Given time + relationships, you will end up hating your church, which is when you can most learn to love.

When you find a church you embrace, the first few months will be the honeymoon period. When that's over, you'll find faults and flaws all over the place. It's inevitable, and like a devoted wife or husband, this is when we must persevere.

I'm not talking about if the church uses you, abuses you, or goes sideways theologically. You can walk out on those. I'm talking about negotiating all our personal preferences. Those are bound to be bruised, and though it's not wrong to have them, they're not reliable.

In other words: *Prepare for the season when you begin criticizing your church*. Get ready to start being judgmental about the praise team, the sermons, the mission, the people. Sure, it's good to be discerning, but Satan is constantly trying to divide us, so be on guard when you have an overly critical eye. That's when you will learn to love — not when things are fine, but when things go sour. Love bears *all* things, and if you're committed to your church, you've made a vow as solid as marriage.

3) Finding a church is like finding a spouse: one bad experience doesn't mean they're all bad, but there is *one for you*.

Not every church is for every individual, but there *will* be a church for you. Which means, please don't be too offended if a church doesn't seem to accept you. It doesn't make them all bad; it just means you haven't found the one yet. Around the corner, there's a church who will absolutely love you just as you love them, flaws and all.

A really good handle on this is to *see how they serve.* Some churches only exist to perpetuate their programs. You'll find others that really go out of their way to serve others, however imperfectly.

4) A church culture is bound to feel threatened if you're culturally different – and you'll feel threatened by their feeling threatened.

Please hang with me on this point.

Every single person is bound up in their cultural ethos — upbringing, background, tradition, beliefs — and the second you walk into a church, you are bringing *your* culture into theirs. So collision is bound to happen. Whether you are an "activist," "creative mind," "liberal," "introvert," or "hipster," you will clash with some and be welcomed by others. We all have a spiritual sensitivity that does not immediately embrace different walks of people (Romans 14).

The thing is, I used to believe that we could transcend this sort of stuff. I thought every church should be for everyone. But I don't believe that anymore. *I believe certain churches exists for certain contexts within certain cultures in their era.* Some churches will be diverse; others more homogenous; and God is using them both.

God celebrates unity *and* diversity, and that can't be made more clear than in His own Trinitarian nature.

This is why I'm no longer impressed when someone bashes the mega-church, because a small church can be just as greedy, moralistic, and hypocritical. One of my dear friends is being trained as the next keyboardist for an internationally known mega-church, and I have to say: my friend is one of the sweetest, most wonderful Christians you'll ever meet, and her church has done fine by her. No one can convince me otherwise.

Sure, many churches will appear cold, but usually it's just their culture colliding with yours. Unless they're called Westboro or Nazi Crossing, all the clique-ness is part of our human nature to identify with a similar culture, and this doesn't always mean that a church lacks grace.

It means that God has the imagination to interlock different shades of paint for unique paintings, and it takes time for certain hues (like yourself) to find each other. Some churches do this better than others, but let's not rag on that process nor wait for perfection.[22]

I'm all for being racially and spiritually diverse under one roof. It has nothing to do with "ethnocentrism." I still believe that even after Jesus comes back to reign, we will be ethnically diverse. But I believe we can find a church where your identity as a whole is not merely tolerated, but *celebrated*.

5) The church is full of crazy, which is exactly why we need the church.

Please remember: as much as the church is *a lot* to put up with, so are you. So am I. So are we all.

My first pastor endured me for years. I was a rebellious, arrogant, woman-hunting atheist, but he loved me anyway. And as disappointed as I have become with the modern church, I myself am so much more disappointing to others — because we are imperfect people clinging to the mercy of a Perfect God.

One of the main reasons for church is that God puts a whole bunch of idolatrous people together to learn patience, grace, empathy, and love — and without that sort of rock-tumbler environment, we would never have a mirror to understand who we are. We would never become polished jewels in Christ. God aims for us to crash and collide until we can

---

[22] Paul touches on this in 1 Corinthians 12 and Ephesians 4.

see each other as He sees us: broken, thirsting, and beloved. That's when God is glorified, through a people who love each other anyway.

At times it will feel like you're being crushed instead of polished. It will indeed feel like other "Christians" are making this too hard. But what God really wants is that you begin with *you*. If you really want a revival in your corner of the world, it won't begin by pointing fingers or the blame-game or setting up "us" versus "them."

It begins with you and Him.

Chapter 3.5 —
Interlude: When You're Too Quick To Dismiss That Guy, You Can't See What God Is Doing

Sometimes I'll look at a dude and instantly judge him — *"There's no hope for that guy in a million years"* — and I have to slap myself, because I was that same guy a million years ago.

I think it's easy for us to throw around labels like "lost cause" and "damaged goods" and "bad for business" because we're just lazy. It allows us to sit back and judge from a distance. It's easy to like people who are likable, but really dang hard to get involved with emotionally draining drama queens.

Everyone loves the idea of compassion until it costs them.

I tend to time-stamp someone on how they used to be, because it's more comfortable for me to presume "at least I'm better than that guy." It physically bothers me to think this person could change. How could everyone *like* him now? I want to say things like, "But I know how he really is" and "People don't change" — but then I'm revoking the very chance I've been given.

I've seen Christians casually dismiss other Christians down the street, pastors dissing pastors, churches entering into fierce tribalistic nationalism claiming a moral standard above the curve. I've been wounded by the venom because I have a past, and no one has honor in their hometown. Sometimes I desperately plead my side to be heard, but some people have their mind made up about you. You're the bad guy no matter what you do.

Really though: *We just don't want to get into the broken mess of other busted people.* It's dirty work. It requires standing out of our chairs, rolling up our sleeves, entangling with slobbery flailing lives, even forgiving them. It's not our nature. It hurts. It costs.

But this is what God did, against all odds: because God sees people as they **could** be, not as they *should* be.

Whenever we dismiss someone as incapable of change, we instantly sucker-punch the sovereign grace of God. We are downsizing His sovereignty to those people and not these. Then we're no longer talking about God. We're just exposing our laziness.

You know what I mean. I see a person on their first lap of faith and I make assumptions; I see 0.5% of a person's life and somehow predict their future; I see half a story and presume the whole thing. But this is a sort of evil that holds back potential, that undermines growth, that destroys a child's dreams. It's an ugliness that I've experienced too, from those who wouldn't give me a shot, who wouldn't see past their negative filters and accusations and condemnations, who saw me as a deadbeat nobody with no hope of a turnaround.

But occasionally, love would cut in and open a door. It grew my heart. It embraced me in.

Love sees a greatness in someone who cannot see it in themselves. Love keeps no record of wrongs. It hopes in all things, it does not rejoice in evil. It perseveres.

God saw you from a cross over a distance of two-thousand years, *and He loved you enough to stay there.*

I hope we have eyes to see that God is doing something we cannot see. This takes discipline, but we have help. God has a vision far greater than my sight. He has an imagination that infinitely outweighs mine. He can take a murderer like David and crown him the king. He can take a terrorist like Paul and breathe holy words into Scripture. He can take a beat-up dude like you and me and baptize us into saints.

We think a person is an impossible case, but God is in the business of the impossible.

After all, He saved you and me.

— J.S.

Chapter 4 —
The Deep End of Icky Awkward Issues: Sexuality, Society, and Politics

I have never, not once, heard a nuanced argument on political and social issues. There's too much emotion, too much bias, too many agendas, and all kinds of personal anger disguised as passion. We quickly demonize, rationalize, and polarize. There's always some guy who never says what he means, and on the other end, the guy who waves picket signs at funerals.

Both extremes fail to acknowledge the *actual human beings* caught between the issues. Abortion and homosexuality and government policies do not exist in a vacuum of abstract concepts, but actually involve living breathing souls with the same hopes, dreams, and hurts as you and me.

God is not in the business of hammering people into His own belief system, so it would be foolish for us to attempt what God doesn't. God sent a bridge called Jesus, an actual human being who lived among us and loved us. Many disagreed with him, and they crucified him, but Jesus continued to pour out love over sin, even on a cross.

Let's do the same. Let's be a people whose love is so great that it cuts through sin, both yours and mine.

1. Ten Thoughts on God and Homosexuality

"What's your opinion on gay people? I believe in God. Everyone says that homosexuality is wrong and it says so in the Bible, but they're people too, and I think God loves them. I don't think someone chooses to be gay, and I don't think gays are going to 'burn in hell' as some people say. I just wanted to know what you think? I just need a real answer from someone."

Dear friend: Here are a few thoughts to reflect on.

1) God loves you, end of story. If you say, "God loves you, *but*—" then we're not talking about God, the Gospel, or grace.

2) It is *not our job* to convert someone to anything, ever. Don't even. God never says, "Change first." God loves first.

3) Your sexual identity is *not* the only thing about you. So both the national news anchor or that angry preacher-man who keeps bringing up this issue are equally narrow-minded sensationalists. And let's stop using the words "bigot" or "liberal" or "homophobia" if we don't first care about the subtlety of rational, two-way conversation.

4) I want to apologize on behalf of the Westboro "church" and brimstone preachers who tough-talk the pulpit to "stand up for what's right," and for the church at large that has diminished the humanity of *real living breathing human beings* who have homosexual feelings.

5) The church likes to stand on what we're against instead of what we're for. You can tell me what I'm doing wrong all day, but unless you show me something else, then we're still at square one, ground zero.

6) When I talk with gay friends, I've realized the church has *never* offered another option besides, "Stop it." And even when we try to hold up traditional marriage as the bastion of righteousness, most Christian marriages are so messed up that we've revoked our own right to speak.

7) When Apostle Paul wrote about marriage, I bet he was thinking that Christians would show the best marriages ever — because up to this point, women were treated as cattle and men were given free reign with no rules.

Paul called for a revolutionary love-based marriage, for husbands to give their lives for their wives like Jesus and for wives to serve their husbands like Jesus. But the church has fragmented this beyond comprehension.

8) I wish I could share the awesome joy of Christian marriage with the whole world and to be able to say, "See how cool this can be?" — but that's been a failed dream. It's no wonder that more and more people are not seeing "traditional marriage" as an option, because it's not looking that much different than the ruined home they grew up in.

9) This is a global issue — because before the church can really present their case, they need to have one first. No, we're not called to be perfect, but I think saying "I'm not perfect" becomes an excuse to be lukewarm. No one wants perfection; they just want real. That starts with *you and me,* dear Christians.

10) One day, your homosexual friend might come around to the beauty of a biblical marriage between one man and one woman. One day, your friend might understand that you respect him or her no matter *what*. One day, your friend might look at your marriage and want something like that, if there's something worth showing (oh church, if you'd only see yourselves). One day, your friend might be hit with the true heart of the Gospel and experience the total grace of Jesus — one day.

But whether or not that happens, you keep loving on your friend. Dang it, we better love this world like crazy. No one is a project. We are not "superior" to them. We are not the harbinger of justice or Advice-Robot 2000 or the fixer of all things wrong. You are one flawed human being who is called to love another flawed human being. We love them. Jesus died for you and for them too.

2. Sexuality Is Not Everything

"I've always wondered what would happen if we were wrong about homosexuality. I struggle with this. I've prayed for years but nothing has changed. I have major depression and general anxiety disorder. If we're wrong, then I've wasted years of my life. But I'm also afraid of being right. Would God condemn someone who studied the Bible, prayed, but simply came to the wrong conclusion? I want to get married and I want a family, but I'm not attracted to women."

First I must say, you're very awesome for your honesty and your candor and for saying what most Christians are already thinking. I only wish the church was half as honest as you are.

I have to say again that *it's not the church's job to persuade anyone of anything, ever.* The church is not my platform; it's His.

I believe what the Bible says on all the tough issues, but I also believe it's my priority to love you, care for you, pray for you, and serve you regardless of your preferences, race, sexuality, intellect, past, status, or face.

I love you, Jesus loves you, and that's that.

For anyone who did not help you to experience the unconditional love of Christ, I'm sorry it went down that way. I'm sorry for the horrible approach of the church to suffocate this one issue beyond sanity. Despite what anyone tells you, there is no prerequisite or "standard" for the grace of God, and that's why it's the grace of God. For any time you were ostracized or abused or left hurting, I'm so very sorry.

There is probably a ton more I could say here, but I'll boil it down to this —

Please do not determine the course of your life based on what you think is possible today.

You might feel like you're stuck in a rut or circling a doubt or anchored to a feeling, but the thing is, I would never put it past God to uppercut your life. He can, does, and will. It's not my job to persuade you of anything, but I can tell you that when God is in the equation, mountains get moved and any kind of heart in any condition can surprise itself.

We can't really claim that your current slice of life right now is how you will always feel. Please don't take a tiny percentage of your journey as a reflection of the whole thing. Please be open to the possibility that God will do *anything* He wants through you.

God loves you, and that love is going to jumpstart a process in your heart that will take you places you never could've imagined. Take any Christian like myself and spin the clock back five years, and they could *never* have guessed how God would place them today.

No one in a billion eons would've thought this self-centered, overly horny, fist-shaking atheist would be a Christian blogging pastor. Let's never underestimate God on that.

Please allow me to add one more thing.

Your sexual identity is not everything about you, because you are a God-created individual who is much more than your urges and appetites and desires.

Both the secular talk show host and the red-faced preacher who set a laser-sight on our sexuality are just squeezing attention to their platforms while reducing human beings to human do-ings. That's a no-win.

You're not just based on who you want to have sex with. I don't mean to diminish the issue, but it's possible we've blown this up out of proportion and made it some cartoon monster. You might have supersized your issue to consume your entire vision, which always robs us of our true purpose: to love God and love others in this race of life.

God does call us to something beyond the singular fight with our natural fleshly nature.

In my flesh, sure, I'd love to have mindless sex when I feel like it, and I can swim in self-pity all day long. Or I can lay that aside and realize I'm *way* more than this. I'm not just my impulses and gut instinct and physical needs and selfish tendencies. While they're a part of me, they're not the only thing. And I won't let self-pity be a secret doorway to settle for less.

God made me for something so supernaturally outside my flesh that this struggle, while still present, gets left behind in the adventure.

So let's put aside the question for a minute.

If this was not your only issue, *what exactly do you think God would call you to do?*

Maybe no one at church has ever asked you this question.

Maybe you've only been told what you "shouldn't do," and they're leaving out the part where God calls us to an incredible life-fulfilling all-glorious mission that's actually the handcrafted purpose of our lives.

I would totally look into that.

I love you times a million and I'm throwing prayers your way.

3. Reaching Out To The Gender-Diverse

"I was wondering what your views on gender identity are; I live in a very gender diverse community, including transgender and other non-gender people and just sort of realized that their lifestyle is something that simply didn't exist in biblical times. If you have any thoughts on how to deal with that theologically, I would appreciate your insight!"

I'm no expert on gender identity, but the Bible is pretty simple. Just love people. **Love is your first priority above all things.** I don't care if that sounds old or generic or repetitive or easy. This is a timeless truth that transcends all the differences of our cultural history.

When you say that things were different in "biblical times" — you're right, because they were worse.

A little history: While Apostle Paul was writing the Book of Romans, there was an Emperor named Nero who was using Christians as torches to light up his front lawn and he was involved in at least two known homosexual affairs. If you ever read on the Roman Empire, there were all kinds of "master-student relationships" between old dudes and young boys that today we would call pedophilia and statutory rape. Orgies of every kind were rampant. Cross-dressing and gender-diversity were not uncommon.

So please consider that Apostle Paul was writing on sexuality during an upside-down time when he could be impaled with a wooden pole and lit up like the 4th of July, and he told the truth. Read Romans 1. He does not hold back.

Yet Paul's every motive was guided by the overarching love of Jesus Christ. Nowhere in the Bible does Paul say, "Hey, you only get Jesus after you clean up your junk, then come find me." God doesn't give the Ten Commandments to the Israelites until *after* He rescues them through the Red Sea. That pattern is all over Scripture.

Apostle Paul loved people, period, and we're called to do the same *no matter what*. Paul knew what Christ saved him from — the murderous ambitions of a terrorist — so he understood people with baggage.

He actually loved them so much that at one point in Romans 9:3, Paul says he wish he could go to Hell so others wouldn't. Just think of that for a second. Eternal flames. Who would ever do this? Except Jesus? Honestly, probably not me — so I have a lot to learn about love. I want to love like Paul did, who loved like Jesus.

I bring that up because we get this backwards. **We often preach morality first before Jesus.** We preach God's commands before God's glory and His story. So the church has been especially good at attacking things like homosexuality or abortion or evolution but has totally lost a love for real souls created by God.

That's why we even ask questions like, "How should I approach this kind of person?" — because we think it requires some kind of unique special approach like slipping a truth-pill inside a nice-guy-mask inside a theological homing missile. It really only requires you being there, and you being how God has called you.

Have you ever talked to any of your community face to face? If you have, you're already ahead of the curve. I've had the privilege of speaking to friends with homosexual feelings, and being one-on-one with them is where all our dumb preconceived notions go out the window. They have hopes, dreams, hurts, passions, insecurities, and anxieties, like all of us do.

At this point, in case you're thinking, "But what about the truth?" — **The modern church is terrible at offering a better alternative than "You just stop it."** It's like we can't get past the issue into offering *more* and *better*.

Right now in your neighborhood, there is 1) a dude who doesn't know the awesomeness of marriage with a woman, 2) a fifteen year old pregnant girl who feels like she only has one option, and 3) a confused kid who can't think for himself on the origin of life because both sides are yelling in his face. What these three people are *not* doing is thinking of church as the place with all the answers, because most of us have been one-sided narrow-minded jerks.

I can't say that gender-diverse people are any different than me. **I would love them just like any other created human being.** My job is not to persuade anyone of anything. Only God opens eyes and changes hearts. Not by picket signs or angry blogs or stupid arguments. If I ever want to be heard on any of this, I must earn that right, and it's only possible by way of love.

I must also offer a caution here. I've been guilty of using poor people as props in my own Savior-Narrative. Sometimes when a gay person walks into my church gathering, I consider it a "victory." I can take pictures on a mission trip or at an orphanage or a shelter and suddenly, I'm a social media hero. Yet I forget that *no human being is my personal charity project.* I don't do this to "win points." Even in the way I'm writing this, I sense a danger in sounding like a cool-laid-back-nice-guy, when in reality, to actually love people is way harder than my pretty words. I truly struggle with this, because I know I must check my own motives in my compassion for others. I don't want to do this to look credible. I want to do this because I really care. The only way this can happen is when I see the selfless, one-way, unconditional love of Christ.

By the grace of God, I'm going to spend time with anyone regardless of what they do, who they are, or what they desire, because this is exactly what Jesus did, and I always want to be where he is. Jesus died for every person, every group of people, every individual, including those we disagree with and those who make us uncomfortable. That's love.

4. So About Abortion — I'm Pro-People
"May I ask your views on abortion?"

Disclaimer: This is a painful, dividing issue that involves so many variables that I can't hope to fully cover all of them in the following. Whether we agree or disagree, my hope is that we keep the mothers and their children (and fathers) at the forefront of our prayers and discussion.

This is a huge topic that equally wrenches and infuriates everyone involved, so I know in advance that I might upset you. So again, my heart is not to bring you to "my side" or bash the "other side," but to show grace for the people in-between.

I can safely tell you one thing. No one in the history of anywhere has ever thought, *When I grow up, I would really like to have an abortion.*

This isn't some childhood dream, and no matter where we stand on this issue, no one celebrates abortion or has abortion parties or gives abortion-bouquets. It's a painful decision that many real living breathing human beings have endured.

I don't mean to be glib here, but we've turned a very sensitive personal issue into a splashy sensational front-page political position. We force one side or another, but forcing by coercion dehumanizes.

If my female friend were considering an abortion, I would do everything in my power to suggest a reconsideration of that option, but if she ultimately decides to get one, I'm not going to lose respect for her. I will not love her less, I will not shame her, I will not treat her differently. I will be there for her.

If my friend does heroin, eats glass, injects alcohol, kicks animals, and plays with grenades, I will do everything in my power to suggest something else (or possibly call the police), but I'm not going to pick up a sign, stand outside a rehab clinic, and picket a bunch of people who are already suffering through situations that I can barely understand. That's called "subtle as a sledgehammer." It's to diminish and minimize our humanity.

What our world has done is what it always does. It take a human issue, forces two sides against each other, comes up with all kinds of wonderfully articulate arguments, and ratchets up the volume.

All this screaming from pro-this and pro-that and "two-sides partisan" stuff is just a small cross-section of bullies with bullhorns expressing their political ideology, and underneath that is mere self-promotion and vanity. Satan is laughing his butt off over this.

Forget *all* the arguments for a second. Does anyone see how crazy it is that we're arguing *at all?* Most people can only see in such binary pigeonholes because it's all they know. All the yelling ignores the teenager who has to make this life-shaping decision. None of us are coming together *for her.*

We also set up a microscope over a tiny slice of the problem. Abortion is like a tiny link in the chain. How about pro-infancy? How about pro-children? How about making adoption a viable option? How about education on pregnancy and relationships and better parenting? And if a woman were to choose abortion, how about not shaming them? How about giving them choices for counseling and offering grace through Christ? And to preachers: how about not condemning them as if they are in a different category of "sin" than you are? How about the church unite to help the healing process?

When I'm asked if I'm pro-life or pro-choice, I've often described myself as **pro-people** on the issue. I get hate for that because it appears elitist, hipster-ish, and liberal. It sounds like I'm being soft or dodgy. I would counter that "pro-life" or "pro-choice" are actually soft and dodgy. They hardly accommodate for the real life stories of lifelong realities. The "debate" on abortion deteriorates into a focus on a specific window of nine months, which is the most shortsighted viewpoint on any issue ever.

I wonder where Jesus would be while hate-mongering criminals are blowing up abortion clinics and killing abortion doctors. Jesus would be in the clinic, with the women, with the doctors. He'd show them their options but love them the same. He would not be outside in the ridiculous noise of nearsighted fist-shakers who enjoy the sound of their own voices.

I want to be where Jesus is. I want to be the church that opens doors, not waves signs.

I don't want to condone abortion. I believe every pregnancy should have a chance. But if you step back and look at what we've done with the issue, it is downright upside-down insane. Every woman who is considering abortion or has already had one *also has a story, has hopes and dreams and a purpose like every other God-created human being.* Let's love her. Let's help her to consider other options. But let's love her regardless of what she chooses.

5. Church Vs. State: How A Christian Fights For Policy Reform

"I agree with everything you mentioned in the post about abortion, but do you think it is unloving to believe abortion should be illegal? I've been told time and time again how it is not sensitive to the woman in the situation to not give her a choice, but for the sake of innocent lives I personally believe it's the government's job to protect them. Is this insensitive or unloving as a Christian?"

I wish I could give all sorts of nuanced guidelines about how to fight for changing laws and government policies and social trends, but I lack the intellect and information to really weigh in here. I can only tell you what I believe about it.

Everyone will be called to fight a different battle in their Christian walk, whether it's abortion or poverty or injustice or disease, and I can't speak for your personal calling. But here are some things to consider, both general and specific.

1) The separation of church and state is crucial to maintain freedom and humility.

Let's pull it way back and see the big picture. Once the "institution" of church starts to gain a foothold in the government, we begin to impose our values on the world. That means we are revoking the human right to choose, which can only increase rebellion.

I'm not saying that fighting to change laws is wrong, but I'm suggesting that making it "illegal" could be religiously oppressive. People do not play nice under oppression (e.g. the Prohibition) and any sort of sweeping-policy change has a profound effect on society that requires your full long-term attention to consequences. That means following up on anything you fight for, which many of us never do.

Let's say you win and abortion does become illegal. Suddenly the women who want one are going to back streets, paying exorbitant amounts to some so-called doctor who could be a fake, which puts women at risk. That's not uncommon even today. Even if you changed the law, the law does not change people.

Laws about homicide, theft, and violence make sense because they are mostly universally agreed upon. Even then, these laws don't always deter criminals. It makes the worst of us more clever to work around the law. So with a much stickier issue like abortion, where not everyone sees eye-to-eye, making it illegal will encourage a lot of backdoor crime.

That's not to say that we should legalize everything and let people run amuck, but just to consider how complex the abortion issue really is. It's not a clear-cut black-and-white decision. Not everyone thinks, "This law against murder is so lame," but some people would think, "This law against abortion is forcing my hand."

If the church is also going to step in every time they think a law is "wrong," this not only squeezes freedom but will destroy our humility. Church history has proven this over and over; when the church is given worldly power, it has hardly ever done good with it. Which brings us to the next point.

2) The church must be a safe haven of grace for sinners, not a platform for political culture. Only a gracious church could possibly hope to shape the cultural landscape.

While laws will change according to the demand of their times, the church must be an irreplaceable beacon of hope and healing for those who have been culturally burned.

Let's imagine for a moment that the culture is one individual. How do you introduce this person to a new way of thinking? By hammering them with law reform and picketing them and shouting at them through a bullhorn? No; you love them like Jesus does. However you would act on a micro-level, you can work that at the macro-level. Social reform begins with the individual.

Some would say, "Oh that's so ideal, come on. We live in the real world." But why should we abandon the ideal just to settle for a devalued "real"? We can still pursue an ideal while we deal with the pain of reality. No one was ever helped by settling for less.

3) Great men and women who fought for social reform always stayed at ground level with the oppressed.

It's cool if you decide to run at Capitol Hill over some laws you disagree with. What's even better is to open your home and your church to rape victims, the homeless, war veterans, the mentally disadvantaged, and single pregnant teens who need guidance. If you really believe it's the government's job to protect the unborn, then you also better make it your job to provide for real hurting people. Otherwise, and I say this out of love: you're like every other hypocrite.

If you do feel called to fight for what's right, it cannot only be to change laws. The great historical figures of our time, for all the faults they had (because they were human too), also endured with the people they were fighting for. They were not just great speakers. They were in the dirt and grit and mess of oppressed lives. They were willing to die out of love for others.

I want to be careful here because I know some of us can name bad examples of overzealous people who died for the wrong things and fought the wrong way. But a stark difference is always in how someone reaches out. Mother Teresa was involved directly hands-on with the poor in Calcutta; Hitler made eloquent speeches while killing millions of people he hated.

Screaming for policy-change is easy. It's like every other annoying church out there who idolizes principles but neglects their community. When a government can see a church who actually cares for the broken and is genuinely pleading for better laws, that's when those who influence policy actually take notice. While you might disagree with abortion, if your church loves on women who have made that choice and guides pregnant women towards healthy decisions without judging them, you will stand a chance to be heard.

The raving religious is *never* heard, and if you're just another voice, you'll be thrown in with them. Do both. Fight humbly for what is right, but help those who have been wronged. Your voice will only be heard if your heart is moved and your hands are moving.

6. Can Doctrine Become Idolatry?

"It seems that too many Christians make 'agreement with the right beliefs' into yet another work they use to save themselves and an excuse to hate other Christians (especially liberal and progressive Christians.) Do you think adherence to correct doctrine can become an idol?"

Hey my friend, I don't mean to sound like an alarmist, but pretty much *everything* can become idolatry. Especially doctrine.

A few years ago, I was really caught up by the Reformed Calvinist movement and their "Gospel-Centrality," and while I still mostly agree with the theology, I no longer self-identify as a Calvinist.

Mainly it was because their heads were stuck inside the *implications* of the Gospel instead of the author of the Gospel Himself, so there was no real relationship with the Living God. But it was also because most of the Calvinists I've met were insufferable jerks who yelled "heresy" from a distance on their super-blogs while hardly loving God or people.

I know I'm undermining my own point here, and God has grace for them too, but my friends who are actually good Calvinists do not wear the label. In other words, if I can't tell a Calvinist is a Calvinist, he's probably doing it right.

The Christian life is often about maintaining a balance between tensions. So while we absolutely want to have correct doctrine, we also want to be in the mess with people and love on them. While we adhere to the discipline and law of God, we are also motivated by God's grace and mercy. While I believe in predestination, I also believe this reconciles with free will — and I don't claim to know how, because my brain is too small and I'd likely catch fire if I knew. When we swing too much to either side, it becomes **doctrinal idolatry**.

Let's break this down a bit. The reason why Christians resort to shutting each other down is because —

1) People always default to **a false dichotomy of "for" versus "against"** so that we can maintain a distinction and act as if we're championing a particular cause. Even people who say, "I don't label myself" are already labeling themselves. Everyone picks a side and demonizes the other. We naturally tend to define ourselves on our differences in the most negative way possible. I might have done it in this very paragraph, because it's inescapable.

If you've ever witnessed the debate on marriage or abortion, then you know it doesn't even sound like anyone on either side cares about the people. They end up yelling about abstract issues or hogging up the political square to get attention.

2) Every facet of culture ends up categorizing the other, so that we live in a **reactionary culture** in which every category is simply born out of aggression towards another. Basically, the Protestants came about this way. Most sermons and Christian books are built on the thesis, "Don't be like that one guy."

Many ministries are simply just a response to being hurt somehow by another ministry — but any church built this way will eventually succumb to passive-aggressive attitudes, resentment, fear, tribalism, and graceless theology.

From the mega-church to emergent churches to hipster churches and urban ministry, we're all in some way fighting back against "The Institution," which is some false straw-man of what we do not want the church to be. Certainly there's some wisdom in fighting off bad methodology, but if we're solely built on this, then who is "winning?" Pretty much just Satan. This is why so many Christians end up hating other Christians right down the street.

When you combine all this, we get a toxic church culture that dehumanizes and cannibalizes. But I'm not blaming anyone. This is the way it is, and it's extremely difficult to escape the vortex of our fallen human nature. The only thing we can do is have some humble self-awareness, to fight against these instincts by the grace of God, and get under the authority of the Holy Spirit. Anything less will inevitably cause us to categorize the other.

Jesus was really hard on the Pharisees because even their own namesake meant "the separated ones." They would pray things like, "Thank God I'm not like those other people." There was no room in their hearts for the tax collector, prostitute, the blind, beggars, demon-possessed, and born-again disciples. Jesus had no such categories and loved them too.

I don't mean to be hard on the Pharisees. Then I'd be categorizing again. I mean to say, Jesus picked on the Pharisees the most because they had utterly lost the point. I'm sure Jesus was sick to his stomach about this. Part of Jesus's death was to demonstrate *there are no unique categories of people and that he came to die for us all.* Jesus, at the cross, demolished our right to grade other people to a standard. As John Stott once said, *"Nothing in history or in the universe cuts us down to size like the cross ... At the foot of the cross, we shrink to our true size."*[23]

But when you meet people who still categorize in black-and-white, even those people who pretend to be nuanced and smooth-talk it by

---

[23] John Stott, *The Message of Galatians* (London: Intervarsity Press, 1968), p. 179

saying, "We should pray for them" — they all need grace too. Do not hate the hater. **Do not idolize anti-idolatry.** Be patient with the impatient. Embrace the tension and maintain the balance. It's easy to think we're superior to Reformed Calvinists or Arminians or hyper-grace guys or mega-churches or those N.P.P. dudes, and it will be a lifelong temptation to look down on them — but they are fellow human beings whose lives continue long after we've bashed them, and they need Jesus like you do.

Philippians 2 tells us, *"Consider others better than yourselves."* This doesn't mean we roll over and play loose with theology. This doesn't mean we water down the truth. It means we go for the same heart that Jesus had when he took on flesh, became one of us, and gladly died for you and for me. If you squint your eyes at someone and feel the categorical anger in your bones — remember, Jesus died for that guy too. The sooner we embrace this, the more free we shall become, and perhaps even work together across our doctrinal differences.

> *"My generation is gruesomely lonely, but in response, we don't need another handout, another kind gesture, or a better bible study. We don't need more people that will merely know our name and address or care for us sporadically and at arm's length. We need big, reimagined, Jesus kind of love, and people willing to sacrifice themselves in order to live it with us. We need people who will love us enough to get messy.*
>
> *So be deeply involved. Be covered in someone's tears. Be the person who gets the call at midnight. Be the person who hears the gory details when someone's marriage or career falls apart. Be the person who tells someone the hard stuff that they need to hear but no one wants to say. Be the person who repeatedly gets someone else's mud and blood all over you. Be the person who goes home a little uncomfortable at night, not because of your behavior and thoughts, but because you've been near enough to someone else's. Be a family member to the lonely, messy people of this world, and to my generation"*[24]
>
> — Josh Riebock

---

[24] Josh Riebock, *mY Generation* (Michigan: Baker Books, 2009), p. 90

7. Racism: The Not So Invisible Elephant

"What are your thoughts on how a Christian can graciously engage in dialogue about racism and injustice with someone who isn't justice-oriented? I find myself trying to walk the line of challenging them while not breaking relationship trust. I'd love to hear how you approach that situation, and what things you keep in mind."

Hey my dear friend: First I must say that I'm grieving with the entire community on every side of this. As always, before I even talk about issues, I want to talk about the *people* inside them. I don't ever want to forget that people have actually died in these racially motivated crimes, and that courtrooms and juries can't ever bring them back. My heart is breaking profoundly for us as a people who have gone wrong and been wronged.

My heart also equally grieves for the ugliness of the internet community and how quickly we devour each other over race and justice. On one hand, I believe each of our communities must examine ourselves first, but on the other hand, I'm so dang tired of explaining that racism exists.

Please allow me to suggest three things upfront. Each one will probably make someone else mad, but we need more self-honesty and not less.

1) Most bloggers who talk about Social Justice don't actually care about the oppressed, but about going viral and getting high-fives from other bloggers.

2) Those who don't believe "racism exists" cannot be convinced by snarky sarcasm, but only by patience and reasoned sharing.

3) Change can only happen by entering the structures already in place from the inside, not by slamming on it from the outside.

The problem with bringing up racism is that it instantly becomes a magnet for horrible messages. It's not that I want people to agree with me, but it's that we're way too quick to say a problem *doesn't* exist instead of acknowledging that someone's pain could be real. If my body keeps hurting somewhere, chances are it's a diagnosis of something bad. In the same way, we need to diagnose the culture, too — yet nothing enrages people more than talking about race and justice, mostly because people can't stand to face the ugliness inside and to say, "I'm wrong."

There's always going to be someone who's disappointed in a "racially charged view of the world." Speaking as an Asian minority, I've been verbally and physically attacked directly because of my race; I don't think it's some kind of delusion. Racially based motivations are real. If I've "bought into" a myth, I suppose my bruises can speak the truth. And none of that even marginally compares to the racism that many of my friends face for their own families every single day.

It's almost impossible to gain any traction with this online or even face-to-face. No one's interested in a conversation; we're all yelling as loudly as possible to point at our own platforms. And I'm saying this for *every side.* We all do this. I think the majority of "Social Justice Bloggers" are making it worse.

Most bloggers are using Social Justice and "cued buzzwords" to go viral and get attention. It doesn't help anyone and it only diminishes the actual issue of racism. It turns it into a circus carnival, and I'm begging you: if you're another blogger who randomly writes on these matters with zero context or care, then please stop. We need more depth and not shallow sound-bites. You're actually parodying the whole thing into a laughable hand-wave.

There are really three groups of people here:

1) Preaching to their own choir.
2) Silently oblivious to larger issues.
3) Trying to reach across the divide.

Unfortunately, most bloggers are only preaching to their own choir. It's full of overbearing, snarky, sarcastic bravado that only speaks to the people who already agree. Sass is fun, but it never works. Sarcasm and sneering and passive-aggressive commentary don't convey ideas, but division. It's not a conversation, but a circular fist-bump.

I hardly read any "activist" blogs these days because they're all the same. Someone says a "burn" type thing, it gets passed around thousands of times with #preach or #ooohhh, and that's it. No one does anything. Mental agreement and assent do nothing. Of course, I believe awareness is crucial and important, even life-saving. A few might actually donate or reach out to the people in authority to affect change. There are still thoughtful people who offer solutions and get involved with the people who are hurting. But my guess is that 90% of the online community doesn't really care. They just want to impress their other tribalistic buddies and it's an isolated echo chamber of point A to point A. I'm not okay with that.

It also does no good to stay silent. We must reach across the divide. Here's what I suggest if you're talking to someone who might be racist or blind to their own racism. I use a modified hybrid of Aristotelian philosophy and Jesus's approach to wealthy upper-class men.

We can ask two questions.
1) **What do you mean by that?**
2) **Why do you believe that?**

You see: When you only make propositional statements from your opinions, you immediately put another person on their automatic, pre-programmed defense. I'm not above this; I do it too. It goes nowhere. We can't possibly peel back years and layers of racism in another person during a heated exchanged of ideas versus ideas. But when you ask *questions* about a person's belief, several good things happen. You then put the other person on **equal footing** so they can explain themselves, and instead of defending, they're now **confessing**. The hope is that they'll hear their own ideas out loud as you continue to ask "what" and "why," and they'll realize that their own ideas are not as sound as they had once believed. It'll start to sound silly, even to them. I can almost guarantee you that most people have never been openly challenged this way and have only perpetuated their ideas with like-minded people. By questioning them, you are entering softly while still turning over stones.

This is not a trick, by the way. People can tell when you're pulling a fast one. People can tell when you don't love them or you're using a formula or you're being a smug jerk. So don't be a smug jerk and do love them. Please be open to hearing them out, because maybe they have a painful story behind their anger and prejudice. Maybe they simply need to tell it to be set free.

You can see why the entire blogosphere is completely anti-productive to dialogue, because you can't really ask questions and share stories back and forth. The internet is made largely for propositional statements. That's why you see the most hate online: because arguments escalate into competition. No one has ever changed their minds online, and if they do, it's only to look smart and not because they're becoming smarter.

The reason why I believe Martin Luther King Jr. had such a sweeping effect on our national psyche is because he managed to be both **compassionate** and **just**. He asked the right questions and navigated with the right surgical touch. He reached across dividing lines to the people in authority and was able to negotiate without haranguing them. Of course, he protested and raised his voice and he was fiery and passionate and occasionally had to be angry. We have the right to be outraged for our wounds. Yet all these responses were controlled, focused, and had a direction. Systematic change began when someone entered the system through wisdom instead of slamming against it from the gates, and I believe we can be wise enough to do this today.

Unfortunately, many of us don't have the patience or perseverance. You won't find the nuanced thoughtfulness of both MLK's eloquence and firm confidence within one person. We're all either too brazen with nothing to say or too scared to say anything. If MLK was a blogger today, I think he would be embarrassed and ashamed to see that no one was trying to reach outside their polarized box; he would see a lot of unorganized choirs with zero consensus squabbling for each other's attention and then closing their browsers to watch the next episode of the Kardashians. MLK, Gandhi, Thich Nhat Han, Mother Teresa, and Jesus would all see *blindness*.

It's easy to stand up for something. There are enough soapboxes to go around. I'm waiting for the guy who will actually kneel down with me in the trenches, roll up his sleeves, and hurt with me. I'm waiting for the guy who will listen to my story as a victim of racial abuse and prejudice. I'm not interested in debating, because talk is a cheap dress that you can buy with a free blog in your basement, and I'm done with people preaching pretty words without doing what they preach first. Even true content is false when it's not backed up by movement and momentum. Quoting famous quotes doesn't help me: you only need to get to know me and maybe we can turn this all around.

I hope we can each take a long real look at our own platforms, and then ask, *"If the 'other side' had my exact tone and argumentation and methods, would I even care to read them? Would I even listen to myself?"*

Of course, I don't expect anyone will honestly do this, because I'm a cynical person. Everyone hates to change or to challenge themselves or to hear the hard things. No one likes discomfort or self-confrontation, because we like coddling and triumphalist self-affirmation.

But maybe, just maybe, a few of us might take an honest look at ourselves and examine what we're really shouting about, and perhaps find a better way than the shouting. And maybe some of us will reach up to those who are in power who actually want to help, because there are still good people in charge who want to do the right thing, or maybe the few of us in power would actually wield it for good instead of swinging it for our own acclaim. I have hope to see justice in my lifetime, and it starts outside our room past the front door.

Chapter 4.5 —
Interlude: The One Thing We're Not Doing About Injustice

Every time I go online to read about another tragedy, I grieve nearly as much over the ugliness of our online banter.

I read all the polarized back-and-forth shouting, and it makes me sick to my stomach — as it always does. It's a whole lot of yelling, but none of it does anything, nor does it influence anyone who could. Most of us yelling on our blogs are only trying to go viral and look relevant and be sassy instead of actually caring about the people involved. You can tell, and we can see right through it.

I believe in the right to peacefully protest. I believe blogging for awareness is good. I believe we should leverage our social platforms to speak up for the voiceless. I believe even "trolls" and "haters" have the right to speak, because the least dignified person is afforded the dignity to speak their mind.

But I think there's one thing we keep saying that we'll do and we simply don't. We say we will, and we're not.

I keep seeing, *"We need to pray."* I keep hearing that over and over. I've probably said it too. *"Pray for our country."* It sounds nice and it's true. But I wonder how many people are actually doing this. I wonder if they realize the potential magnitude of what they're saying and what prayer can actually do if we went for it.

How about if the billions of people who tweeted and preached and blogged and sassed about injustice actually did pray? I don't mean to sound uppity or self-righteous. I'm preaching to me, too. I'm not telling you what to do with your anger; I'm also angry. But imagine: if we all got on our knees together daily, even just a few hundred of us, and sought to commune with God and reflect on each other's needs and thought about how to serve one another. Imagine taking five seconds to have empathy, and what that could do for the whole day.

A few months back, after reading too many cruel comments online, I felt driven to my knees to pray. To be truthful, I haven't done this in a long time. I consider myself a "Bible-believing Christian" — but prayer is hard. I usually do it in the car, between places, always on the go. It's totally different on my knees. At first I thought, "This will make a great blog post." It took a while to really be in silence. I was too self-conscious, and I expected it. Something in us resists the spiritual. Even those who want to pray find it hard to focus. But I pushed through. Soon — I ran through the fog of my own distraction, and I knew He was there. I knew He was grieving over us. And I could only say, *"We're so screwed up right now. I'm screwed up, God. Please help us. We need your help."*

Maybe it did nothing. But at least God and I, we had a good time together. I felt a sober peace. The light outside felt brighter, sharper, new.

If there really is a God and He has the power to intervene and change hearts and orchestrate human structures, then I don't see how we could be doing anything else *but* prayer. If God does exist, and I believe He does, then we need nothing less than His divine power to heal a hostile, weary world. We need action strengthened by prayer.

I'm only asking that we would ask, *"If I really believed prayer worked, what would I pray for the world right now?"* Then maybe some of us would go do that. A few of us might cross the line and really pray to the God who can do what we can't. And even if nothing changes, then you did, and if we all did, then there's a chance we could turn this whole thing around. I have hope for that, even in a world such as this.

— J.S.

Chapter 5 —
Why (Me) God? Doctrine on Disasters, Death, and Staring Down The Devil

When the world goes crazy and life gets upside-down, it's really hip to say, "Just be there for someone" — and you're called a jerk if you say anything else. This is the new quip-ster cliché, and it's now its very own legalism.

I understand this, because it's insensitive to preach cold abstract theology at hurting people. Anyone who does this is thrown under the Religious Nut Bus. Defending God over cancer and car accidents and earthquakes often feels like I'm punching the air. For some of us, the evil in this world is the single largest hang-up we'll face to faith, even more than bigoted hypocritical Christians. We might part ways here and it's easy to be cynical. And that's okay. We're free to disagree.

But I wonder if most millennial Christians only resort to "Don't talk about God, just-be-there-for-them" because they're afraid of backlash from mainstream opinion. I wonder how much of our talk on "relevance" is a cowardice in offering a clear lucid theology on the pain of a broken world. The church has definitely messed up this conversation in the past, with bad platitudes like "He moves in mysterious ways" and "Just-wait-until-heaven," but when we're done apologizing for where we got it wrong, the Bible still has something good to say. If we can get past the fear of ridicule, there's a rich, robust, roaring framework of faith that can endure the worst that life will throw at us. Even when we don't believe it to be true, I find myself *wanting* it to be.

While I'd be the first to say that we can't fully answer such huge cosmic conundrums, we can at least wrestle with these real life concerns in humility and sympathy. I believe God graciously receives our venting. More than that, there's an untapped wealth of resources that I believe

Christianity gives specifically for the brokenhearted. I can't hope to answer the divine *Why* questions, but we can find out what to do here at ground zero.

Of course we need to be present to love, to listen, to learn. Our "being-there" has priority over theology. I'm not going to bring up my systematic outline of God's sovereignty at the moment of your collapse. But at some point, I need to give you more than a hug. I need to respond to the hurt, and no one wants a pat on the head or a pat response.

I truly believe that the Christian faith has the most coherent, cogent, competent worldview on suffering. **Christianity offers both the *pathos* and the *logos*, both a presence and a reason.** On one hand, we keep silent vigil when a friend suffers; we are loyal by their side. And on the other hand, we talk it out. We vent our frustrations. We seek wholeness.

I believe, like Job, that it's absolutely acceptable to struggle with the nature of God's goodness, and that it's okay if we're never fully at rest with pain. We can keep asking: *Is He truly good? Is He really in control? How much am I allowed to doubt Him while still holding onto Him? Do I have the grace to question Him?*

Even if God never tells us *why* we go through tragedy, we can still ask Him —

What do we do now?

Christians believe this is all going somewhere. We don't always know why, we don't always know what God is really doing, we don't always find it easy to trust Him.

But I don't want to be ashamed of my theology.

After all, my theology is alive, risen, and here.

1. How Do I Know If It's God or the Devil? On Pain, Evil, and Suffering

"Would God purposely put His children in a situation where they would be hurt in any way (rape, kidnapped, something like that)? Or is this the work of the devil? I don't think He would, but I don't know."

My dear friend, there's probably a huge list of questions I'd like to ask God the second I see Him (right after I collect my eyeballs back into my head). So right upfront, I'm not sure why God allows certain atrocities to happen. I'm not sure why the devil is given such a long leash. I'm going to ask about it, probably with my arms crossed and wings folded.

The Question of Evil has not been adequately answered by the greatest philosophers of history, and I probably won't be the one to crack the code on that either. Even if I did have some solid theology on why certain atrocities happen, I still doubt it would satisfy the victim of rape and abuse and slavery and oppression, no matter how much "logical sense" it makes to the brain. If I concluded, "All the bad stuff is really Satan," then a suffering person could only reply, *"So now what?"*

I can only offer a few thoughts that might help you on your journey here, because the perpetual tension of *Why-do-bad-things-happen* will never be resolved by any single answer. **Anything we say on pain will always be inadequate for the actual suffering person.** No such all-encompassing answer from any belief system really exists. I can only say that I believe the Christian perspective best *accommodates* the problems we see today. And please know, I would never, *ever* enumerate these reasons out loud the moment after a person has been seriously damaged. There's a time for that, but it's on their time-table and not mine.

1) Our current world is not the way it ought to be.

The Bible tells us that our world is fractured by sin. *Sin is not just disobedience against God and how we're made, but also a disconnection from the all-fulfilling love of God.*

We were all once perfectly aligned satellites to channel God's glory, but kicking out one satellite disrupted all the others like collapsing dominoes.[25] Ever since the Garden, we've tried to find God in things that are not God. That's how our internal disconnection manifests into external disobedience. In other words: a legitimate need to seek comfort can lead to alcohol addiction or codependency or a string of shallow one-night stands, because we're exiles looking for home.

We end up abusing people as "obstacles" and using people as "vehicles."[26] We build a kingdom of self because we're apart from our True King. We attempt fulfillment through stuff and people and experiences — and though not all our seeking is wrong, our methods get us burned. **We try to squeeze from people and things what only God can give us.** These expectations crush others and crush ourselves, and in a way, it crushes the heart of God. The elevation of self-satisfaction leads to an authoritarian tyranny of self that no one could possibly bear, including ourselves.

Sin not only causes problems between people, but also Personal issues (like vanity and insecurity and greed[27]) and Planet issues (which is why our earth doesn't function liked it's supposed to; even inanimate creation cries out for rescue[28]). At every level, *our whole world is shriveled by the disease we call sin.*

---

[25] Genesis 3:17-19
[26] "Paul Tripp Interview," http://vimeo.com/32163117
[27] Mark 7:20-23, Romans 7:21, Galatians 5:19-21
[28] Romans 8:19-22

From God's point of view, He's working with a world that is in every way completely disarrayed. It's like walking into a room where someone has flung paint and glass all over the place.[29] Where do you start cleaning up a spill like that? And beyond this, the Bible tells us there's a devil who exacerbates our struggle, so that we're getting mixed signals thrown into our already turbulent mess.[30]

Before we even talk about why God allows evil to happen, I hope we first confess that a part of the problem is *us*. The devil only pokes at our pre-existing selfishness. We marred the world with dirty paint; we chucked the shards of glass at God's creation. We're each accountable for our portion of the problem. If you think, "That's not fair, Adam and Eve started it!" — well, imagine you and me in that perfect Garden. How long before each of us would've done exactly what they did? Even if it took a million more years: we would've been the same exiles looking for home.

I know that knowing this won't be very helpful when a tsunami strikes Haiti, or in a courtroom waiting for a verdict on your son's murderer, or at the hospital bed with your wife for the tenth time. But the very reason you're upset about these things points to *the very heart of God Himself*, because you know that something is very wrong with everything.

As C.S. Lewis said, *"Nothing is yet in its true form."*[31]

---

[29] Inspired by Andy Stanley's message "Sea of Glass," http://northpoint.org/messages/starting-point-series/sea-of-glass
[30] 2 Timothy 2:26
[31] C.S. Lewis, *Till We Have Face: A Myth Retold* (FL: Harcourt, 1956, 1984) p. 305

2) If this world is not how it was meant to be, then not every pain is meant to be God teaching us a "lesson."

Since our world is broken apart from its original design, this also means that *God suffers with us when we suffer.* God doesn't stand by waiting for us to "get" some kind of epiphany. Very often, pain is just pain, and it sucks, and it doesn't need to be spiritualized.

When Jesus taught us to pray, "Your will be done on earth as it is in Heaven" — this implies that *God doesn't always get what He wants.* This might sound blasphemous to you, but this means **God is just as angry at injustice as you are.** He's looking at the human story with all the anguish of a single mother who lost her only child, with all the betrayal of a church's lying pastor, with all the hurt of a father who prays for his prodigal son.

I'm not sure if God purposefully leads us into bad situations. But I do know we're all walking through an irretrievable maelstrom of death and loss and permanent "gone-ness," and at every turn we are wading through an innumerable number of consequences that began in the Garden. God is working through this infinite number of misaligned imperfections in our universe to write (and re-write) His story the best He knows how. From His throne, I can't imagine how difficult His job must be to guide the best possible options for the human story while never infringing upon our free will.

When Job's friends try to tell him, "You got wrecked because you sinned," at the end God drops by in a storm and says all of Job's friends are wrong. God shuts down this business of connecting our hurt with some kind of "unconfessed sin." At the same time, God doesn't give a simple answer about life and pain and lessons. Probably because no human words could accurately resolve this tension between what is and what ought to be.

3) If God were to intervene every single time, there would be nothing left.

It does seem like God could step in at any time and stop evil.

I just wonder at what point God should do this. At the level of action? At the level of thought? Of atoms? Of free will? If God were to electrocute us every time we intended for evil, we would all burst into flames.

God allows our cycle of consequences to unroll, mostly because this is what makes us human. And even then, God does often relieve us by His grace over and over. That brings us to the next point.

4) God has probably saved us by an innumerable amount of close calls.

Whenever someone asks, "Why couldn't God have prevented this one?" — I always want to counter that God *has* prevented a lot of stuff, and that the world is not as bad as it possibly could be.

I can't count all the times I was almost into a car accident or was steered out of an explosive situation or found random help at the exact right time: and from God's point of view, we never thank Him for this stuff. We just explain it away as "coincidence" or "serendipity" or "good luck." An earthquake happens in the ocean and it's a "weather pattern." When it happens on land, we call it an atrocious oversight by God. But maybe this says more about us than God.

In the Book of Acts, the account of the early church, we find out that Peter and James are both arrested for their faith (Acts 12). James is immediately beheaded but Peter is kept alive. Try to imagine this happening in your church. "Did you hear? Pastor Peter and Deacon James were arrested for being Christians. James was killed and we don't know about Peter." Imagine James' family. They would be going crazy, asking God why He let James die, and perhaps secretly wondering why God let Peter live.

We never find out why. It feels cruel when you read the passage. God prevented Peter's death, but in some sense did not intervene for James. *Yet both actually could've died, because evil men were killing Christians by their own free will.* And when Peter and James were arrested, their church thought they were both pretty much dead. It's only a miracle that Peter actually lives, and I hope we can celebrate that. I hope we can see that God's gracious hand is still at work. It's definitely awful that James died; I never want to diminish that. But I also imagine the families of both Peter and James comforting each other throughout the whole ordeal, pressing each other on in faith.

5) God did send an ultimate provision to upturn evil.

Here's why I believe in Jesus.

Because at some point in human history, God became one of us and reversed the human condition. Just one place, at one time, in the dirtiest sand-swept stain of a city, He healed our entropy: and He invites us into that better story.

In the cross and resurrection: Jesus absorbed the cycle of human violence. He showed there was a better way than self-centered tyranny and retaliation. He paid the cost of sin on our behalf. He reversed the ultimate consequence of death from the first Garden by turning death backwards in a new Garden. He bestowed that same death-defeating power into those who believed his story. He identified with us by taking on all the harm of sin, though he never sinned himself. He promised us a union with Him by uniting us to the Spirit of God. He inaugurated a new kind of kingdom where the weak can win, the poor can succeed, and all our survival values are flipped into sacrifice. Jesus redefined what it meant to be human by creating an upside-down kingdom where the humble will be elevated and the prideful would be melted by love.

Jesus essentially stepped into the glass and re-did the paint. He went into the fragments and re-created the pieces. He doesn't answer why bad things happen, but he gives us a love stronger than all that does.

All this means that *a victim doesn't have to let their circumstances define who they are.* We don't have to let what happens here on earth to say who we are forever. While I don't know *why* God might "allow" these things to happen, I believe that God doesn't want these things to be the final word about us. I want to believe Genesis 50:20 is true, and that the devil has limits, and that even the worldwide permeation of sin is no match for the healing work of Christ.

A last note. If your friend is going through some horrible pain right now at the hands of another person, it's not our job to explain this within the box of our theology. That's a harsh thing to do. Jesus never did this: he only wept when he heard of Lazarus, he wept over Jerusalem, he stayed at the homes of lepers and demoniacs, he fed the hungry multitudes. More than our persuasion, our friends need *presence*. This is what God did when He became one of us, and this is how we embody love — by mourning when others mourn, by giving space to grieve, and by allowing joy to find its place at the right time.

2. If The World Is So Evil, Why Fight For Good?

"What's the point in living? There's going to be judgment day, the world's going to end anyway. ... If there is an end, everything we do would be useless ... Maybe one's purpose may be to make this world a better place. Forget it, the world's going to end. ... If I want to meet my Father in heaven, I can just kill myself and make my life much easier.

"I hate this world. Why can't I kill myself to go to this place? Why would I go to hell if I killed myself? Why am I working so hard to survive in this world? ... I'm sinful. I'm guilty. I'm not happy at all. I'm not grateful for being alive. ... Why should I live in a world that ruled by the devil? The prince of this world is the devil. Instead of living in the devil's world where I could get tempted and go through pain and suffering, I just want to leave this world. Wouldn't I be more happy in the heavenly world with my Father and Jesus with me?"

I've asked myself a lot of these same questions. I think all of us have. When I meet elderly people who come to Christian faith late in their lives, they always ask, "Why can't God just take me home now? I'm too old to be chasing Jesus."

I don't have the catch-all formula for this. Anything I say on this will be ultimately disappointing. But I do know that 1) God originally created the world in perfection, 2) the world now is not as it ought to be, and 3) the very fact that we can struggle with these things means we're alive, which means our lives have already launched into being, so we must choose.

When I say **"our lives have already launched,"** it's like when you begin playing a song or giving a public speech. You're now in the middle of it. You've started and now you must finish, and there's a constant tension of how it will end. But since it's been launched, you must choose to do something with it. So we can either give into pessimism, or numb ourselves with optimism, or keep some healthy balance of both.

Some days I'm overly optimistic. Other days I just want to yell, "Screw you people." **But every day, I choose to fight**. I fight evil, oppression, injustice, sin. I fight for happiness, for joy, for fellowship, for the things of God. Why? Some days I don't even know. It doesn't always feel worth it. Sometimes I choose the right thing and I get screwed over, and I see people do the wrong thing and get rewarded.

But given the current reality of our world and the fact that my life has already launched, I would rather fight on the side of good. I would rather know for me (at the very least, and for God at the most) that I'm giving life, not taking it, and that I used my life to give it away even when the odds were against me. That's ultimately and ironically how we find peace. By fighting for it.

I don't think "dying to go straight to Heaven" is a viable option. To be blunt, it's selfish. I don't want to quit in the middle of a song; I would rather finish badly than not finish at all. I believe there's work to be done here while I'm alive, and I want my friends and family to go with me when this story is done.

I also believe that God's final victory is the biggest hope for us, because this story has a happy ending. It means we're in the middle part of the story, and God has given us the free will to choose whether we want to be part of the happy ending or be part of the other side. If it's between the two, I don't want the other side.

I know that sounds trite right now, because it's such a churchy thing to say: but that doesn't make it less true. We live in the "Now/Not Yet," when God has already made all things good, but we have yet to see it complete. And at some point, we must resolve ourselves to be okay with that. Maybe this is not what you wanted to hear, but please pray about a renewed spirit to care again. You have a part in this story to heal your corner of the universe. You still have a life to give life. I pray that you do.

3. What About All Those People That Never Got A Chance With God?

"I have been raised in a Christian household & attended a Christian school my entire life. However, I only started taking my relationship "seriously" with God after graduating. Why did God choose *me* to know of Him and place me in my aforementioned environments? What about those who live life never knowing about God? Why doesn't God reach out to them? Since I know God, is it my duty to spread His Word? What about Catholics/Muslims etc.? Am I just blessed? But Isn't that unfair to the nonbelievers?! "

Hey my dear friend, thank you for your very sensitive gentle heart about this. As an Asian born in America, I know that I could've easily been a Buddhist in Korea or a Shintoist in Japan or a Confucianist in China. Or even a Communist or Marxist or Socialist. Or a tribal villager living on a Filipino island. Or one of those Tibetan monks in the mountains who only eats apricots and lives to 120.

This issue has always bothered me, as I found it rather disturbing that God would geopolitically confine Himself to one people-group for millions of years, and only recently branch out in the church era. Even then, I would think a "loving God" could offer every person an opportunity to hear about Him, at least once, if He truly loved us.

So let's consider a few things, some which we might disagree on, which is okay. This is only from my own limited understanding of doctrine, the church, and our culture.

1) We actually have no idea how God is reaching people in the world right now.

I think a Westernized Christianese churchgoer tends to assume that evangelism is a package deal in which we make a specific offer, and if someone "accepts Jesus in my heart," then it's a closed deal. Like this is the only way to go. This is very much a post-Enlightenment idea in which all information must be transmitted by systematic form, line by line, until we can regurgitate it verbatim.

Yet if we think Jesus can only be shared by the confines of human language, then our view of God is much, much too small.

While I'm 100% supportive of mission teams, evangelism, and preaching the Gospel as much as possible, I think we're limiting God when we box Him inside an academic Western checklist. The Bible makes clear that God can speak through dreams, circumstances, images, visions, and in one case, even an ass. We simply have no idea what our creative God can do with the limitless spectrum of people in this vast world.

Of course I don't rely on this to dismiss evangelism, and at the very least, our faith must contain words. But you've heard those stories of isolated tribal villages that have received dreams about Jesus and are now faithful Christians, without any contact from the outside world. It could be crazy, sure, but I don't ever want to downplay it either. And the only way to find out this happened is to visit them, and if you find out they don't know Jesus, then dear Christian: it's suddenly on you.

In the end, I would never put it past God to reveal Himself in an imaginative number of ways that do not fit our tiny paradigm.

2) It's difficult to determine whether a person has "enough knowledge" to "be saved."

I've always said that the Gospel is simple enough for the five year old and deep enough for the eighty-five year old. The criminal who hung next to Jesus was saved in the last minutes of his life; a man like Nicodemus who knew about God his whole life was more lost than the prostitutes and prodigal sons.

This must mean that someone who dies in a school shooting and calls out to his bare little knowledge of Jesus could be saved. A child in a tsunami or a person with Down syndrome or a man who's lost his memories could still, at some point, understand the Gospel and not merely be saved, but *safe*.

I don't mean to sugarcoat this whole thing and say that a tiny head-knowledge will work for everyone. I wouldn't bet my life on it. I just want us to ask: *How much faith is really enough to get saved? At what point must our lives prove what we really believe? Where is the cut-off for saving knowledge and how do we even determine that? Is there some point where our faith activates salvation? Or is our faith truly given by grace and more about the object of our faith than the amount?*

Romans 1 tells us that God shows Himself through everything, so that none are without Him. This could be a stretch, but I might even say that *God sees our faith by the grace He apportioned to each of us, so that we're each accountable for what we individually know*. A teacher who tests his students on untaught material is a bad teacher, and maybe I'm being too soft here: but I don't believe God is a bad teacher.

3) Not just anyone goes to Hell.

Prisons aren't built for people who don't believe in the police. They're built for criminals. I know this analogy is not perfect, but the concept of Hell is simply justice for those unrepentant people who've been a part of rape, genocide, oppression, slavery, and abuse. I'm sure it makes God sick to His stomach: but if He was not a God against injustice, then He wouldn't be loving at all.

4) Seriously, God chose you. Which is both good news and a wake-up call.

I believe that we must absolutely rejoice that God has called us. **If you're a Christian, I hope you never get over it.** The God of the universe knocked on the door of your heart and said hello, *to you*. This is nothing to be ashamed of or to be guilty over, because contrary to church culture, God *does* want us to feel good about some things. As if Christians need one more guilt-trip to be all somber and morbid on Sunday mornings. So be joyful that He chose you, my friend.

But also know: *Growing up in a "Christian environment" is not the blessing we think it is.* In the West, being a "Christian" is as easy as praying a scripted prayer or sitting in a pew one hour per week. In the East, being a Christian can usually get you killed in a variety of slow unpleasant ways. I've hardly ever met a lukewarm Eastern Christian: because their environment has already weeded out the uncommitted.

If we ever think, "Oh I'm so lucky to be a Christian in America" — we're not only disrespecting every other country and Christian in the world by assuming a better culture, but we're thinking too much of ourselves. Certainly there are advantages to our country, but there are so many slick subtle disadvantages: which are the most dangerous kind.

Trust me on this: Most Eastern Christians are appalled at our abuse of religious freedom in America, and would laugh to tears at the entertainment culture within Western church. I don't mean to sound like a superior snob here, but I'm saying: **being an American Christian is *more reason* to give, share, love, and talk about Jesus, because we have the freedom to do so.** I say this with all grace for you, but if you feel sorry for third-world people who might never attend church like you do, then that exposes a blinded arrogance and a wrong presumption about our "Christian nation." We must both rejoice in our faith and be humble in our fortune.

I'm saying this because I love you more, and not less. Before we weep for some concept of the faithless person in another country, we so-called lucky Christians must first weep for ourselves. Tears of joy, yes, and tears of grieving love for our neighbors who don't know Jesus.

4. How Do I Respond To My Friend's Suffering?

"How do you respond when someone says 'If God is good then why did my sister die, why does he let people suffer and why does he let all these bad things happen in the world?'"

You know, I've read tons of books on God's goodness — even one that was over 500 pages long — with tons of great arguments and stories and victories and apologetic defenses, and I always agree with all the points. I've heard great sermons about God being in control and I can "amen" them all day long.

But when the hard times roll in: all my ideas about the goodness of God fall flat on their face. When the trials come, my rock-solid theology evaporates. When life punches me in the gut, I double over and I don't get up for a long time.

In the face of real pain, life gets too messy for one-liners, tweet-able slogans, and well-meaning doctrine. Life *in the moment* tends to throw the Bible out the window.

If someone were to ask me, "If God is good then why did —?" ... I wouldn't even try to answer that one, because we're not looking for some kind of logical rationale.

I believe there are good answers, and I believe them most of the time, and we could sit down over coffee in our comfortable sweatpants in an air-conditioned room and discuss those reasons in calm collected voices: but when you experience the cancer, the car accident, and the phone call that changes everything, you're not hearing me about God's mysterious ways.

I say that not to avoid the question, but rather to confess: *I am completely inadequate to explain to you every part of God's Plan for your life.*

I don't know why God makes some of the author's choices that He does. Not every story ends with a musical. The Bible is the same way. We don't get to see all of God's reasons in this lifetime. Sometimes life just sucks, our hearts hurt, bad things happen, and *it's okay to be pissed off.*

Do you know who else is angry at our hurt? God is. Maybe that's no comfort to you, but God is *right there in your trial and He completely understands.*

This world is broken, fractured, fallen, and hostile. We live in a condition called and we feel the effects of it every day. God is angry *for* you. He hurts when you hurt. In the worst moment of your life, your Heavenly Dad is cradling you with all His grace available, even if you reject Him.

But: None of this is God's "Plan B." Somehow, God is sovereign and writing this story from beginning to end. God's not falling asleep at the control deck, and He's working all things together for a powerful, glorious good. I've heard Corrie ten Boom, a Holocaust survivor, say, *"God uses what He hates to achieve what He loves."* In other words: *God uses those Fridays at a bloody cross to bring about Sundays at an empty tomb.* I hope I'm not being too cute here. Yet if I can trust God on Friday, I'll trust Him to see it through until Sunday.

The most important thing here is that if your friend is hurting, to avoid listing the "Ten Reasons Why God Is Good." Please don't carpet-bombs with clichés to rush along the process of healing. Too many preachers do this too quickly, pack up their sermon notes, and hope that we can store this back-pocket theology for a rainy day — when all the while, the hurting congregation just needs someone to be engaged.

Your mission is to be in the flesh for your friend and to hurt right along with them. It's to get Romans 12:15 all over that.

Jesus did the same. He suffered what we suffer. He was crushed not only to exchange our sins for joy, but also to heal our hearts with a peace beyond our circumstances. He reminds us in his resurrection that this world is not our final home. And we're called to go to our friends with this kind of love, hope, patience, and wisdom — because it's enough.

When life gets hard, often the only thing I really have is this simple shred of belief that God is with me: that He came to rescue me from this broken body and is daily ushering His Kingdom into my weary soul. And God has blessed us with a community to reinforce His work in me. I'm continually overwhelmed by amazing friends who hear me vent and weep and hurt, who encourage me and cheer me on and cry with me, and I'm reminded of how Jesus made us His Body to experience such wholeness. It's this Body that points me to the simple presence of Jesus, which is just enough for one more step.

We're not short of reasonable theology for the goodness of God, but when it comes to the gritty ordeal of life — the best theology is you.

I consider that our present sufferings are not worth comparing with the glory that will be revealed in us.
— Romans 8:18

And we urge you, brothers, warn those who are idle, encourage the timid, help the weak, be patient with everyone.
— 1 Thessalonians 5:14

^{15} Instead, speaking the truth in love, we will in all things grow up into him who is the Head, that is, Christ. ^{6} From him the whole body, joined and held together by every supporting ligament, grows and builds itself up in love, as each part does its work.
— Ephesians 4:15-16

5. Does "Everything Happen For A Reason"?

"Hey, I'm not sure how to ask this but lately I've been wavering in my faith and trying to come back. But one thing I've been struggling with is the concept of 'everything happening for a reason.' What are your opinions concerning that? Also, what are your opinions on rape and who it occurs to and why?"

Hey there my dear friend. Thank you so much for your kind message.

You know, over the last few years, I've come around to no longer believe that "everything happens for a reason." I think it's a very cute proposition that might help us for a while, but it starts to fall apart when you read the news or there's an earthquake that kills millions or your friend is sexually abused or your dad has chronic pain for the rest of his life.

To pull lessons from these things minimizes our humanity.

If you talk to anyone who's involved in such a huge tragedy, you can't say those cute clichés like "Pain forces you to grow" or "God has a wonderful plan for your life."

I believe more and more that *not every pain has a lesson.* I think sometimes that pain is just pain, that life can be a mystery, and it's all part of our weird wild crazy human experience. Pain is part of being human. We don't need to spiritualize everything. We don't need to wrap things up with a bow-tie. Sometimes there is unresolved tension and we need to let it bleed.

However, here's why I believe in the Christian faith.

I believe in Jesus because his life means *God actually showed solidarity with us in our pain.* I know that doesn't solve pain right now. But when I'm hurting, I don't need a lecture or a connect-the-dots-theology. What I need is a friend who will stay with me side by side and hear my venting, embrace my shaking, love me through my slobbery flailing mess. I need a *presence* who both understands my pain but is just enough above it to lead me through it.

And if I believe the narrative of Jesus, then we have both a person who has been through what I've been through and a divine presence who can help pull me through the worst of it. Jesus on a cross showed an unresolved tension that bled — but Jesus out of a tomb showed there really is a bow-tie to this whole thing, a far-off nearly imperceptible light at the end of this tunnel.

Maybe we will find out the "reasons" one day for why everything happened. Maybe they will satisfy us, or not. But by then, the answers probably won't matter anymore. Because we'll be face to face with the God who was with us all along, the only one who never left us in our mess and who *truly understood us as we are, venting and angry and hurting and all,* and we'll find out He really did love us despite us, and He suffered infinitely more than we could ever bear to face on our own.

I hold onto this hope. It feels foolish some days: but on those days, it's all I have and all I need.

6. Optimism Vs. Pessimism Vs. Hope

"This may be a strange question-is it against God to be pessimistic? In light of the S. Korea ferry tragedy, I pray that more survivors are rescued. But deep down, I don't believe much more made it (although I hope I'm wrong). I feel bad for thinking this and I feel like I'm disrespecting God. Thoughts?"

Hey there my friend, first of all: thank you for caring about the South Korean ferry incident. I know that's been far removed now from our collective minds because it's no longer in the news, but I do appreciate you acknowledging them. I don't mean to sound snobby there, but we're just so quick to forget about tornadoes and tsunamis and Trayvon Martin and so we move on to the next trendy thing.

I believe the nuance of Christian faith calls us to realistically assess the brokenness of the world while *at the same time* knowing there is a better hope above our circumstances, a hope that we can experience in the middle of our tragedies between heaven and heartache. I don't think the Christian needs to pick one or the other — we reach for both.

Scripture gives us the mental weaponry to legitimately face off against evil, suffering, and sin, calling out the world as it really is: a fractured fallen place of entropy. So no Christian could ever be so optimistic that there is denial. Yet we're also called to persevere triumphantly amidst the mushroom cloud because nothing that happens on earth is the final word on our story. No Christian will ever be so pessimistic that they're hopeless. Nothing here gets to write the conclusion on our lives. You are never what happens to you.

Tragedy is very real, of course. For long seasons, it can knock us out of orbit and we will eat dust and tears. These are all the right responses. The prophets in the Old Testament were a sad dramatic bunch, and I'm not making fun at all. They tore their clothes and cursed at God and wore burlap sacks over their heads while screaming on street corners. It wasn't a pretty Oscar-worthy performance; we're talking straight maudlin vomiting from all the horror of the world. They were pessimistic a lot of the time, and they were right.

If you read Lamentations, written by Jeremiah, he's describing a war-torn Jerusalem. The streets are full of lawless riots. No one is burying their dead, so corpses litter the streets. Mothers are getting ready to eat their children. And in the middle of this massacre, in all the fuming wreckage, Jeremiah writes a remarkable passage:

[19] I remember my affliction and my wandering, the bitterness and the gall. [20] I well remember them, and my soul is downcast within me. [21] Yet this I call to mind and therefore I have hope: [22] Because of the Lord's great love we are not consumed, for his compassions never fail. [23] They are new every morning; great is your faithfulness.[24] I say to myself, "The Lord is my portion; therefore I will wait for him."

In other words, the Christian perspective is that *we are the most sorrowful and most joyful people of all.* We do not deny our humanness and we fully feel pain, yet we experience the highest of highs. We live within an unresolved tension by closing the loop where we can, bringing healing to the best of our ability, knowing that the door can close but that nothing is truly over yet.

I'll leave you with a quote here:

"Look at Jesus. He was perfect, right? And yet he goes around crying all the time. He is always weeping, a man of sorrows. Do you know why? Because he is perfect. Because when you are not all absorbed in yourself, you can feel the sadness of the world. And therefore, what you actually have is that the joy of the Lord happens inside the sorrow. It doesn't come after the sorrow. It doesn't come after the uncontrollable weeping. The weeping drives you into the joy, it enhances the joy, and then the joy enables you to actually feel your grief without its sinking you. In other words, you are finally emotionally healthy."[32]

— Timothy Keller

---

[32] Timothy Keller, *Walking With God Through Pain and Suffering* (New York: Dutton, 2013), 253.

7. Why Did God Make Me This Way?

"How do you stay confident in a good God when He has 'fearfully and wonderfully' made you with depression? I can't understand why He'd watch His kids live with chronic unbalanced neurochemicals that make them suicidal."

Hey dear friend, as a fellow lifelong fighter with depression, I think there are really two ways to look at this.

One is that God created everything in history, including death and disease and disasters, as a big ball of yarn that will one day be un-done by His glory. The other is that God created a perfect world of perfect yarn, but it became frayed when sin and death entered the picture and we now live within the stream of a disarrayed universe, which will be re-done by His glory. (If you're a doctrine-nerd, the first view is called "supralapsarianism" and the second is "infralapsarianism.")

The problem with the first view is that it assumes God is the author of evil and tragedy. The problem with the second view is that it assumes God is out of control somehow, as if He didn't see this coming. It's hard to reconcile either idea, and both of them have good points while bringing up tons of problematic questions.

For me: I'm sort of balancing it out right down the middle. I believe I wasn't made with depression. I don't think we were meant to be sick or starving or dead. And at the same time, I believe God is the author and He's totally in control. I don't know how both of these things can be true, but it's beyond me to understand. I live within the tension of a fallen imperfect world and a perfectly loving God.

What I won't do is moralize or spiritualize any of this to say that "pain is a lesson" or that God gives everyone a "wonderful plan for your life." I don't know why such evil exists. I think it scares some Christians to say "I don't know," but I can't pretend to draw lines between my depression and some epiphany. Our pain is going to be bad, and there's nothing else I can do but let it bleed sometimes and let it be part of our story.

I can be certain of one thing.

When I'm hurting, God is hurting with me. God is just as mad as you are about the pain in this world. He was so mad, in fact, that at one point in history in a sand-swept city of blood and retaliation, He entered our pain, side-by-side and face-to-face, and died for me. He suffered not only for us, but with us, and jump-started a healing in a tomb as a glimpse of the glory for where we're headed.

I can either believe all this pain is pointless, or that all this pain will one day be rectified and compensated. It's not easy to believe the better story. It feels crazy sometimes. I still have a lot of questions, and I'm going to ask Him every single one. But my hope is a future memory of everything set right by a glorious God who has already answered our hurt in a cross, and has healed every wound in a tomb.

The thing is, I do see glimpses of healing today. Even when my depression is so heavy I can hardly see, it's undeniable that knowing *I am loved* permanently by a cosmic constancy is the one thought that pulled me through another horrible day. The hurt was still there, but beauty was louder. His glory out-shines my suffering. Of course, I do believe that medicine is acceptable and we need community and counseling and therapy. Yet if I were completely healed today, I would still need to know what all this is for. I would still have to tap into the pulse of divinity to do something with my limited time on earth. And maybe some of that is to let other people know, *You're loved, no matter what's happening.* If you're hurting, I'll hurt, too. I'll do it for you, just as Jesus did it for us.

8. Why Don't We Care More About Persecuted Christians?

"Why isn't anything being done about ISIS? The Muslims I know are silent, & we're all just living our privileged little lives. As the days pass I feel more depressed & farther away from God. I cry to Him about it but I hear nothing & I'm afraid. And every time I see a cheerful Christian post about God keeping us safe, I feel bitterness and anger and I can feel my emotions slowly shutting down and I don't want that but it just hurts. So. Much."

My friend, honestly, your question very much stirred me and disturbed me and convicted me. It broke my heart.

Because I think I'm part of the problem. I post prayer requests about ISIS or some other atrocity or disaster or tragedy, and I question myself. *Am I doing this to show I care? Do I really care? Can I do more?* If there are 27 million slaves in the world and 26,000 children who die every day of preventable causes: how could I stay on this computer? *How could I even think about anything else?*

It's so discouraging. To be truthful, it keeps me up at night. I'm not saying that to boast. We live in a painfully broken world where even a single glance at it could eat us alive.

There's another layer to this guilt, too. Sometimes I think I use poor people as a prop for my own "savior-narrative." Or I become a pseudo-Social Justice Warrior, or I try to be a Google-Expert about statistics that I haven't double-checked. I donate money to various charities every month, but maybe even this is because I look around my home and I see wealth, and it disgusts me, and I donate out of a self-loathing heart. I want to boycott a billion different things, or say to everyone, "Your problems are dumb, because kids in Somalia are dying and there's still genocide in Iraq and 80% of the world lives on less than a dollar per day."

The more news I read, the more it kills me inside. The more I see mocked up selfies, and cute Christianese slogans on Instagram, or these theological debates that only theologians care about: the more I get angry, frustrated, hurt.

How can we break free from this cycle?

I have no simple solution for this. The only thing I can actually say here is that each of us, by God's grace, have a limited amount of resources and ability and knowledge, to do what we can, where we are, with reckless abandon. We cannot save everyone, nor can we fully "move the needle" on poverty and slavery and oppression, nor can we make even a small dent in all the injustice of the world.

But each of us have a part in our brief little time here on earth. Each of us participate in the divine nature, in the history of the universe, and each of us individuals are just the one endangered species of our own kind, who can do something in the world in such a unique way that no one else can do.

I think most of us will ignore that burning hot passion to do justice, and we'll go back to Facebook and our phones and our planners and laugh it up. And maybe we do that because we're afraid to face the horror. But I also believe that many of us are scared of our own ability, and that we actually *can* do something great, and we just don't want the responsibility of such God-given power. I believe we are more scared of the light than the dark, because it's so much harder and more terrifying to do good than evil.

My friend, I cannot rebuke everyone for their lack of sympathy. I can't yell on my platform to make others do something, or this will only be an external apparatus that forces behavioral change. I can only be changed by God myself and go do justice, and act justly. I can donate to churches abroad and pray for persecuted and raise awareness. And if God does call you to become involved at the government level or to be a missionary or to lead the charity efforts, then my friend, you are much braver than I, and I hope others such as myself will join you in every way that we can.

The hard part is not to get bitter or overwhelmed or to presume over others. But to simply do our part.

I pray you will receive this in a spirit of gentleness and love, because I want to encourage you and nothing else. You have a special burden in your heart for a certain people, and I pray you will find every way you can to be God's instrument for them, and that others might join in your wonderful journey.

Godspeed and God bless.

Chapter 5.5 —
Interlude: Around The Corner, A Second Wind

You've been in meltdown before, when the world felt unusually cruel and your insides collapsed and there weren't enough tears to cry through your heaving, convulsing sobs. Like the wind was uppercut out of your soul.

It's not pretty. Not like the movies. It's not dramatic or cathartic or ironic or Oscar-worthy — it's ugly, snot all over, face puckered in fifty places, bowled over with all kinds of noises spewing from your guts.

I was reading John 20, and Mary Magdalene was there too.

Now Mary stood outside the tomb crying.

I read this and grew horribly sad, imagining her hunched over and hopeless. Her world was punched through. I knew how she felt.

The man they called Savior, who had rebuked seven demons out of Mary and had been bathed by her family's precious perfume, was now just a cold lifeless body in an airtight tomb. Along with his body were the dreams of a different future.

Mary was demon-possessed: so she wasn't allowed to shop, marry, have friends, go to the Temple, or travel freely. She was one of those fringe losers on the edge of everyone's radar. Maybe Jesus would've changed all that: but they killed him on a dirty wooden cross.

Only — around the corner — something was happening.

The dream was not dead.

Mary turns to see two angels. They ask why she's crying. She laments over her Lord, whose body she thinks has been stolen. She doesn't understand yet.

She turns again and there is a gardener. He asks why she's crying. She thinks he knows where the body went. She doesn't understand yet.

Some of us live in this space — *we don't know yet*. We are sitting outside a broken dream weeping into our hands and watching the sand fall through tired fingers. It's gone. We can't possibly know how it will get better.

God understands this. It's partly why He sent His Son — to turn back the clock on every fallen grain of sand.

Jesus, in a miraculous meta-cosmic reversal, finished the sentence of humanity with his resurrection. Entropy died. Tragedies no longer defined the end. On the grandest scale, hope weaved itself into broken human hearts and we were revoked every reason to fear.

Then on the smaller scale: for Mary Magdalene, and for you and for me — we await the miracle around the corner.

We lost our dream in a garden once. But the gardener is here.

He is alive: and so now, are we.

It could be that nothing around you gets better. But He is there, extending grace within the swirling mess of a hostile world.

It could be that people around you don't change. But He is there, growing you to change when others do not.

It could be that you get stuck at that obstacle once more. But He is there, having already removed every obstacle between you and Him at the cross, empowering you for so much better than you think.

In your crushed swollen chest where the hurt pulls in: Christ comes to fill the broken places like so much water in cracked earth, new breath stretching your lungs, so we may thrive and bloom and stand on our shaking feet again.

Turn. He is there.

— J.S.

Because I live, you also will live.
— John 14:19

Chapter 6 —
Extreme Trauma:
Stressed, Depressed, and Stuck

Triumphant, inspirational preachers can inadvertently leave the destitute in the dust. When the Gospel sounds more like a pep talk for daily living instead of God's Rescue Mission From Sin, then those with lifelong trials are left wondering, *How could God ever understand me?*

I've seen the looks on faces of the abused, suffering, and physically wounded in the midst of churchgoers raising their hands in victory. The hurting are disconnected in their mourning; the church is ill-prepared for those in grief. The front row is singing and jumping and hooting with the disco ball and fog machine; the back row is somber, disillusioned, detached from it all.

They don't need another cheerleader rally. No clever words or cute slogans will speak to them. Only real talk about Jesus, who is both a holy sanctuary and a safe haven, will ever really reach.

The long arm of the Gospel convicts the comfortable and comforts the crippled.

All must be accounted for.

1. I'm Suicidal and I Just Hate Myself

"There are times where I just want to die, sometimes I just want to hurt myself, sometimes I curse myself, sometimes I cannot look straight in the mirror because I hate how I look, sometimes I call myself names so that I would never feel good about myself. I am a Christian and I tried so hard to tell this to my church-mates but no one really cared."

Dear beloved friend,

I totally applaud your bravery and honesty in writing this. As much as you might not hear this right now, please know you are loved, we care about you, and many of us have struggled with the same exact self-doubts. You're not alone, and I'm praying for you even now as I write this.

To feel this way does *not* make you a bad person. You have a worth and value and dignity apart from what you think about yourself, and certainly apart from what other people think. Though you might expect a Christian like me to say this, *the Creator absolutely loves you and wants you and cares for you*. I know we don't always feel that way, but it's no less true. God proved it on the cross.

I'm speaking from a place of understanding this more than you could know. I tried to kill myself ten years ago[33] and there was a season of self-harm that I thought would never end. I still struggle with depression and severe bouts of doubting God.

The one thing you need to know is that *this will pass*. It always does. The thick fog you feel right now might prevent you from seeing it, but *it won't always feel like this*. The clouds always part and the light breaks through, and it's our choice to look up.

Often for people like you and me, we believe a false narrative over our lives that we've rehearsed for a long time. Call it a *devil's script*. My

---

[33] http://jspark3000.tumblr.com/post/79502372694/ten-years-ago-i-swallowed-a-bottle-of-pills

false narrative is, "Everyone always leaves." This narrative is built on true things that actually happened, but I lay that on top of everything else.

So when I disagree with a friend, I assume the friendship is over and that something is wrong with me because "everyone always leaves." I misinterpret very harmless actions and become self-loathing because I've believed this narrative for so long.

Part of me wants to believe that *I suck* and *I'm no good* and *I deserve this* — because it's actually harder to believe that I'm loved, I'm accepted, and I'm on God's mind every second of everyday. I'd rather punish myself to make up for my own shortcomings because that feels measurable. It's so dang comfortable and familiar to stay inside the darkness of depression and self-hate, but so unpredictable to be within God's grace. It's so difficult to say out loud, *Jesus loves me, I am infinitely adored, I have a love I don't deserve.*

All this might sound corny to you, but the devil's script is one of the very reasons it sounds that way. It makes us feel like we can't be positive, that we can't smile, that we can't embrace our reflection, that we're not allowed to have joy — but the truth is, God is seeking for your happiness this very second. God has a better script.

My beautiful friend: **Eventually your season of darkness will pass, but please don't go into the next season with your eyes closed.** Don't fall for a false narrative by continuing to beat yourself up. Please don't let the lies of the enemy lodge into your heart. God has a plan for you, a purpose, a destiny, a handcrafted journey that is beyond anything you could dream of. Leave behind the imprisoning expectations. Expect to fail and fall, but look up, because Jesus is right there with you. If you can hold on to even a sliver of that truth, you'll keep moving forward, even if it's a simple stumble.

Please also be willing to get help. Find a mentor, counselor, an older brother or sister in Christ, and talk it out. Vent. Reconstruct your story. It's okay to find encouragement. It's okay to cry with a friend. If one person lets you down, give them another chance or try someone else. This won't go perfectly, but be proactive.

Don't let this be the only thing about you. Find a need and serve a need. Plug into a ministry that serves the least-of-these. You'll see some tough problems you've never seen before, and you'll be able to help those who feel what you feel.

Call someone and get a hamburger and Haagen Dazs. Rent from Redbox and scroll through #lolcats on Tumblr. Go to a church event, a Bible study, visit a new church. Try a dance class. Enjoy your one precious God-breathed life.

Finally, brothers, whatever is true, whatever is noble, whatever is right, whatever is pure, whatever is lovely, whatever is admirable—if anything is excellent or praiseworthy—think about such things.
— Philippians 4:8

2. About Cutting and Self-Harm

"Any advice for someone who suffers from Self Harm? Or a Christian that suffers from depression? It's so difficult talking to most Christians about these things because of the stigma attached to both situations but keeping it inside feels bad too."

First I want to say, I'm really sorry, because I know how much it sucks and also how bad the church has been about honestly approaching this issue. And believe it or not, I did go through a season of cutting before. I hardly ever bring this up because many people assume this is just an "entitled American problem," but belittling an issue doesn't make it any less real or hurtful.

Self-harm can boil down to a coping mechanism, a way of life, a release, a form of punishment, an outward expression of inner-loathing, or a relief.

I won't pretend to know all the psychology behind it, but on some level, people hurt themselves because it helps somehow. Otherwise we wouldn't do it. It's not the right kind of help, but it's trying to help *something*.

When someone verbally beats themselves up or goes down the spiral of self-condemnation or looks in a mirror with hatred and loathing — it's a comfortable place with familiar contours and a cozy sign on the door. It feels safe, even as it keeps destroying you.

The problem with self-harm, just like with porn or substances or shallow flings or impulse-buying or trophies or religion, is that *it doesn't work*. It doesn't cover the universal emptiness that we're all trying to fill.

And however you think you deserve it, you don't. However it makes you feel, it only relieves you in the moment. However you think it's an option, there is so much better and so much more. You and I know it's just not working, and you'll have to consider leaving behind that comfortable place and finding something else that does.

I don't believe any of this is your fault and it does *not* make you a bad person. It could just be that you haven't known another way. I wouldn't ever claim there's some easy process to quit, just like depression can be a lifelong battle. This will take time, effort, good mentoring, good friendships, and better options.

If your situation is making it worse, I know how tempting it is to run to the nearest release to take back control. But please believe me: it won't give you the control you want. A blade doesn't give, speak, feel, hear, heal, or understand.

The next time you're about to take up that blade, you'll have to make a conscious decision to tell yourself, *I know God loves me*. As corny as that is, even if you don't feel it, even if you don't want to believe it's true, even if every ounce of you is pushing it away, *please see yourself as God sees you.*

Just a glimpse. You are loved, God wants more for you, you are His child, you are co-heirs with Christ, you have been saved by the King of the Universe, you are friends with the Creator, you're redeemed by an unbreakable love, you are better than all this, you are made for more, and you *can set that thing down and walk away and step into a different sort of world you never thought possible.*

Today, just today, you can be free. And tomorrow, we'll worry about that when it comes. Each passing day, this can be farther and farther in your rear view before you know it.

I know things might be falling apart around you and maybe you're waiting on a miracle, but God Himself is working on that through *you.* Believe it.

That's not to pump you up or fill you with pep talk. That's to widen your vision a little. You're made to love God and love people. Find ways to do that. Go serve, get plugged in, find a need, go love. That's what you were designed to do.

And hey, it's totally okay if you go looking for encouragement. Go look for positive voices. Look for people who will build you up. Look for the one or two honest friends whom you can tell everything. Please seek a new safe place, where God's grace is present and overflowing.

3. Everything Is Killing Me

"How should I go about my life when self-pity, anger, jealousy, anxiety, depression, and severe stress-related health problems have taken over my life to the point where I am paralyzed inside my own home? I'd like to think that I believe in God, but I am beyond confused and I'm at the point where I am losing touch of reality."

You got to know I love you, so please hear me speaking in love here.

1) Seek help. Now.

If you haven't already, don't even for a second be embarrassed to find help. I know plenty of great Christians who get therapy, have prescriptions for antidepressants, and need recovery groups to get back to functional. Don't delay on investigating your options.

We live in a broken, sinful, fallen world, and often medicine helps align some of the chemical brokenness in our brains. I'm not okay with psychiatrists who hand out pills like candy, but no one should be ashamed to get that sort of help if they're desperate beyond reality.

I've struggled with depression and suicidal thoughts for as long as I can remember, and I've had great counselors and a great community to walk me through it. While ultimately they can't decide for me, nor can I depend on them so much that I push God to the fringes, it would be crazy to think I could've gotten better on my own.

There needs to be somewhat of a weaning process too — a counselor's goal should be to work themselves out of a job and get you functioning on your own — but relapses can happen and we shouldn't be afraid to pick up the phone in tougher moments. Whatever you have to do, find help.

2) Start telling people.

If they don't know already, you need to confess all this to your family, friends, and church. It doesn't matter if they ridicule you or reject you. Keep finding people and tell them what's up.

Of course, it's easy to turn that into the Pity-Party Show, so your motive must *absolutely* be to get better. It needs a direction. We can't use "honesty" as a permission slip to do worse, and some of us will find ourselves in a vicious cycle when friends pamper our every "mistake."

However this works for you, you'll need accountability. I know that sounds unfair, especially because in your current state, your friend's rebuke might hurt even more. But as hard as it is, self-pity and anger and all the things you're going through are *not* what God wants for you, and you'll need to talk through them regularly as they pop up. Your friends might point out that some of your issues also stem from idolatry, selfishness, a need for approval, or straight-up laziness.

Again I understand that's harsh where you're at right now, and I do empathize with everything that you feel. But you have a broad mix of concerns that will need both encouragement *and* rebuke. Please be willing to hear the love and the truth.

3) Fight for your joy.

If you want to feel sorry for yourself, then you will. If you want to get better, then you will.

I've had friends that dealt with schizophrenia and depression, and there's a huge difference in how they deal with it based on their attitudes. At times, I believed even if my friend didn't have schizophrenia, he still would've been weighed down by his bitter negativity. One of them would lose a job but bounce right back; the other would lose a job and blame everyone and play video games for a week while barely filling out applications.

You have to want to get better more than anything else you've ever wanted in your life. God wants you to get better too. I don't mean your performance or achievements or status. God wants you out of that pit so you can experience real joy. He loves you no matter what you choose, but He'd much rather you experience His love too.

I'm praying that you'll throw self-pity out the window. It can't make decisions for you. It's a liar. When you're up to the edge of that fountain full of true relief and happiness, then I hope you drink as much as you can. Splash in it, bask in it. You're so much closer to this breakthrough than you think. Everyone has access to this life-giving well to quench their thirst, but so often self-pity holds us back from risking the edge into joy. Please don't turn your back on it thinking somehow you don't deserve it. None of us do. It's God's freely given gift. And that's *more* reason to fight for it, and not less.

Once again, **effort is not legalism.** In other words, you're not earning God by trying harder. But we must choose to receive all He has for us. Maybe that doesn't make sense to you, so I'll say it like this. *God loves you. Believe it. Fight for it.* Whatever you have to do, believe that God loves you. Put that truth over your feelings. The healing will come. But so you must choose.

2 Peter 1:3-8

³ His divine power has given us everything we need for life and godliness through our knowledge of him who called us by his own glory and goodness. ⁴ Through these he has given us his very great and precious promises, so that through them you may participate in the divine nature and escape the corruption in the world caused by evil desires.

⁵ For this very reason, make every effort to add to your faith goodness; and to goodness, knowledge; ⁶ and to knowledge, self-control; and to self-control, perseverance; and to perseverance, godliness; ⁷ and to godliness, brotherly kindness; and to brotherly kindness, love. ⁸ For if you possess these qualities in increasing measure, they will keep you from being ineffective and unproductive in your knowledge of our Lord Jesus Christ.

4. Helping A Friend With Depression and Anxiety — What To Do and *Not* To Do

"Could you share some practical advice for the friends of those who are struggling with anxiety and depression? What should we do and what should we not do to best encourage our brother/sister during such dark seasons?"

A great question, and thank you for caring to ask. You're already an awesome friend for it. Thank you also for not diminishing the issue. Anxiety and depression are very real, not just "in your head," and can be completely debilitating.

Much of this will be common sense, but since I also struggle with depression, I have a bit of firsthand knowledge of being on the other side.

A huge disclaimer: This is a topic that spans so much bigger than my words will allow. I'm inadequate to cover every angle here. Much of the following is what worked for me, but is by no means a comprehensive treatment for you or your friend. It might help some but not others. No two people are afflicted the same way. There's no single scientific formula to fight this, and if even there was, we each require a unique approach that will not fit a simple diagram. I never want to make light of this issue, and nothing I say here is a "cure." I can only offer a battle plan.

Another huge disclaimer: If you sense that your friend is suicidal or extremely unstable, please intervene as quickly and gently as possible. While not all the signs are the same nor easily detectable, a few signs include: your friend gives away their possessions, they become more withdrawn and unwilling to talk about themselves, or they speak in tones of finality. If you're questioning whether to "give some space" or to move in closer, it's always better to move in closer. Please don't second-guess that one.

First, what not to do.

1) Please, no inspirational pick-me-up cliché lectures.

In fact, let's also skip the innocent sharing of Bible verses. Doing this at the wrong time can be so much more hurtful than helpful. When someone is anxious or depressed, there's a crazy-thick shell around their ears that deflects nearly everything, or will somehow reverse words into something worse.

Bring yourself. Bring silence. When Job got totally blown up and lost everything, the best thing his friends did (until they began to lecture him for thirty-something chapters) is sat with him in silence for a week.

Please do not jump immediately to spiritual, practical, biblical monologues. Please do not try to instantly relate and say, "Yeah that reminds me this one time when I also ..." Don't point to a website or a book or a doctor (there's a time for all those). It can be very insensitive and it's also a huge reason why Christians in particular look like robotic cheerleading machines.

2) Invite them out to something fun.

Most people who are Type-A "Fixer" personalities assume that when someone is hurting, then that's *all* they should talk about. Most Fixers presume that if they just dig enough, use surgical words, have a caring tone, and press persistently, then we can get to the "root of the issue" and be done with it like a math problem.

While part of this is very true and noble, an anxious or depressed person is *not* only composed of their issues. They're a whole person with likes, dislikes, wants, needs, dreams, hobbies, goals. They also sometimes just want to eat a burger, watch a dumb movie, replay a YouTube video, listen to loud music, lose at bowling, fall down at a skating rink, catch a frisbee, run a mile, or drink hot cocoa. Ask them: *If you could do anything right now, what do you want to do?* Then go do that with them.

Eventually you can get to the root stuff, but keep a holistic picture in mind. When I was at the bottom of depression, I didn't talk to the guy who kept poking at my hard heart. I opened up to the ones who brought me candy and their dog to my house. This is *not* shallow, because real human beings need a day off, even from their own brains.

3) Overjoyed cheerfulness to compensate does not help.

I've met some people who assume that an opposite attitude will lift someone out of anxiety and depression. So "confidence" can somehow counter an anxious attitude, or "super-cheerful-perkiness" can attack depression.

I understand the reasoning behind this, but in the long-term it's actually very painful. If you told me you wanted to cut yourself and I said, "There's a sale on belts at Saks!" — that's absolutely insensitive.

It's okay to get on the same wavelength even when you don't understand their pain. I learned a lot of great things from my psychology degree, but my biggest point of disagreement was that I was taught to remain distant, detached, and emotionless when I counsel. That doesn't help either. It's okay to cry together, to agree that life sucks sometimes, to feel their anger, to share their concerns. It will drain you a bit, but that's part of being a friend and a Christian servant.

Here's stuff to consider that you can do:

1) RTP — Rock The Prayer

When the time is right, pray for them on the spot. I know many of us say, "I'll be praying for you" and then we forget, so just pray for them right there. It might feel awkward, but most times people *do* want prayer and don't know how to ask. Some people feel selfish, often thinking, "Oh don't pray for little old me, there's bigger stuff out there." Take the initiative. Show them you care, now. You'll also be secretly teaching them how to pray.

2) Firmly speak truth that looks forward.

At some point, the truth has to be said. We cannot stay in Pamper/Coddle/Spoil mode forever. Let them know that even if they don't feel like it, they *cannot* stay crippled by their feelings forever. They're also not allowed to use you as a whining board for too long.

You know how when someone gets a cold, they act a bit sick even when they've recovered? I don't mean to say that anxiety and depression is the same way, but there has to be movement forward regardless of feelings. When someone ends up quitting school, their job, their family, their church, or any number of commitments, that's allowing the problem to win. When someone can keep going *despite* their feelings, then they have won another day. Help them towards that victory, a day at a time.

Sooner or later, they must move into a new season of their life, because life goes on. Anxiety and depression might be a lifelong struggle, but that's more reason to move forward and not less.

This can be tricky, because we want to be sensitive yet at the same time call out childish behavior. Don't enable anyone to go backwards into pity-party reflexes. This will require a lot of discernment, but please don't feel like you're being mean if you eventually have to pick them up with both hands.

3) Dig it out with heart surgery.

While clinical depression and diagnosed anxiety are formidable unreasonable beasts (see the next point), there are usually tangible reasons why someone is depressed or anxious. Let them know first that it's *not* a sin and it's *not* wrong to feel this way. But at the same time, there's also an elephant in the room (or a circus of elephants) that needs to be confronted, or else they will be paralyzed.

The best way to do "heart surgery" is to ask questions and to listen. Sometimes when things are said out loud, that's already halfway to a solution. It could be family stuff, a stressful lifestyle, a secret sin, a past trauma. It could be a lie they believe. Let them let it out.

Once you want to tell your friend to confront something, suggest the options. When someone lays out options for me instead of directing me with commands, I almost always figure it out myself. And when someone can figure it out on their own, they're more willing to follow through *and* believe in what they're doing.

4) You can always refer them.

Please never assume you're the only one who can help. I always appreciated it when my friends told me they didn't know how to speak to certain areas of my depression; I would rather they confess ignorance than make up a bunch of fluff. Sometimes we're in way over our heads. If it gets very, very bad, you can always suggest medical and professional help. Let them know there's nothing wrong with seeing a counselor. They can go to your pastor, an elder, a deacon, an older Christian brother or sister. I have my own counselor, and really, the world would be a much better place if we all got regular counseling. Nothing wrong with it *at all*.

Please do this with sensitivity, too. It might look like you're "passing them off," but remain available. I wouldn't suggest this as a first resort, but I know when I've met my limitations as a friend. I myself have been referred to other counselors as well.

If your friend agrees, tell them you can go with them for the first session or so, even if that means waiting outside. Maybe it won't work for them or it won't be the right counselor the first time, but that's okay. This is not a one-time thing. Persistence and patience.

5. Is Depression and Anxiety A Choice?

"A lot of hurting young people on my blog. Is depression and anxiety a choice? My pastor believes it is. 'Generational curses', 'biblical strongholds', etc. Thoughts?"

All right. I don't mean to bash your pastor here, but I'm flipping on the police lights and pulling him over and putting him in time-out in the booster chair with everyone else who's grossly misinformed about mental illness. I've been saving this one for a while, but *this is why we can't have the nice things*.

While someone might misuse the words "depression" or "anxiety," this does *not* mean that depression or anxiety are any less real or debilitating. There are some of us who live with a switch inside our hearts that flips up and says, "Now you're going to be depressed," for no reason. While some depression and anxiety probably is a choice, it's dangerous to say that all of us can just "will" ourselves into wellness.

This will sound mean, but most people who do not suffer from depression or anxiety just don't get it. It's like telling someone you have a migraine and they hand you a glass of water. You sort of want to punch their hand off.

Pseudo-biblical language that doesn't speak to reality only shortcuts a huge issue. You can tell me to "rebuke it in Jesus' name" all day long, but I need some actual help.

Let's get this part right. While not all our emotions point to legitimate choices, having feelings is *not* wrong. You're allowed to feel your feelings, all right? It's okay to be a human being and no one should ever blame you for that.

If you're denying your emotions, you're also denying your humanness. Even the spoiled little princess on the latest reality show gets a fair hearing on why she flipped a desk about getting the wrong-colored car (hint: it's not about the car, but her emptiness). What's important then is to examine *why this is happening* and how to react *in the moment.*

People go through different seasons and occasionally experience severe internal weather patterns that you don't just "choose" your way out of. We can't always "pray away" everything. There's no easy off-button for those cloudy emotional fogs that suddenly overtake you. A lot is at work here — upbringing, situations, spiritual warfare, personality — so blanket-answers will not help.

But for a moment, let's assume that depression and anxiety are "curses" or "strongholds" or whatever. *You still need to know how to battle it.* That's where this kind of thinking falls short. If I told a depressed person, "Just snap out of it" — that could work for a day, at most. If I told them, "Pray off that curse" or "Refuse the stronghold," that's not equipping anyone for the daily war of the heart.

I've had a lifelong struggle with depression, and can I tell you what works? Having a great community of friends who are there for me, who can handle my craziness, who still love me through my humiliating, whiny, ugly, slobbery, overdramatic bouts of unfiltered emotional explosion. And in the end, they're unafraid to speak the sobering truth.

I'm grateful for friends who sometimes force me to get dressed and get out of the house and get ice cream and love on me way beyond what I deserve. They sit next to me without lecturing me or throwing around verses or saying trite pick-me-ups. Jesus is the same way. He doesn't condescend when I'm depressed. He loves me right through it and meets me where I am.

What also works is just straight worship, and talking with Jesus out loud, and exercise, and re-listening to that one sermon that encouraged me so long ago, and serving in a place of broken people. To do what you're made to do will move you past the hurt, even if it's just one step.

The tough truth is that actually battling depression is a messy task of digging deep and getting dirty. That's why a lot of ministry workers use half-baked language to escape the gritty work of diving in the deep end. Almost no one naturally moves towards a depressed person because we think, "Well he's rich, he's good-looking, she's got it together, why would she cut herself, why would he be on meds" — and that's really a way of saying, "I'm too selfish to serve that person. I only serve people that are nice and clean and pure. I'm too lazy to understand."

The church is called to be *the safest, most gracious, loving place on the face of the earth.* No one should ever be shamed for their brokenness. No one can be left behind. No one's sin deserves more or less attention, and we all have equal access to the Heavenly Father by way of His Son.

It was Jesus who stepped into the mess without qualifying anyone, and he calls us to do the same. He didn't just tell us that our sin-broken condition is bad. He showed us a way out and a path forward towards him, to the greatest joy. If you can help someone make even a step in that journey, they will be grateful forever.

6. Fighting Off That Stress

"Hello! How are you doing? I wanna say, thanks for answering people's questions and concerns on here. I was wondering how you deal with stress. I've been more stressed lately than I have been in a while, and it's starting to affect me physically. I'm continuously praying because the effects are scaring me, and I've already set up a doctor's appointment. If you have any tips on dealing with stress and trusting God through it, I would appreciate it greatly. Thanks, and God bless!"

Thanks for the awesome question and for your very kind words.

You know, I've heard plenty of teaching on stress and I'm a Psych major, so mostly I hear the same thing. *"Are you stressed? Well, stop it."*

But I know that doesn't help. It also doesn't help to try that same technique on anger, lust, greed, jealousy, grief, or loneliness. It's like trying to stop a bus with your body weight.

The other thing I hear is, *"If you really knew the peace of Christ, you wouldn't be stressed out!"* I wish it was that simple. Even when Jesus and I are the most tight, I can still get anxious like crazy.

The thing is, stress is completely unavoidable. I think people tend to get stressed about getting stressed, as if somehow they "shouldn't be stressed if they're in Christ." But with all the demands, deadlines, and due dates of life, it's completely understandable that you'd feel an anxiety between *what needs to be done* and *what is not done.*

That's just life. Half the battle of fighting stress is to simply **anticipate** your bodily changes and to recognize what's happening. That's true with temptation, with conflict, with fear of the future. To be able to say, "Here it is. The pressure's on. My body is freaking out, right on time. I'm on to you." And then the other half of the battle is to move forward anyway.

There is plenty of practical stuff I could say here. You probably already know about —

- To-Do Lists
- to have some kind of a written planner
- to have a mentor or an understanding friend
- to find stress-relieving activities like exercise or drawing or skydiving or sword-fighting
- to prioritize your tasks with what's most time-sensitive (do stuff that's due soon now, don't do stuff now that's due later)
- to not look at tasks from left to right, but front to back (because a stack of dominos left to right will psychologically overwhelm you, but from front to back means you take care of things one at a time like a deck of cards)
- and to foster good habits like taking a scheduled break or jogging the same time everyday or using mouthwash (because good habits foster other good habits).

Yet even all these only reduce the stress. You'll still need to push forward with the task at hand. The cool thing though is that *very act* of starting your priorities will undo a lot of the anxiety, because **the human mind releases tension as it moves forward into tangible action.** That's a lot of fancy talk to say, *Start anywhere, but just start.*

About prayer: You're totally right to pray, and even "secular prayer" or a time of meditation is known to have positive effects on the body. But prayer, as we all know, is hardly a fix-all or genie or magical potion. That's not even the point of it.

What I would also pray about is asking God **"Why."** *Why am I doing this right now? Why is this so important to me? Why am I stressing out about this?*

I know that sounds overly existential, but I believe when you spend time with questions of *purpose*, you'll be able to 1) re-affirm your purpose in Christ to move forward with God's call on your life and 2) downgrade things that are *not* so important in your life.

There are tons of stuff we do that have no other point besides routine or indulgence or extra layers, which we could all cut from our life with little loss. Knowing where to say *no* will cut unnecessary stress.

To name some examples: Christians sometimes write daily in a journal, as if this is just as important as reading the Bible. But "journaling" is not for everyone, and if it stresses you out, don't do it. Sometimes we make a huge deal about making our bed perfect, or studying every scribble of lecture notes for the exam, or knowing someone's whereabouts at all times, or being a Nazi whenever someone is late to a meeting or praise team practice or worship service.

Prayer can help you sort through these things to see what's critical in light of eternity. The longer you spend in, *"Our Father, who is in Heaven, hallowed be your name—"* then the more your relationship with God and with people will take the main stage in your heart.

A last thing. As I said before, stress is often caused by seeing *what needs to be done* and seeing *what is not done*. So to close this gap, some of us become perfectionists. We become high-stress because of a need to make things perfect, even when we know it's killing us.

Then stress becomes a means to *conform reality to our desire*, as if stress will somehow bend things into shape. While there is such thing as "good stress" (called eustress in psychology), most likely we feel *distress*. There might be a death-grip for control that you'll need to let go of each day.

Let's accept some imperfection. **It's absolutely right to strive for your best, but we're called to trust God with the results.** When I let go of expecting perfect results, that actually cuts most of my anxiety immediately. It also allows me to love people for who they are instead of how I'm trying to mold them.

I had to remember too that all the results *are always in God's control*. Not were, not will be, not can be, but *are*. On one hand that's a little maddening, but on the other hand — I can relax.

I can stop trying to squeeze everything into my will. I can let go of stressing myself into a twitchy neurotic mess. I can repent from the hostility of being so controlling. If God is in control — and He is — then I don't have to be. Since He's good and all-knowing and He loves me, then when things go bad, He's still good, and He *will* work it out for my good. It does not mean I won't be stressed, but it *does* mean that no matter how stressed I am, He's still in control.

I'll throw you a prayer. Love you, my friend, and so does He.

7. I Feel Bad For Being An Introvert

- "Any tips on how to embrace my introversion and just be me? I've always felt misunderstood my whole life. I just want to be comfortable in my own skin without letting society's standards pressure me."

- "I'm starting college this fall and it seems the closer it gets, the more anxious I'm becoming. I'm an introverted person naturally but I want to be confident about making new friends. Even so, I end up doubting and convincing myself that everyone is just 'better' than me just because they are outgoing. I even get anxious that I didn't choose the college God wants me to go to, which is dumb. I want to have faith in his plan and become secure based on the fact that God loves me, but I feel stuck."

Hello fellow introverts. I'm glad we found each other.

You need to know first that God made you this way for a good reason, and you can trust Him on that one. As I've heard a pastor say, *God made you the way you are because He wanted to say something to the world that He couldn't say through anyone else.*

Some time ago, I wrote a post on introverts that unexpectedly went viral.[34] I honestly had little idea that so many felt the same way: hamstrung by over-thinking, taking a long time to process things, staying quiet in Bible studies and small groups, and feeling sort of ashamed about it all. I'm not really into labels, because they can force us into unlikely binary categories, but many, many people self-identify as introverted because they're not sure how else to explain themselves.

Unfortunately, churches and society at large have a tendency to applaud extroverts and be biased against introverts. It's bound to happen. Extroverts are seen as cheerful, passionate, go-getters, and friendly, while

---

[34] http://jsparkblog.com/2012/12/13/14-ways-to-handle-a-christian-introvert/
http://jspark3000.tumblr.com/post/37804515166/14-ways-to-handle-a-christian-introvert

an introvert will be called moody, depressed, emo, hermit, indecisive, lazy, lethargic, apathetic, uncaring, and the ever dreadful *shy*. But really, we're just misunderstood.

Over the years, I've come to accept my introversion as a part of God's design. I've come to see that introverts can do anything that extroverts can do too. We can be pastors, praise leaders, business owners, doctors, rock-stars, or the President. There's no magic-switch for any of this; we'll just go about it in different ways. An extrovert can use his connections and I'll just have to work hard. I'm stereotyping here, but this is seriously an extrovert's world.

My friends, all this is really a two-way street. On one hand I hope we can love on introverts a bit more and find that they need time to think, they need to rest longer, and they do want to share their brilliant thoughts when they're comfortable. On the other hand, introverts need to allow grace to bring out the best in us. The irony here is, *you'll have to overcome your introversion to explain your introversion.*

At some point you must open up to share what's going on inside. Please know that it takes a while for most people to understand how hard it is. You'll have to explain some of your habits. Every introvert is different, so you'll have to explain your particulars. But don't worry if someone doesn't understand right away. Be persistent and consistent about explaining yourself. *Explain your heart completely without letting anyone interrupt you or overpower you.* This is important. Please don't avoid this conversation, because you'll need to communicate like this your whole life. It hurts to be vulnerable, but that's why we have grace. We have the permanent unfailing constancy of Christ as our anchor.

If your friends or family reject you or ridicule you, it's fine. You tried and you can try again. Other Christians need to learn that God wires people very differently for His purposes, and this will be a chance for them and for you to see it.

You'll also need to sift through your own motives and recognize that introversion *cannot* be an excuse to cover your agenda. It's true that we take time to process things, but that can't be an excuse for laziness or inaction. It's true that we remain quiet in group settings, but that can't be an excuse to remain cynical and sour. We can't hide behind "dysfunction" to cover for crappy behavior.

As for gaining confidence: I feel like we set unfair standards on ourselves about what confidence really means. We see a macho muscular dude who appears so sure of himself and then we play the comparison-game — but we don't know what's going on in his mind, either. For all we know, this guy could be faking his grin or stuffing his shirt.

Have you considered just embracing your awkwardness and uncertainty? And then just making decisions anyway? I really don't know anyone who is 100% for-sure on anything, and I doubt *any* of us have waited for some confidence-bar to fill up all the way before making decisions. Not even the macho buff dude does that.

Maybe you don't know if this new person you just met will be your friend. Take the chance anyway. Maybe you don't know if this girl wants to have lunch with you. Take the chance anyway. Maybe you're scared to hit up that church event. Go anyway. You don't have to wait for the fear to subside.

Fear is often obliterated by the very act of deciding and doing. The more you can act in spite of yourself — you'll suddenly find that none of your worst fears are all that bad. The sky doesn't fall on you and your pants don't spontaneously disappear (if that's happened, I'm so sorry). *True confidence is just going for it anyway.* Emotions are a good fuel at best and unreliable at their worst. Your emotions are real, yes, but they can't determine your decisions. As determination wins, it gets easier every time.

Whether you fall on your face or not, *God loves you*, and no conditions apply. He sent His very own Son for you to cover your sin, to defeat the devil, to secure you back to God, and to give you daily grace for all your anxiety and afflictions. In Christ, God doesn't see your performance or the insecurity or the clumsiness or the doubt. He sees you wanting to come out to play, and He is graciously calling you forward to receive His joy and peace. So come out to play. Don't wait another minute on that.

Who God has called you to be is the you that you've been wanting to be all along.

"It comes the very moment you wake up each morning. All your wishes and hopes for the day rush at you like wild animals. And the first job each morning consists simply in shoving them all back; in listening to that other voice, taking that other point of view, letting that other larger, stronger, quieter life come flowing in. And so on, all day. Standing back from all your natural fussing and fretting; coming in out of the wind."[35]

— C.S. Lewis

---

[35] C.S. Lewis, *Mere Christianity* (New York: HarperCollins, 1952, 1980), p. 199

8. Overcoming The Constant Fear of Failure

" I've really been walking this submissive path in my life and it's this constant fear of failure. It seems that there are things that no matter how much I try, I keep failing and it seems to become an infectious disease to my self-esteem. I ask God for help but I feel like I'm asking a strange request that I don't even know where its coming from. It's been a silent cry for years as a young boy and I'm over it. I'm so tired of failing so often and I want God to help me end it."

You know, the fear of failure has been one of the most debilitating fears of my life.

I am constantly, *constantly* afraid to try new things, because I only like to do things I know I'm good at. If success is not a possibility, I make up some lame reason why I don't want to try.

I could probably tell you all kinds of wisdom like, "Go for it anyway" or "God is with you" or "If at first you don't succeed ..." — and while these are true, I know how scary it is. When you fail once, it crushes your soul to powder, and it makes every next attempt that much harder.

The only way I've learned how to personally deal with failure is to *stare defeat in the face and wrestle it to the very end.* This is different than just telling yourself "I'm a winner" or "I'm loved." This takes a little extra work, and it's worth it.

For me, when I totally fail a sermon, later that night I'll take out my notepad and write all the places I went wrong. I'll write all the missed opportunities, the awkward statements, why this or that didn't work, how I failed to tie it together and land the ending. It's just *brutal,* and it feels like I'm punishing myself.

But you know what? After I'm done, I feel a million pounds lighter. And suddenly I have a clear picture of what I want to do next time. I gain a little hope amidst the defeat, and I realize that *I can do better*. And even if I still feel terrible, at least I'm now *moving in a direction*.

You'll have your own process for this, whether it's writing it down or going on a walk or drawing a diagram or talking out loud. But however it happens, it's best not to skip this process.

Unfortunately what most people do is, they call everyone they know and look for validation in their failures, they text a million people fishing for a nice response, they blame their environment or other people or their sad-story or their busy schedule, they avoid or deny or whine or wallow — but there's no direction to any of this. *They haven't confronted what went wrong.* They're using friends as a sounding board instead of examining themselves first. They don't bring that stuff to God for healing.

We tend to beat ourselves up over some amorphous concept of low self-worth, so then we're defeated over being defeated. I want to be done with that.

Many of us also think *all* pain is *always* bad, but even if that were true, we still need to ride through the middle of it instead of avoiding it altogether. What I mean is, *if we're going to be hurt by the inevitable failures of life, I'd rather learn something than nothing. I'd rather move forwards than backwards*. Surprisingly, most people choose not to learn from it, which is like gaining XP in an RPG and then deliberately not saving your game.

I'm making this sound easier than it is, and I know it's a gut-wrenching ordeal. But life goes on, and so must we. Whether it's education or your job or your marriage or raising kids or heading a project: *We need to expect failure and be okay with the emotions that arise — and then not waste those failures, but use them to plan and prepare.*

We get better by being specific in our honesty, and then asking God for wisdom and grace on the next go-around. Otherwise, we'll go crazy turning ourselves inside-out. At some point, the self-confrontation also needs to end. When we get it on paper, it needs to be released. And we move forward. We can't stay in that place of evaluation too long, and even if we fail again, God has grace for that.

I have to add too: *I don't think the feeling of being an insecure little kid ever completely goes away.* The hesitation and uncertainty and awkwardness are rooted deeply, and I'd even say that people spend most of their adult lives compensating for the lost little twelve-year-old kid inside them. So you're not alone there. It's okay to feel like a big goober sometimes, and it keeps me humble. No matter how rich or buff or successful I get, I'm still a little boy who needs my Heavenly Father. I'm as dependent on God as I ever was and will be.

Search me, O God, and know my heart.
Test me and know my anxious thoughts.
See if there is any offensive way in me,
and lead me in the way everlasting.
— Psalm 139:23-24

9. Struggling With Loneliness: How Is God Enough?

- "In the book of Genesis, there's a verse where God said that it was not good for man to be alone so He will make a helper for him. I think this extends even beyond marriage to say that we were made to have close relationships in our lives. What's confusing is how this applies when we feel lonely? It's not all about us & what we want but, how do we cope with loneliness when we were made to have those close friendships to walk through life together but also know that God is all we truly need?"

- "Hi, I have struggled with loneliness for a very long time. God has been healing me but I still have problems with it. During my lonely times, I would listen to sermons, sing praise songs, or just do activities I enjoy but sometimes, I just get wrecked and end up sinning. I belong to a church and try to catch up with friends but because relationships are like revolving doors. They come and go, it doesn't really help. How can I trust God when I am an emotional wreck."

Hey there dear friends. Thank you for trusting me with such a huge important issue. I think it's very rare that we get to hear about a theology on loneliness and companionship, and while I know I can't possibly remedy all your concerns today, we can chip away a few layers of this together.

Please first know that *loneliness is part of who we are and it's not wrong or bad or sinful.* In other words, being lonely actually shows you're human, and not anything else.

To quote Timothy Keller, he says —

"Adam was not lonely because he was imperfect. Adam was lonely because he was perfect. Adam was lonely because he was like God, and therefore, since he was like

God, he had to have someone to love, someone to work with, someone to talk to, someone to share with. All of our other problems—our anger, our anxiety, our fear, our cowardice—arise out of sin and our imperfections. Loneliness is the one problem you have because you're made in the image of God."[36]

But of course, it's not just as simple as walking into a party or a college campus or a church and suddenly finding all you're looking for. Here are a few things to consider.

- Having a lot of people in your life doesn't guarantee you'll be any happier. You can constantly be where the action is but never actually make a connection.

- Intimacy requires an intentional effort. You probably saw this coming, but it's totally okay to put yourself out there and find people with a common ground and likes and interests. It might feel embarrassing to "look for friends," but it's absolutely okay to pray about finding some and then putting yourself in environments to meet them.

- Intimacy doesn't work with everyone. We're not obligated to be friends with every person we meet. Friendship is a privilege of trust and permission and healthy boundaries and shared joy.

- Some friends are for a season, and then they go. As painful as it is, friends can inevitably drift in distance or direction, and occasionally those friendships need to be let go. Some of your friends will be lifelong, but many others will have less of a place in your life as life goes on.

- *We're not meant to walk this spiritual life alone, as if being alone is some kind of "qualifier" for how much you're relying on*

---

[36] https://www.facebook.com/TimKellerNYC/posts/621239534582603

God. There are some of us who are convinced that being in solitude all the time is so righteous and godly and pure, but this is crazy and unbiblical. The love of God becomes so much more real when you're amidst other God-loving people who love you. It's why 1 John 4:12 says, *"No one has ever seen God; but if we love one another, God lives in us and his love is made complete in us."*

Of course codependency and people-pleasing and caving into unfair demands are all harmful. But it's also a bad idea to assume that our godliness is measured by how much we "de-idolize" people in our lives. To idolize anti-idolatry is still idolatry, and it's not healthy. God made us for face-to-face, eye-to-eye, chair-to-chair encounters with people, as much as we can.

- Try to know your own rhythms and whether you lean towards introversion or extroversion. I know that being an "introvert" or "extrovert" is not exactly a dichotomous clear-cut science, but it especially helps to know if you're an introvert who needs to recharge from people, or you're an extrovert who needs to make connections everyday. Extroverts will become more lonely more quickly, and will need to find the line where they're becoming too needy. Introverts will tend to push people away, so they'll need to find the line where being a snuggie-wearing hermit is getting a little weird.

- God has specifically put people in your life to love you, lead you, help you, and root for you. Many of us have our eyes closed to this, because we're looking for a cool attractive person to fall into our lap who meets our invisible standards. But it's also possible that God wants you to have real time with the 80 year old grandma in your church or the quirky professor or the older married couple or that one kid no one will talk to. Sometimes we're not really lonely, but our standards for companionship are too high and awfully shallow. We'd be surprised to encounter some very awesome people when we step out of our own safety.

- Friendship is not about fighting loneliness, but finding life.
Friends can't be about "filling a void." That's like eating cardboard when you're hungry. Friends are about sharing life and laughter and love together, and if you can correctly estimate both their limits and their needs, you'll be much healthier in how you interact with them and spend your alone-time as well.

- No matter what, intimacy with God is the priority.
There might be long stretches of time when you won't have a real connection with anyone, and it'll be painful. There might be seasons when people reject you or you're ridiculed or the rumors make you a pariah in your own town. You'll be misunderstood or ethnically in the "wrong" place or there will just be a secret dividing line between you and the inner-circle, for all kinds of unfair reasons. I've been there. It's almost unbearable. And it's these times I had to dig my heels in the ground and preach to myself that my dignity and identity cannot be wrapped up in other people. Because they're just people. It's crazy that I would even let human opinion dictate my own value. It's not that I dismissed them or got prideful or stuck up my nose: but I recognized that they're not my glory, that they do not have qualitative weight over my worth, and they cannot control how I feel about me. I was able to love them more but need them less. I was able to connect without being clingy. I was able to let go of friendship and validation as a pseudo-savior, and instead trust that God was my one unchanging constant.

We cannot expect our friends to die for our loneliness. They cannot be everything we need them to be all the time. But Jesus loved us enough to die, that he might be with us always, that he might meet all our needs. When you begin there, you'll have the strength to stand with friends and to stand alone: and you will find, you are never truly alone.

10. How God Heals
"How do you let God heal you?"

Hey there my wonderful friend. Before I even answer with a whole lot of functional details, may I just say that if you're going through anything right now, I got crazy love for you. Here's a prayer even as I'm writing this, and after too.

The thing about healing is that it hurts, sometimes even worse than the original wound. Most people think healing is just a "matter of time" or "don't bring it up," and while that's partially true, it also involves an active confrontation with yourself to get where you want to be. When a bone breaks, you set it. When you get scraped, you use peroxide or alcohol. When you get bruised, you endure an ice pack. I don't mean to take the metaphor too far, but if you only allow "time to heal," then you could end up with a mangled bone or an infection.

If you're talking about someone who has hurt you, then forgiveness will hurt even more. It's a daily process of letting go of what they did to you. It hurts because it'll feel like you're letting the person "get away with it" somehow — but without absorbing the pain and releasing the debt they incurred, then you let the person who hurt you to keep hurting you.

Forgiveness is *not* a one-time deal. Some days you'll have to forgive them a hundred times just to get through it without punching a wall. And that's okay. You can scream and cry it out and yell in your prayers. It's better than dancing around it. It's why Jesus says forgive as many as seventy times seven. He's talking about *one person* here.

God knows that forgiveness is not so much a gift for them, but a gift *for you*. It's not denying the sinful act that was done to you, but it's robbing that act of its power by saying, *"This will not define me or twist me or push me around. I will come out better in the end, not bitter."*

If you're talking about healing from self-loathing or sustained trauma or some bad choices (like a bad relationship), all these things feed off the same lie of self-condemnation. We easily fall into a false narrative of decreased worth based on what we've done or have gone through, as if some poor choices stick to us like tar and cooties. The lie is always, "I am what I've done" or "I am what's been done to me."

I know this lie is hard to shake, because maybe there was some responsibility in where we ended up. *But punishing yourself to pay off your own guilt can never work, and unless you've been violated against your will, denying any guilt at all is equally impractical.*

This means healing here will require both 1) owning up to your part (which unless you've been molested or robbed or jumped, you have a part), and 2) letting your heart rest in God's truth about you. Avoiding those things will only make you more prideful, more bitter, or more depressed.

Resting within the truth of Scripture is tougher than you think, because it means allowing God to contradict you. Since we're inclined to use our pain as an excuse to retaliate or escape, God will constantly try to revoke this from us. Part of His healing is to remove our "right" to be reactionary. I heard a pastor once say that true meditation on God's Word is *allow the Scripture to argue against every part of you that is antithetical to His truth.*[37]

In other words, **real healing begins when you scoop out the lies of your distorted thinking and replace them with God's truth about you.** This will hurt. But it's the only way to real freedom and peace and joy. Everyone will naturally resist this because it feels corny or intrusive, but more than that, it feels undeserved. When we're so comfortable with the dark, we squint at the possibility of things getting better in the light.

Yet God is so willing to rub the salt of His Word on your wounds so that you can wake up from your own self-loathing. He's the well of cool

---

[37] This is a paraphrase from a sermon by Timothy Keller.

water for your bruised tired hands. He's the only love who could fulfill you enough not to overreact to the pain. God really does want you to know that you are *not* what has happened to you nor what you've done. Jesus came to take your wounds into his own hands and feet, so that you may live. He did this for our final victory in eternity, but he also did this for you today, in this moment, so you may experience a foretaste of that wholeness. And God is going to move at your tempo, never rushing, because He knows that your healing will take a step at a time. So we must be willing to hold up those truths to our naked hurt, because healing begins with honesty.

> *The Lord is close to the brokenhearted*
> *and saves those who are crushed in spirit.*
> — Psalm 34:18

11. Why Did God Even Make Emotions?

"Hi! What role do my emotions have in my [spiritual] life? I know my emotions don't change who God is to me, or my responsibilities in living out my life for Him. However, when it comes to making decisions and daily living, it seems that emotions often get cast aside as a non-factor. God has made us to be emotional beings, yet how do we embrace our emotions without being naive or blinded by our feelings?"

This is a great question and I love your balanced approach. Let's start from the ground-up and see why God gave us these pesky colorful shades of feeling, and then see if we can draw some left-right boundaries.

1) Emotions subjectively point us to an objective reality.

If you are one of the four people who has read *The Abolition of Man*, then you'll remember C.S. Lewis describes how a sunset evokes a certain reaction. The same with a child's laugh, the screech of a chalkboard, the sight of blood, the smell of ice cream. Somehow, our experiences tell us that everything has its own value that stirs something in our soul.

Unfortunately, it's also the current trend to rip the value out of things so that nothing is really sacred or worthy of awe. Essentially we learn in school that stars are merely observable bodies of gas and people are just a fleshy globs of molecules, which isn't academically wrong, but it devalues the wonder of the world. Logic is a great thing until you're scorching the human heart into a wasteland.

Emotions harken back to an original design, where G-major makes sense with E-minor, where waterfalls enchant you, where two humans are not merely in transaction but sharing real life together. To ignore emotions is to ignore our humanity.

2) Emotions don't always make a great engine, but do make a good catalyst.

I remember learning in social psychology that emotions have a biological directive, much like pain: it tells us to move. When you put your hand on a stove, your body feels pain to prevent physical damage. It says, "Your flesh be burning."

Happiness says something is good; grief says not good; confusion says find answers; frustration says find another way; even depression is pushing you towards something better. God wired us with feelings for positive action.

In general, the principle is that emotions are not necessarily good motives nor purposes for any of your goals, but they can push the process along. If your only goal to get married is for total blissful happiness, you'll be even less happy, but it's definitely a good thing to fight for happiness in marriage everyday by doing what makes you happy together. It's a very fluid truth: at times we persevere in spite of our feelings, and other times our feelings remind us exactly why we persevere.

I've also noticed that usually *action* leads to *feelings,* so that if you just love on someone regardless of their response, you'll soon develop actual loving feelings towards them. These feelings will then be the catalyst for more action. It doesn't usually happen the other way around; I can't always muster enough feelings to go do things.

C.S. Lewis helps again here: *"Do not waste time bothering whether you 'love' your neighbor; act as if you did. As soon as we do this we find one of the great secrets. When you are behaving as if you loved someone, you will presently come to love him."*[38]

---

[38] C.S. Lewis, *Mere Christianity* ((New York: HarperCollins, 1952, 1980) p. 129

3) It's okay to feel your feelings. They can just happen.

This is where we get hung up the most. Feeling your feelings is *not* wrong and does not make you a bad person. The Bible is full of gritty, perverse, unglossy, non-Photoshopped people that complain, throw things, and never hestitate to make a slobbering scene by tearing their clothes and putting sackcloth on their heads. Read the book of Lamentations or any two of the Psalms — no one is "normal" in the Bible.

Some of us think if we're depressed, then something's wrong with us. That somehow anger, anxiety, or grief points to some horribly deep trauma — and while that can be true, it doesn't help to numb that with a bottle of pills or one-night stands or a pat on the back.

Nearly every life-stage is marked by some emotional change. People are just a raging bag of hormones, childhood trauma, mental dysfunctions, menopause, neurotic quirks, and mid-quarter-life-crises. In-between that are seasonal, monthly, weekly, daily, and hourly moods. We are all a mess and some of us are barely hanging on. We must take the good with the bad. The sooner we can embrace the insanity, the better we can tackle our haywire feelings.

4) Christians: It's also okay to be happy.

Some Christians think that "happiness" is wrong somehow, as if our entire emotional state of bliss can only be wrapped up in God and church and that twelve minute window when the praise team plays the latest generic song.

But if I ever win the Lottery, you know what I'm doing? I'm going to shake what God gave me hollering at the top of my lungs giving high fives to random strangers up and down the street. I'm taking those feelings all the way to the bank.

Inversely, if one of my family members passed away, I don't care how many times you say, "It'll be okay" — it's not okay. Let me be not-okay, okay? We don't need a billion people saying, "Be strong, keep your head up, look on the bright side." Sometimes I just want to say, "This sucks" and totally let God handle that one.

You can't help having some feelings, so instead of dismissing them, it's better to find healthy ways to handle them. A truly embraced anger says, *"I'm going to talk this out with God and a close friend and a mentor and be honest about my craziness and see what I actually want."* Which brings us to the last point.

5) God has a plan for your emotions.

God ultimately made emotions because it's what makes us entirely human. We get to feel the whole spectrum of every intense passion in the world. The hottest volcano churning out molten lava doesn't compare to a spouse scorned.

The trick is not really to harness all your emotions and dumb them down, but to red-line them the right direction. God has a plan for that.

We all know the person who follows their feelings way too much with zero thought, like when someone thinks every cute face is instant marriage material. The emotion itself is not wrong, but God wants to take us somewhere good with them: and it's not going to be towards every attractive person in a five foot radius.

King David is the perfect example of both right and wrong emotional tides. On one hand, he feels so much respect for Saul, who's trying to kill him, that David doesn't touch him when he's given the chance. On the other hand, David sees Bathsheba naked on a roof and has her baby, tries to pin it on her husband, and then kills the husband.

Since we're in that condition called sin, sometimes we work through our emotions in illegitimate ways (that's putting it mildly for David). So instead of working rightly through our anger by honesty and prayer and healthy counseling, we tend to numb all that in drugs or "vent" it by fighting and throwing fits. Instead of divinely designating our sexual urges into the God-ordained plan of marriage, we can get carried away by our lust into empty, meaningless flings.

The best I can tell you here is to be thankful you feel anything, to bring those feelings to God in total honesty, and remember that feelings do not always determine truth but they can sometimes tell you what's true. You are *not* your feelings, but they're still a part of you. We prioritize truth over what we feel, but part of the truth *is* the emotional element, and we can surrender both sides of that to God's authority.

You might be surprised how often God will say, "I feel you on that one, too. My Son knows everything you're going through, and He's right alongside you."

"Don't bother much about your feelings. When they are humble, loving, brave, give thanks for them: when they are conceited, selfish, cowardly, ask to have them altered. In neither case are they you, *but only a thing that happens to you. What matters is your intentions and your behavior."*[39]

— C.S. Lewis

---

[39] C.S. Lewis, *The Collected Letters of C.S. Lewis, Volume III* (NY: HarperCollins, 1950-1963, 2007) p. 127

12. Four Thoughts on Finding God's Will

"How do you know if what you're doing is part of God's plan? How am I supposed to know I'm doing the right thing? I just applied for an internship for my favorite company and I'm anxious. Will I get it? Do I simply wait and trust God? Does He approve of it? If not, then how do I know I'm even in the right direction? I can't tell/feel the difference between making my own decisions and making the ones based on God's will."

Finding God's Will is the church's Holy Grail, and our obsession with "hearing from God" gets us to some weird places.

This over-complicated sort of magical approach doesn't begin to answer the questions you posed. What if there needs to be a snap decision and we can't survey the entire Bible on the spot? How do we know it's the Holy Spirit and not our own voice? How do we interpret "signs" and circumstances? What if we come between two impossible decisions? What if both are equally good, or equally bad?

While we could ponder forever on these things, let's consider some thoughts on His Will.

1) God's Will is not necessarily about predicting the future, but about the person you're becoming.

While it's tougher to discern "God's Plan," which is His sovereign will, we have His commands, which are His moral will.[40]

You've probably read Psalm 37:4 before, which says

Delight yourself in the Lord and he will give you the desires of your heart.

---

[40] Inspired by James MacDonald's teaching, "The Way of Wisdom."

Preachers often misinterpret this to say, "If I enjoy God, He'll give me what I want!" But actually it means *if* you're delighting yourself in God, He will implant in you *His own desires.* Try reading it one more time.

When you are pursuing God, your heart will begin to default to Him. To make it simpler: If you follow God's moral will (His Law) you can be sure you're following God's sovereign will (His Plan). If you are becoming the True Self that God has called you to be, then **out of who you're *becoming* will emerge the *doing*.**

You build a momentum as you follow Jesus, however imperfectly. So if you have an important decision coming up, try to see *what is most consistent with your momentum in Him.*

This is actually easier than you think. Pick the internship that will be an opportunity to grow and fulfill His mission. Pick the campus where God can best work through you. If you have two equally good choices, pick the one you like. If you have no good choices, wait. Simply ask God, *Why this place? Why me, here? Is this truly me?* God has an answer.

2) God's Will is not always comfortable.

I hear Christians in a circle say, "I felt peace about that." But I've never understood what this means. A peace where the stars aligned? A peace in my storm? A peace that feels warm and fuzzy inside?

I actually heard of a pastor who kicked out his wife and shacked up with his secretary, all while saying, "I felt peace about that." I mean dude, sometimes God's Will is common sense.

First Peter 4:12 reads,

Dear friends, do not be surprised at the painful trial you are suffering, as though something strange were happening to you.

We should expect that following Jesus means we lose some friends and to be ridiculed and rejected. I don't mean to go after a "poverty gospel" — but if you love Jesus, it won't be rainbows and puppies.

Following God's Will isn't always a romantic brochure. Serving the homeless and being a missionary in Africa are awesome, but not always pretty. So the *real peace* is knowing you're the real thing, that you're giving your all to Christ, that you're giving your life away despite what's happening around you.

3) Look for good mentors who will guide you.

In addition to Scripture and the leading of the Holy Spirit, seek godly Christ-centered people who are *already chasing after God* and ask for their wisdom. It doesn't have to be, "Hey you, mentor me." Just ask questions. Tons of wonderful, annoying, curious questions.

Good mentors will cast big visions for you, always saying, *You can do this. God will do big things in you.* And if you mess it up, they will be there to say, *You're better than this, so let's get up and go again.*

4) The Holy Spirit doesn't always "speak," but He confirms in hindsight.

A lot of us expect God reveals His plan in neon lights the second we pray. But God knows we are time-bound creatures who learn by experience, so God's Will is often confirmed in hindsight.

Usually the Spirit guides *as we are already moving.* Galatians 5:25 says "let us keep in step with the Spirit" — and doesn't say that God will make a yellow brick road.

So if you get started on a path and you discover you're not wired for it, **it's okay to move onto something else.** It's okay to try a few things until you find the right thing. Sometimes finding God's Will also means finding what is *not* God's Will. This doesn't mean you can just experiment everywhere, which is why Scripture and mentors are important.

The Spirit is most likely not going to be an audible voice and won't be writing on a wall by a glowing hand. Usually you know it's Him during or after the moment is over.

Notice in Acts 18 that the Ephesians ask Paul to stay, and he replies, "I will come back if it is God's will." He sails to other places to preach, but eventually comes back to Ephesus and stays for three years. The way I see it, Paul felt funny about leaving the Ephesians so he came back. That funny feeling was most likely the Spirit's prompting.

This happened to Paul quite a lot — and it will to you, too. Was Paul 100% sure? Maybe. But he was 100% sure *he was called to share Jesus,* and 100% sure *in hindsight* that the city of Ephesus had a great need.

I've known friends who went to medical school and hated it, so they quit. They had so much guilt about quitting. A lot of the guilt was from parents and self-doubt, which I understand — but they had to learn it was okay to quit med school *after* they went to med school. They are happier now doing what God has actually wired them to do.

I hope I haven't exploded your head by now. Simply remember that just as your parents or mentors or counselors have given you an *inner-voice* of wisdom, then as you saturate yourself in the Word and fully press into the Gospel, the Spirit will be your biggest voice. And unlike anyone else, the Spirit is perfectly good, perfectly righteous, and perfectly rooting for you.

Chapter 6.5 —
Interlude: Mistakes Don't Say Everything About You, And It's Okay To Make Them

At times we can be so suffocated by the mistakes we've made that we think we're too incompetent to get any better.

There's a terrible whisper in our ear: *You're just not good enough at this. You're not smart like those other people. You'll always screw this up.*

Or you might have had a certain picture of your life by now, but you've somehow irreversibly ruined it all and you're picking up the pieces of a dead dream. You see your friends further along in life with less effort and you wonder when you'll ever get it together. You thought the new improved "you" would happen any time now, but "any time now" was five years ago.

My dear beloved friend:

- No one is really as confident as they let on. Most of the macho bravado you see in the streets and the business world is just a false pumped-up cover that consumes more energy than it creates. I don't mean to compare and demonize, because God grieves for them too. But this is *not* sustainable, because confidence doesn't come from covering a lack of one.

- No one really has it all together yet. We force so many self-pressuring parameters on our performance that most of us are neurotic, twitchy, over-productive busybodies with no real destination. In a culture where we celebrate only victory and are scared to talk about defeat: please don't measure yourself on an impossible grading scale. Don't measure your private moments with everyone else's highlight reels.

- **Mistakes are how you learn.** Everyone is afraid of failure: so we protect ourselves by bargaining with the teacher or begging for extensions or ensuring we never get a scraped knee. Such a pampered coddled culture will keep you feeling safe for a while, but it'll also keep you sterile, shrink-wrapped, and cold. It's a lifeless journey. *It's okay to make mistakes, and occasionally it's even better.* Scrape a knee, brush it off, get up and move on. Learn from the past and laugh with it too.

- **You're doing better than you think.** You're in the middle of your motion, so it's hard to see where you are. But so long as you've been taking one heavy step forward after another, no matter how awkward your stumbling, *then this is worth celebrating.* Every moment you've done right is a miracle in itself.

- **Be willing to pursue a new dream.** Sometimes we try so hard to grab our old dreams that we're not open to new ones. We look too long in the rearview instead of what's ahead of us. I've missed a lot of opportunities this way. But keep your eyes open for open doors, and be flexible enough for a new vision that will be even better than the last.

- **Dear Christian: Your confidence is in Him. We are works in progress looking towards the work finished, Jesus.** We believe in a God who *knew we couldn't ever reach perfection, so perfection came to us.* If you feel like you've failed today, the very reason Jesus came was to take on your failures, your ego, your pride, your pain, your sorrows, your sin. And He'll keep working on you until glory. Everything good in you is God in you: and anything bad in you, He's working on that.

This is His grace.

— J.S.

*"Be confident of this,
that he who began a good work in you
will carry it unto completion
until the day of Christ Jesus."*

— Philippians 1:6

Chapter 6 and ¾ —
Forgetting How To Be, Reclaiming How To Breathe

I met with my counselor the other day, a semi-famous mega-church pastor here in town, and I had really forgotten what it's like to be around someone who is so comfortable with himself that it made *me* comfortable with myself.

My counselor is one of those cool pastors who smokes cigars and uses dirty words and he used to be a rich drug dealer, so he owns this huge house and hosts these extravagant church parties with hundreds of curious people looking for real spirituality. He does this without even really trying to impress anyone, and with sort of a wink. Once I was leaving his office after a meet and he yells down the hallway of his church, "I'll keep praying about your porn problem." The very conservative staff glanced at me and I ran and he couldn't stop laughing. My counselor reminds me of Jesus.

So I told him everything. How I blew up on someone the other day. How I was juggling multiple ministries plus a growing blog. How dissatisfied I was with the mainstream church. How I haven't talked to my dad in over a year. How I was fighting anger and unforgiveness and lust. How I always felt like I was pouring out of an empty cup, and that the same grace I preached for others was almost never reserved for myself.

I told him I had this monster inside me, barely underneath the surface just coiled around my guts, and just when I thought I was making "Christian progress" and it was dead, it would lash out and destroy everything I love and then go right back to hiding. I wanted this thing inside me to really, truly, eternally die.

Then he looks at me and says, "You're not really walking with God." I was almost offended. But he was right. He went on.

"You're doing so much, just *do,* and you lost who you are. You find who you are, then you can do again."

"So what do I do now?" As soon as I said it, I heard it. I said "do" again.

He said, "Pray. I mean we're both in ministry, you already know that. But you see how we're talking? How you can tell me anything? How I can just be me around you? That's prayer. Praying is like breathing. It's a way of life that can happen all the time. That's walking with Him."

I think I was trying not to weep. I remember when it was like that, when I felt like I was walking with Him all the time. When being with God was like breathing. I did want that again. And it was not a matter of doing, but being.

He said, "It's okay to pour out when you're empty. You can't do that for a long time, but that's grace. You can preach grace all day and be a legalist to yourself. Quit listening to yourself and listen to Him. And don't preach too far ahead of yourself. If it's been hard, then preach that it's been hard."

We hugged for a long time. He told me he loved me. Before we parted, he said, "I wish I could tear that monster out of you. Let God inside, and He will."

—J.S.

Chapter 7 —
Heaven, Hell, Heresies, and The Hairy Mess of Religious Objections

I skip the hard stuff that Jesus says. I pretty up Jesus to make him more convincing because I don't think he's enough on his own.

I do this because I'm scared, I'm nervous what you'll think about him — and I have this other idea of God that will go down smoother to answer all your doubts and concerns.

Doesn't this make me a liar? Or disingenuous? Or a magician? Or a bad movie trailer?

I end up saying, "Jesus is actually saying —" and then go into a detailed explanation of the Greek to gloss over the really hard things he said.

We don't like to wince. We cringe at the tough stuff that doesn't mesh with our modern Western sensibilities. We are *sure* that Jesus meant something else. So we dress him up, decorate his words, and exegete the edge off him.

In Matthew 13, when Jesus says what he'll do to evil people — he'll *"throw them into the blazing furnace, where there will be weeping and gnashing of teeth"* — I fail to see how this is a gentle, generous, by-golly Jesus who gives free hugs and high fives.

In Luke 12, when Jesus says what the master will do to the wicked servant — *"He will cut him to pieces and assign him a place with the unbelievers"* — I can't turn this around by saying, "Jesus is *really* saying, 'I will never stop loving you.'"

In John 6, Jesus preaches a sermon so hardcore that every single follower except the appointed twelve end up leaving him. Jesus asks the remaining dozen, *"Do you want to leave too?"* I don't see this in any church growth books or discipleship workshops.

In Matthew 10, Jesus says plainly with zero disclaimers: *"I did not come to bring peace, but a sword. For I have come to turn a man against his father, a daughter against her mother, a daughter-in-law against her mother-in-law — a man's enemies will be the members of his own household."* I don't see a hidden meaning in this passage. He said what he meant; he meant what he said.

If you've ever really read the Sermon on the Mount, it's absolutely horrifying.[41] Whether you believe Jesus was real or not, it completely clashes against all our notions of a sheep-petting, halo-wearing, perfect-teeth Jesus.

Can we try to let Jesus speak for himself?

I know that Jesus was absolutely loving to the outcast, the poor, the children, the foreigners, the women, the demon-possessed, the disabled — but are we really skipping all these other parts? He had some hard words for the Pharisees, the teachers, the rich young ruler, and that guy who wanted to bury his dad at a funeral.

I'm not sure if I can keep neutering Jesus like this and still be called a "follower of Christ." What I'm following then is God in my own image. I'm doing both a disservice to Him *and* to you.

There are certainly many things that Jesus said which I don't understand, which I find unpleasant, which tickle my teeth and turn my guts upside-down.

But if he really does love us, he's going to say the hard truth. **Part of love is being truthful, or you're not being loving.** At some point, Jesus pushed up against human sensitivity and ran right through our polite, politically correct paradigms.

---

[41] Virginia Stem Owens, "God and Man at Texas A&M." Reformed Journal 37, no. 11 (1987), p. 3—4. Professor Owens talks about assigning an English essay to college Freshmen about the Sermon on the Mount, expecting a "nodding acquaintance" or "modicum of piety." But to her surprise, the responses were largely anger and hostile dismissal. Timothy Keller also references this article in his message "On The Mountain: The Terrifying and Beckoning God," which you can find here: http://vimeo.com/45466899

Truth is never easy to hear. That's why it's called truth. And that's why it sets us free.

If I were the Son of God and I knew *there was really a place called hell,* then I'd be like one of those scientists in a disaster movie who warns everyone about the impending doom. I wouldn't hesitate to mention the terrible tragedy that's headed for us — and Jesus did the same.

If I were a disciple recording the events of Jesus's life, I wouldn't spare time trying to make the truth-pill go down easy. If Jesus died and rose again for us but never said a nice thing, *he has still proven he loves us by going to a cross and inviting us to eternal life.*

If someone died for me while saying a few tough words, I'm not going to whine about the tough words. I just don't want to chop up the words of *my Friend and King* for the sake of making him look consumer-friendly. I'm not saying we need to be offensive or shocking or colorful about this — but I just don't want to water down my Savior into someone who can't save.

He does love us. So much that he didn't hold back, not once.

I want to let Jesus speak. He is better at it than we are.

"I want God, not my idea of God."[42]
— C.S. Lewis

---

[42] C.S. Lewis, *A Grief Observed* (New York: HarperCollins, 1961, 1989), pp. 78-79
This quote is a famous paraphrase pulled together from several resources. The original quote is, " My idea of God is not a divine idea. It has to be shattered time after time. He shatters it Himself. He is the great iconoclast ... I must stretch out the arms and hands of love—its eyes cannot here be used—to the reality, through—across—all the changeful phantasmagoria of my thoughts, passions, and imaginings ... Not my idea of God, but God."

1. God Seems A Little Crazy In The Old Testament

"Hi, I really love your blog and I love your take on different issues. I'm wondering if you can help me. I have a very intelligent, seeking friend who spends his time learning about different cultures, demographics and religions. He just sent me Genesis 11 and pointed out that God brings division to humanity, and through it war, racism, and other kinds of oppression. I really don't know what to say because that's a really valid point, and I've always been huge on God bringing justice and love."

Thank you for your kind words and for trusting me with this issue. It's a tough one — and you're not the only one who thinks so.

I think deep inside, every single Christian in the world has an unresolved tension with the Old Testament. If the OT were a dinner guest, we'd all be staring at her from across the room as she flips furniture and tells wild stories and eats the entire martini glass. She's kind of hot, but she's also a tad bit crazy.

I don't mean to sound blasphemous, but really, with all these Christian books trying to reconcile the "gracious fairy God" with the "OT monster God," it sounds like we're just apologizing for God all the time. Does He really need all this watered down press? Does He need better public relations? Can we really tame the God of the Bible?

Because if God is really God, then He can do whatever He dang well wants. Fortunately for us, God is "bound" by His very own nature, just as a father or mother is bound to their family. So however you assume God works, you'll see His actions as immediately bad or investing in the good. What I mean is, *God must either be gloriously good or reprehensibly evil,* and wherever you begin with your view of God, you will end up in a place of either peace or suspicion. You'll either see God as a vengeful, mustache-twirling, cartoon villain, or a gracious, grieving, patient heartbroken father. One gloats at us; the other weeps with us.

It really comes down to an issue of *trust*. If I truly believe God is who He says He is — that He is all-wise, noble, righteous, fair, loving, and perfect justice — then I also have to be okay with certain unexplainable actions from God which don't make sense to my tiny limited three lb. brain.

That's not a cop-out, but of course it'll seem that way to anyone who already has an agenda against Him. People love to play "Gotcha" with the OT, but really they're just confirming their own pre-made point of view. We're all biased somehow towards God. I admit my own bias is to trust God, even as I struggle with some really tough things He does. My own preconceived filter is that God is ultimately eternally good, so **He will use even what He hates to achieve what is good.**[43] But for many others, God must be bad, so they've already decided that anything God does *must* be inherently evil. You can't really argue that one, because it takes an incredible amount of trust to say God is good in a broken world.

Your friend might say he's neutral, but the human heart is *constantly* looking for ways to slip out of submission to any higher power. We hate the idea of God unless He does what we want — which is why we pick lesser gods like shiny toys and cheap thrills and friends-with-benefits and mindless distractions. They're easier to control and they can't tell us how to live (even as they enslave us by the soul-sucking grip of idolatry). Even Aldous Huxley, the atheist author who wrote *Brave New World*, declared that he rejected God because "it interfered with our sexual freedom."[44]

---

[43] Inspired by Corrie ten Boom, a Holocaust survivor.

[44] Aldous Huxley, *Ends and Means* (Connecticut: Greenwood, 1969, 1937), p. 273. I understand this quote is often abused by Christians amidst its context, and I don't mean to minimize all atheism as a grab-bag of immorality. The larger point is that we're often predisposed to despise the concepts of authority, the "institution," a higher being, or the supernatural. Since the deck is stacked, it would be wise to consider that no one enters a theological discussion with an objective frame of reference, on either side. Self-awareness is critical.

All that to say: Even if you knew the ironclad answer to all the crazy stuff in the Old Testament, I doubt your friend would say, "You're so totally right! Now I love Jesus." Again, it comes down to trust. Most people don't trust the OT without first trusting God. **I don't mean to say we shouldn't question it — I have *tons* of problems with the OT and I'll be sure to check with God when I meet Him.** But unless your friend is okay with mystery and surrender and not being the main character in his own life, then the OT will always look like X-rated bloody mythology.

I've learned to embrace the tension. I've heard all the logical explanations for the OT, but I find that even academic research does little to make me "trust God more." When we reduce the supernatural to merely dry theology, we shrink God into a deceptively selective box so that we're not really talking about God anymore, but an abstract straw-man that is dismantled by the next best argument. I have a feeling many Christians even like it this way, because they don't have to confront their own sin and can keep a distance from His authority.

So I'll play along and attempt to answer a few things. There are a few reasons why I believe God is still good in the Old Testament.

1) If Jesus is really God, then this validates the goodness of God at the cross. Which means I can trust anything that happens in the OT because it will have been used for the ultimate eternal good. It doesn't mean I *like* everything that happens in the OT, but it does mean that I can quit second-guessing God. In the cross, we see how both love and justice meet together. We see how the futility of man in the OT is met with the perfect mercy of God in the New Testament. The tension is resolved — my sin meets His grace. We don't need better public relations for that, or to tame down the Gospel, or to apologize for such a scandalous grace. The Gospel is enough for me to retroactively believe that every event in the OT had the purpose of pointing to the Cross of Christ.

2) There are countless instances of God's grace in the OT. This even more so than in the New Testament. God consistently reaches towards people of His own initiative, even when people are consistently rejecting Him. Genesis 15, one of the weirdest chapters of the OT, is drenched in God's grace.

3) Issues in the OT like slavery, incest, genocide, wrath, and so-called misogyny are not as clear-cut as they appear to be. Our current Western sensibilities have almost zero context or framework to interpret these things, plus people are always saying, "It's in the Bible so God must be condoning them," which is a ridiculous assertion. God was just as mad at these things as we are. But even assuming God condoned them, I would imagine that God Himself came across some moral dilemmas where He had to pick the lesser of two evils for the long-term good. I don't think it happened this way, but if we're always understanding other people for doing so, then I can understand God on this one too. But really, the OT is full of *imperfect human failure* that doesn't reflect the perfect God.

People like to blame God and religion for everything, but can hardly stand to blame themselves. The OT is very clear that people are the problem and God is the solution. But we pick and choose this to fit our prejudices. A murderer blames his religion and everyone else says religion made him a murderer — but if it's a rapist, let's blame the victim, and if it's some rich white kid, let's blame the parents. This is an inconsistent convenience. It reminds me of how Adam blamed God for Eve, then Eve passed the blame to Satan. We're more civilized now, right? Right.

4) Besides having the right attitude about the OT, I also believe that every single "tension" has a sufficient intellectual answer. For the example of Genesis 11, when the people building the Tower of Babel are struck, God's original covenant was to be fruitful and multiply across the earth (Genesis 9:7). But now these people are trying to be God and staying in one place to build a tower, which would've effectively killed the human race. So God, perhaps in grief, has to divide the people so they'll naturally travel out on their own. Now after that: Were the resulting wars and genocide really God's fault? Or was it a consequence of people not getting along?

We have a way of reading the Bible as black-and-white without nuance, forgetting that the oral tradition of relaying Scripture would add layers that we don't always catch. If you can witness a Jewish reading of the Book of Esther during their Purim festival, there are all kinds of mannerisms that add flesh and depth. Of course, we don't need this extra colorization for the Bible to have power. But if we can put a little humanity in Scripture — to recognize these biblical characters struggled with the same hopes, fears, and hurts that we do — we might read the Bible with just as much reverence as we do for Harry Potter or Sherlock Holmes.

5) Any time God throws down punishment in the OT, God is *accelerating the consequences of sin to display how sin eventually destroys all people.* Sometimes God lets someone get away with sin for a while because God is hoping that His kindness will lead to repentance (Romans 2). But sin will *always* catch up to you, and God cannot delay the consequences forever (Numbers 32:23). Imagine a kind of life where there were no ramifications for anything you did, which would mean God doesn't love us.

Occasionally in the OT, God directly intervenes by opening a hole in the ground or sending an angel of wrath or flying in a bunch of poisonous quails (Numbers 11 and 16, 2 Kings 19:35). I don't mean that God punishes only bad people or rewards only good people or that all bad events are examples of God's punishment. We also can't judge if someone is being "punished" by God or not (they did this in John 9 and Jesus flat-out told them they were wrong). But in the OT, when it's stated that God is punishing someone, like the Ten Plagues, God does it to close the loop between our selfishness and the eventual destruction it causes. I'm sure it makes God sick to His stomach, but He does it in hopes to prevent further human selfishness, just like a good father will punish his kids to guide them in the right way (Matthew 18:14, 2 Peter 3:9).

I know this won't possibly answer all your questions, and I don't pretend to find this easy. I haven't even begun to cover tragedies, disasters, diseases, and other planetary problems. But I continue trusting God anyway, even when it's a tiny thread of trust. I believe God knows what He's doing. When I read the OT, I see a God who gets involved — and I'd rather have a God who gets in our mess and rocks us with mercy and justice, even when I don't understand it.

"... Man interferes with the dog and makes it more loveable than it was in mere nature. In its state of nature it has a smell, and habits, which frustrate man's love: he washes it, house-trains it, teaches it not to steal, and is so enabled to love it completely. To the puppy the whole proceeding would seem, if it were a theologian, to cast grave doubts on the "goodness" of man: but the full-grown and full-trained dog, larger, healthier, and longer-lived than the wild dog, and admitted, as it were by Grace, to a whole world of affections, loyalties, interests and comforts entirely beyond its animal destiny, would have no such doubts. It will be noted that the man takes all these pains with the dog, and gives all these pains to the dog, only because it is an animal high in the scale - because it is so nearly loveable that it is worth his while to make it fully loveable. He does not house-train the earwig or give baths to centipedes. We may wish, indeed, that we were of so little account to God that He left us alone to follow our natural impulses - that He would give over trying to train us into something so unlike our natural selves: but once again, we are asking not for more Love, but for less."[45]

— C.S. Lewis

---

[45] C.S. Lewis, *The Problem of Pain* (New York: HarperCollins, 1966), p. 35

2. Understanding The Reality of Hell

"Hey, I really appreciate your blog. I'm just wondering, but how did you come to terms with the reality of hell? I've known a lot of people who have dismissed Christianity because they couldn't accept the thought of the majority of mankind enduring eternal torment, especially when God claims to be good. How do you navigate through all of that?"

Hey my dear friend, thank you for your very kind words and thank you for asking. I know this is a tough question that divides many people. Here are just a few thoughts on this to consider.

1) I believe most people already believe the concept of Hell, whether they admit it or not.

It often takes the sleepy quiet fences of the suburbs to misinform us about life. Those who have suffered extreme injustice can profoundly understand the need for a final, ultimate judgment. Those who scorn the idea of Hell might as well be saying, "I don't believe in justice for evil." One can't be said without the other. In the end, we have a secret hope that no one gets away with anything. We implicitly want a God who is good and makes sure that justice wins.

I don't think just anyone goes to Hell, but certainly there must be justice for those who continually choose tyranny, manipulation, and oppression. When someone says "There is no Hell," it means they've never faced rape in Rwanda or a murdered child or a national genocide under the Khmer Rouge. It means they never had to watch their relatives shot in the head right in front of them (During the regime of the Khmer Rouge, my Cambodian friend's mom watched all of her brothers executed.). It means they never had to watch their parents get exterminated in an oven. Instead the naysayer's suffering has only consisted of credit card debt or an egged car at Halloween.

If all this bothers you, please keep in mind that most Easterners have no problem with a God who will judge. They actually have a problem with a loving, personal, forgiving God. On the other hand, only over-privileged Post-Enlightenment thinkers who have been Pavlovian-conditioned with Westernized logic could ever say that there's no Hell, because they've never been ravaged by evil. And the only motivation for the victims of injustice to *stop declaring war* is to trust that there is a Hell which ultimately deals justice, so we don't have to.[46]

2) Those in Hell will have tried very hard to get there.

A life apart from God gets us a life apart from God. They will have ended up exactly where they wanted to go. As Timothy Keller says, Hell is merely an eternal extension of self-absorption and inner-deterioration that came from a life of selfishness.[47] To live for only oneself is simply hell.

This also means that there must be *some kind of grace* for people who had no chance to believe, or perhaps threw a prayer on their deathbed, or who are special needs, or who are very young children. While I can't answer all those questions, I believe God's grace covers them in a way that we can't humanly comprehend. We may be surprised in Heaven to see the many multitudes there covered by grace.

---

[46] This idea is from Miroslav Volf, a Croatian theologian who is a pacifist and well understands human indignities.

[47] A paraphrase from Timothy Keller's *The Reason For God*.

3) Jesus paid the price of Hell already.

Here's what I don't hear often enough. *God did create Hell for injustice, but He already paid the price Himself so that we wouldn't have to.*

Most people are saying, "It's not fair that a loving God would make a place called Hell!" But no one ever says, "It's not fair that Jesus had to pay Hell for us!" It's only unfair when it comes to me. No one sees the cross for how unfair that was to God.

Imagine the implications of this grace. Imagine an architect who makes a prison, then you commit a crime, and the architect says, "Don't worry, I'll carry out the sentence for you." No other religion or philosophy or humanism even comes *close* to this radical kind of grace. Which brings us finally to —

4) Without justice, then grace doesn't mean very much.

I know that some Christians would disagree here. But without a theology of justice, then grace is just not very electrifying.

If it cost nothing for God to love us, then His love is just sentimentality. It's a general warm feeling that gives us fuzzies when we look to the clouds.

This is true for relationships. If you only love people who are lovable, then that love is cheap. But if you can love people through the worst of their mess — that love is true, strong, real. It came with a price.

The love of God is a *costly love*. It cost Him everything. God took on flesh and *His whole life was one long crucifixion*. The life and death of Jesus was essentially his descent into Hell. He was tempted with us, suffered with us, grew hungry and tired and thirsty like us, was rejected and abandoned and betrayed and beat up and stripped naked and killed in the worst way possible. He did this, for us, to endure the penalty of our sin on our behalf.

So knowing this, there is no possible way that His love can be an abstract doctrine. When people say, "God forgives me, so the Christian can do whatever they want!" — then they have no idea what it costs God to love us. Grace is free, but it was not cheap. Grace cost Him His all.

I say all this to say, Christianity does not hinge on whether Hell exists. That's not the point, at all. But rather God rescues us unconditionally out of His costly love and invites us into an eternal journey of joy, and when you can know this, then these other doctrines are the very least of our worries.

I hope we can share these things with sensitivity too. I've had relatives and friends pass away without a knowledge of Christ. It's not okay to simply trump this around. I hope we can navigate these things with a loving heart, full of grace and truth. Much love to you in caring for your friends about this.

3. Heaven and Hell As A Motivation For Faith

"Hey man! Love your wisdom & needing some of it. I answered a question about guilt recently & discussed repentance, explaining that God uses love, not fear, to motivate us and draw us to Himself. The anon wrote me back saying that no matter how much I speak of grace, the reality of hell still stands, thus fear persists & remains as a motive for repentance. I don't know how to answer, and would love any insight you may have on the topic. Thanks!"

Hey there my dear friend: Your question has actually bothered me under the surface for as long as I've been a Christian. It's one of those icky things we don't like to think about very much. I've heard smarter people answer this question while dancing around the reality of "eternal torment" and "the worm that never dies," and it's like we mince words or gloss over these realities with tons of verbal trickery. I don't think I'll fare much better. So feel free to make of this what you will.

Please allow me to present my former atheist view on the issue. Basically the problem is posed as:

1) Sure, God offers Heaven through Jesus. But there's a place called Hell, which according to your Bible, is eternal punishment.

2) So no matter what you say about God's love, there is only a binary option with God — Heaven or Hell — and that can't possibly be loving.

3) It doesn't matter that you say "free will," because people either must choose God and be rewarded or not choose God and suffer.

4) Conclusion: Your faith is always undermined by the promise of reward and the fear of punishment, which is a barbaric doctrine that reeks of inauthenticity and materialism and a coercive deity.

But the more I thought about this, the more I saw serious problems in this argumentation. Whether you believe in God or not, at the very least this "binary-choice" argument is vastly Swiss cheese.

1) God doesn't want Hell for you. If Hell actually exists: God already paid the price for you not to go there.

Most people think the idea of Hell is unfair, but mostly everyone forgets that Jesus paid the very price of Hell for you. Again, I don't see anyone saying "It's unfair that Jesus had to die for me." Yet the latter statement is true.

No other religion or philosophy even comes close to this sort of remarkable reality. If God made Hell, He already made a provision for you not to go there. More than that, God *desires* that you be with Him and He doesn't gloat over this by using Hell as enticement.[48]

---

[48] 2 Peter 3:9, Romans 2:4.

Anyone who says, "I don't like a God who would threaten us with Hell" hasn't read the Bible very far. Jesus took it on already. Anyone who says, "God is shaming me with Hell" probably has an ulterior motive for using such a bizarre argument.

2) Our faith is built primarily on a relational intimacy, not reward or punishment.

When anyone says "God uses fear to make people repent," we're still thinking on the wrong premise of reward and punishment. It's not even close to talking about God. **Both Heaven and Hell as a motive for faith present a false dichotomy of choices which is completely outside the faith-relationship of Christian theology.** It's a phantom argument that doesn't even approach the real God, and so remains an abstract doctrine.

God offers everything, most especially Himself. If the richest, most attractive person in the world were to say, "I want to be with you forever because I like you for who you are" — it would be weird to say, "Well what's the other option?" The reality that you'll be alone forever is not some driving force to be with this person. The driving force *is the relationship*, not anything else.

Even "Christians" who turn to God out of fear or reward are not making a real choice. They're thinking conceptually, thinking in a Christianese way about Christianese things outside the actual living God.

The argument that God says "Choose me or else" is actually dead in the water, because even if you choose based on this motive, you still haven't chosen God.

If you don't choose God because you think He's saying "Choose me or else," then that's still thinking in terms of materialistic opportunism. You would be rejecting God based on what He can give you or not give you, which is hardly digging deep enough about the meaning of true relationships. This is all conceptual vague religion which is purposefully meant to keep God at a distance.

3) Hell is a natural consequence of our choices and not a "scare tactic" by God.

Hell is a gradual, eventual deterioration if you go against the way you were designed.[49] Those who don't believe in it still know exactly what it is. And those who don't believe in Hell still want justice for every crime on the planet, because inherently we want wrongs to be righted. So Hell is also a place for those who have perverted justice — and secretly, we do want this. Only sensitive Westerners with a pseudo-political-correctness have a problem with it, until it involves injustice against their family.

As an example: Every relationship ever can go one of two ways.

If you only try to enjoy the "benefits" of the relationship, you turn inward until there is only the lonely self, and this is a private hell (whether the person feels bad about it or not). A selfish person with agendas to gain more will always gain a vacuum of loss, because selfishness always *self-destructs and destroys others*. It becomes its own consequence. This is just a microcosm of what Hell will actually be like.

But if you actually enjoy the other person in the relationship for *who they are* in their essence, then everything else is bonus and you've entered a special sort of bliss. The generous always end up with intimacy, but since even their motive is not to have "more intimacy," they're free to actually enjoy others. It becomes its own reward. This is just a microcosm of what Heaven will actually be like.

When someone says, "Heaven and Hell takes away our free will," this is presuming that "free will" means we can do whatever we want and still have everything we want. Most people will do all they can to slip out from the Christian faith, including accusing God of "infringing on my free

---

[49] Check out *The Screwtape Letters* by C.S. Lewis.

will," when they're really saying that they just want mindless sex and unchecked consequence-less living. That's not free will, but self-will, and it's slavery to the tyranny of self, which is hell.

But in choosing God, I turn over to G.K. Chesterton —

"And the more I considered Christianity, the more I found that while it had established a rule and order, the chief aim of that order was to give room for good things to run wild."[50]

4) A life apart from God will get you a life apart from God, which is an objective choice that is exactly what most people wanted.

If you choose not to get married, you'll be single. No one "threatens" you with singleness, and even if you got married out of fear, you'll be a single person who signed a paper and moved in with someone.

There are certain objective realities that remain unavoidable, no matter how you feel about them. If you don't want God for whatever reason, you'll get exactly what you wanted.

Hell must be at least two things:

- A life apart from God, which is what happens when you choose a life apart from God.

- The endless closed loop of our selfishness <==and==> consequences, played out for eternity — which is also what you will have chosen.

Since God created us to be in a relationship with Him, anything else would be falsely saying that *creation is more important than the Creator.*

No one was designed to live this way. We've all seen what happens when people take creation — whether shiny new toys or political ideology or actual human souls — and use and abuse and neglect and worship

---

[50] G.K. Chesterton, *Orthodoxy* (Chicago: Moody, 1908, 2009), p. 195

them. There are consequences. Again: *When you continually prioritize creation over Creator, you become a more selfish person who will self-destruct and destroy others.* This is an objective reality that is inevitable and will extend into eternity, if you really want that.

This is why Jesus says it's better to enter Heaven with no hands and no eyes than to enter Hell with a whole body[51] (which is quite a superlative, since Jesus was a preacher) — because it's better to have the Creator than the created.

Personally, *I think people who end up in Hell will have tried very hard to get there.*

5) Conclusion: This is a lazy argument that only exposes an entitled mentality. And even then, God has grace for us.

When someone poses the issue of "binary-Heaven-and-Hell," they're only exposing they want the best of all worlds, therefore denying the common reality of our choices. They're trying to say, "No matter what I choose, I want to have it all." It's trying to smuggle in the benefits of a relationship while trying to stay single. Or they're saying, "True love would never threaten me with singleness" — even though singleness is a concrete positional truth that will happen if you do not choose the relationship.

Yet here God is, extending grace even amidst our constant preprogrammed parroted defenses to keep Him away. He gives grace for those who falsely believe He is about fear.

The bottom line: *God did absolutely everything in His power to ensure you would be with Him for eternity, and He even loves us so much He gave us free will to choose it for ourselves.*

---

[51] Mark 9:47

4. Do Christians Have "Stockholm Syndrome"?

"Hello! What do you think about the statement that Christians (and generally believers) have Stockholm Syndrome? I've picked this up somewhere and did some research. It'd make sense and it makes me feel weird about my faith now. Thanks and God bless!"

Hey there my friend. I took some time to read about this, and it seems to be a new form of the argument that "Christians are brainwashed into unquestioning belief and indoctrinated to their oppressive church institutions and cultures."

Like all accusations against the Christian faith, there's *always* an element of truth to them because people are people and we cannot perfectly reflect a perfect God. We're messy creatures with mixed motives in a gray-space struggle.

What I mean is: *Any argument against the Christian faith will make some kind of logical sense, because it will make sense against everyone regardless of their affiliation.* We can blame religion just as much as we can blame human stupidity.

When someone says, "The church is full of hypocrites" — I always say, "Well that's why you should go." Not in a mean way, but I'm saying: There are hypocrites at businesses, schools, hospitals, fraternities, non-profits, and the White House (gasp!), but the difference is, the church is the one place you can admit it and find healing. Yes, hypocritical Christians have harmed many of us, and we need to confess that. But as a tactic to dismiss faith, this is an unthoughtful argument that's a fluffy insubstantial defense mechanism. Most of these arguments have not gone to the bottom of themselves.

So when someone talks about "Christian brainwashing," here are a few thoughts to consider. As always, please feel free to skip around.

1) It's true that the mainstream church has damaged people with cult-like behavior, and we must absolutely be aware of this and apologize.

If Christians can't admit this, there's no point to having this discussion. When someone slams the church, I always end up agreeing with their criticisms. I don't mean that it makes me doubt God, but *their feelings are valid and they've been genuinely hurt by the church.* We have to start there. We need to talk about it. We can't defend all our behavior, because some of it has been atrocious, and we must apologize.

2) We are all indoctrinated into a particular system of belief, no matter where we roll.

I keep beating this drum, but most Western individuals don't realize that they live inside a Post-Enlightenment individualistic "rational" mindset that's Pavlovian-conditioned to reject anything outside of naturalistic explanation. Our dear brother C.S. Lewis called this *chronological snobbery*, in which we believe our current slice of time is far more advanced than other any other time in history.[52]

We're largely a product of our times. We've all bought into paradigms that enforce certain restrictions on our values. Even the value that "I'm above these values" is still a specific constrained worldview. So when you accuse someone of being brainwashed, you're just as brainwashed into the opposition of whatever view you're accusing.

Of course, most Westerners who disagree with Christianity will say "You're a narrow-minded intolerant bigot." A Westernized brain will instantly dismiss the spiritual realm and conservative values. But dismissing an entire group of people because of their ideology is *still* an ideology. To say, "I tolerate everything except intolerance" must deny its very own rule.

---

[52] C.S. Lewis, *Surprised By Joy* (Florida: Harcourt, 1955), pp. 206-207

If you're beholden to your own particular views in fear of betraying your camp or being ridiculed, you're being held hostage, and this takes a blinding self-rationalization that's just like Stockholm Syndrome. This happens with both the very religious and the very secular, and if you deny that it happens with you, you're proving this exact point. *Everyone is a captive to their own particular set of beliefs, no matter where you turn.*

I know what I'm saying will bother most Westerners (and if you've been indoctrinated by secularism long enough, you'll feel you're superior to all this too. You're not, and neither am I). But when I was an atheist, I became weary of atheists because they thought they were so enlightened. When I was a Reformed Calvinist, I became weary of Calvinists because they thought they were so enlightened.

Really, they were both nearsighted and full of preprogrammed defenses for their own little gods. And as an Eastern-Western hybrid, I recognize the arrogant self-important myopia of both sides.

If you're still not okay with this, let's try an experiment. Stockholm Syndrome says, "I understand why he abused me, it's probably for the right motives. I get why he's correcting me, because there must be a good reason." Those are bad rationalizations that could get you killed. But let's take that to the extreme opposite. What if every time my future spouse did the slightest thing I disliked, I suspected a false motive? What if every time my future spouse contradicted me, I shut her down? That wouldn't be a real marriage. I'm demanding a robot.

Someone who says, "I don't want a God who could ever do something I dislike" or "God can't correct me" really just wants a robot-god. And someone who is enslaved to Post-Enlightenment Western thinking has already determined their own robot-god too.

3) God's heart for us is that we *freely choose Him.*

Christianity in its purest form will invite questioning. It's open to deconstruction. If you're frustrated with God, you can yell about it, ask about it, shake a fist and vent. You can disagree and stomp the ground and throw things and yell "Why." Just read the Book of Psalms or Jeremiah or Lamentations. None of the writers were rationalizing what God did, at all. There was a ton of unresolved tension, and some of my first questions in Heaven will be about that crazy Old Testament.

But really, I believe the God of the Bible is open to our challenges. He's okay with all our fist-shaking. As I've said before, *I would much rather be mad with God than mad without Him.*

Also, our entire world of false dichotomies forces you into one fixed viewpoint or another. Most people get upset if you try to re-arrange their bottle of dogma. Most systems of belief are self-contained dominions where nothing goes in or out. A Democrat is expected to act one way, a Republican another.

Which is why Jesus was so wholly unpredictable and angered both sides. Jesus himself was a safe haven who was not defined by dogmatic party lines, but by his gracious solidarity with real human beings caught in the messy crossfire of a broken world. There are no clean-cut solutions here.

I've managed to anger both conservatives and liberals about homosexuality. Take that how you will. The Christian is able to keep multiple viewpoints within tension because *true Christianity does not usurp our identity, but at once draws out the true self while creating a unified ground.*

In the end, God is not holding us at gunpoint here. He wants us to think for ourselves.[53] He also has *our very best interests at heart,* so of course, He would want us to choose Him. If God was the most glorious being in the entire universe, He would be wrong not to point to Himself as the most worthy of all glory. But nor will He ever force that upon us, because

---

[53] 1 John 4:1, Acts 17:11, Proverbs 2:10, 18:15

He gave us the free will to choose. That's what makes us human, and not hostages. God wants the purest relationship with us, without coercion or agenda or even a mutual exchange. How could we ever give to God more than He ever gives to us? When we are with Him, it is always an abundance of grace.

I'll leave you with two wonderful quotes by C.S Lewis once again:

"The happiness which God designs for His higher creatures is the happiness of being freely, voluntarily united to Him and to each other in an ecstasy of love and delight compared with which the most rapturous love between a man and a woman on this earth is mere milk and water. And for that they've got to be free."[54]

"The more we get what we now call 'ourselves' out of the way and let Him take us over, the more truly ourselves we become ... He invented—as an author invents characters in a novel—all the different men that you and I were intended to be. In that sense our real selves are all waiting for us in Him. It is no good trying to 'be myself' without Him ... It is when I turn to Christ, when I give up myself to His personality, that I first begin to have a real personality of my own."[55]

---

[54] C.S. Lewis, *Mere Christianity* (New York: HarperCollins, 1952, 1980), p. 49
[55] Ibid. p. 226. This quote is often paraphrased on the internet, but here is presented in its original form.

5. What's The Evidence For Faith?

"Hi, I'm a growing Christian and I've recently been doing research and gathering info to clarify my faith. I was wondering if you could answer some questions. 1) What is the basis of your faith? 2) How do you support the historical legitimacy of the Bible & New Testament as the true and sacred word of God? 3) How are other religions founded on false doctrine? Thank you so much!"

Hey my friend, I'm well aware that a "secular" or "liberal" worldview will have plenty of counter-ammo for anything I say here. Any Google-Expert can artistically deconstruct this with all kinds of witty semantics, the equivalent to pulling my pants down at a Sunday service. The Bible itself says Christianity will look like foolishness to the untransformed heart.[56]

But I do understand that the Christian faith is a hard sell. Academically it sounds crazy, and spiritually we fight against it. There's also no singular shot of "evidence" here that will be good enough for everyone, and might only dampen your journey of faith into an intellectual exercise. So I must caution that this is not a weapon to bludgeon others in a debate. It might not be the booster shot you were looking for. I only hope these are basic strands you will consider for serious, open-minded thought.

---

[56] 1 Corinthians 2:14

1) Basis of Faith? —

I'm assuming this means, "How do you know your faith is reality?" We would start with which worldview satisfactorily accommodates some of the Big Questions. I deliberately used the word *accommodate* and not answer, because we're not infinite beings with access to unlimited knowledge. We simply follow the clues.[57]

Let's cast a wide net. On one end of the spectrum you have the Materialistic Worldview which supposes there is no God, or one who spun things into motion but doesn't care much, and that there are no eternal souls. Physical processes are then completely natural systems in themselves, and the meaning of life plus morality is self-established with a roughly standardized humanistic dignity. In other words, "I do for you, you do for me, we die happy."

On the other end there is a God who created everything, wants to have a personal relationship with you — loves you, the Bible says — and at some point in human history came down as a man to do what we could not do for ourselves: to bring us to Him. At the very least, we have to account for some dang crazy thing that happened in the first century which made the Jews go nuts. We're then called to love God and love people.

So then: *What best accommodates Ultimate Reality?* As with gravity, what is the explanation that best fits the natural observable law? By what standard can we propose a meaning of life and objective morality? What best suits the Problem of Evil? Looking upon the shape of history and humanity, where does the evidence point after we objectively sift through the data? And after we discard secret agendas?

My agenda for having been an atheist was to dodge authority. I can't speak for every atheist, but for me, I didn't want anyone to tell me, "No (sex)." I also think we must lay down all our agendas about Almighty

---

[57] Inspired by *The Reason For God,* by Timothy Keller

Science, whether we fear it or attack it or abuse it, because science can be such a wonderful element to embrace in our faith. Then there's the emotional agenda, and even saying, "I always felt there was a God who loved me" is not sufficient for a sustainable faith. We each have some layers to peel back before we can really investigate.

In the end, I found the Materialistic Worldview completely untenable with even the most basic principles of being a human being. At first I believed my desires were conforming to a reality that I wanted to be true, yet soon found that Christianity was exactly a reality that I did *not* want to be true. It was terrifying. It also turns out that it most accommodated all those piercing questions.

2) The historical legitimacy of the Bible —

There are much, much smarter people who can go over the historical documents, archaeology, and endless research that has been poured into this field. Every other year, there are more findings in Israel's dirt confirming the Bible (and less than 1% of that area has been dug up). So these are some general, deductive observations of the Bible itself.

1 - The Bible is overly honest.

If I were to make up my own religion, it would definitely not look like the Christian Bible. For example, the story of King David and his affair with Bathsheba, plus the subsequent murder of her husband Uriah, is told with such unrelenting cold detail that no room full of religious conspirators would have left it in there.

The same is true with Peter's failures, the disciples' overall idiocy, Elijah's suicidal depression, Ruth's forwardness, or the women being first to witness the empty tomb (a woman's testimony was not admissible in that day). There's a bald, naked, embarrassing honesty to the Bible that makes the "heroes" look like celebrity mugshots with the worst PR ever.

If I made up a religion, it would be one without any sort of god to mess with me, one where I could hold my own standard of morality that changes at my convenience. In fact, many Christians live this way.

C.S. Lewis says it best: *"I didn't go to religion to make me happy. I always knew a bottle of Port would do that. If you want a religion to make you feel really comfortable, I certainly don't recommend Christianity."*[58]

2 - The Bible claims a Humble God.

The stuff of folklore, mythology, legends, and other religions often describe irrational demigods that are slaves to their own emotions, with limited power, acting inconsistently, committing adultery with witless women (Greek myths are crazy about that), and often abusive and arrogant. In other words, it would be much closer to a religion I would write myself, like a really bad fan-fiction.

The God of the Bible humbled himself to death on a cross, becoming a servant for all and yet remaining a king, offering grace to a broken world. For all the accusations of religion being about "fear and control," that one doesn't stick here.

3 - The Bible reads like straightforward eyewitness accounts.

C.S. Lewis, who specialized in medieval literature and mythology, made a startling discovery of the Bible when he realized it was worlds apart from any manmade ancient literature. Often the Bible reads more like a periodical. The Gospels in particular do not fit any noticeable genre, most especially not the grand sweeping tales of heroic victory and huge clashes. The Bible contains seemingly innocuous facts like a newspaper reporting the events, with little aplomb, perhaps because it really was just reporting the events.

---

[58] C.S. Lewis, *God in the Dock* (Michigan: William B. Eerdmans, 1970) p. 48

Why even add the detail about 153 fish? Why not make Jesus' miracles more sensational instead of as direct as they are? Why have such formal accounts of Moses' travel, battles, and routines? The craziness of Solomon's temple? Or have a book called Numbers with, well, numbers? I find it amusing that what some people think are "boring parts" of the Bible actually enrich the depth of its veracity.

3) Other religions false?

Most religions do not exclude other religions; Christianity has the daring claim of exclusivity. That is, the Bible claims it's the one true faith. I'm always confused by the "Coexist" bumper stickers. I get what they're saying but it's not helpful at all. You'd have to disrespect every religion listed on there.

I won't claim to be a master of all religions, though my grandmother was in a Buddhist cult (*namyohorengekyo*) and when I became a deist, I studied religions more deeply. Being a martial artist, I came to respect Tao (and if I were not a Christian, I might have fallen into Taoism). From my experience, my main beef was that so many religions *make you do stuff to get stuff*.

It's a Consumeristic Contract. You do things to get these things. Like going to a certain store until you find a better store with better prices; that's the consumer mindset. It's safe, shrink-wrapped, deceiving. There's nothing personal or real about it, just a shallow transaction. It's exactly the kind of religion I'd make up. It can also go to the other extreme where you're hustled for your money and your mind or where you keep paying to achieve higher levels. There's no "church" of Scientology in the slums, you know.

There's also the lie that *the better you is in you*. This is why I'm wary of everything New Age — because a billion failed attempts later, it's exhausting disillusionment. It's also selfish and inward, a sort of navel-gazing. Forcing mind over mind is like holding a gun to your head. If you try to control fear, you'll become aggressive; if you try to control anger, you can become complacent. It doesn't work. We need a force outside ourselves to help. And that's an understatement.

Again: *How does a worldview answer the Big Questions of the meaning of life?* We can get convoluted real quickly here, so I'm attempting to keep it as obvious as Occam's Razor. At the same time, I know that Christianity itself *does* sound strange to all bystanders, yet its peculiar oddities begins to accommodate the complicated problems with satisfying answers. It answers a complex reality with truth we would not have made up on our own.

"It is no good asking for a simple religion. After all, real things are not simple. They look simple, but they are not ... Such people put up a version of Christianity suitable for a child of six and make that the object of their attack.

"Besides being complicated, reality, in my experience, is usually odd. It is not neat, not obvious, not what you expect ... Reality, in fact, is usually something you could not have guessed. That is one of the reasons I believe Christianity. It is a religion you could not have guessed. If it offered us just the kind of universe we had always expected, I should feel we were making it up. But, in fact, it is not the sort of thing anyone would have made up. It has just that queer twist about it that real things have. So let us leave behind all these boys' philosophies—these over-simple answers. The problem is not simple and the answer is not going to be simpler either."[59]

— C.S. Lewis

---

[59] C.S. Lewis, *Mere Christianity* (New York: HarperCollins, 1952, 1980), p. 42

6. How Do You Defend Your Faith?

"I am doubting my faith more than ever, from the legitimacy of ancient texts, to the authenticity of the roots of stories found in the Old Testament (as well of those even found in the Gospels) ... So, I guess, my big question is, how would you address some of the biggest 'logical fallacies' or 'errors' found in Scriptures, from texts not aligning, to things being taken from other cultures, to a good deal of scholarly work done by some to prove that Jesus was never a real man?"

There are days I can give you all the "evidence for faith" with a big smile on my face. I did mostly that with the previous question. But on other days, as bad as it sounds, I just want to throw the Bible in the trash and be done with it. Even all those detailed academic answers do nothing for me. I get on some atheist blog and binge-read the hate and all those familiar doubts come creeping back in. They just have a way of twisting my guts around.

I've pretty much heard every single argument there is to hear on both sides, and there is nothing new under the sun. I've watched theological debates between all the best. I don't think I've learned *any* new apologetics in the last few years, and having been an atheist, those guys are not really saying anything new either.

There was a day when I fought valiantly for one side against the other. I've probably hated on Christians just as much as atheists.

Now I'm just a little bored and jaded on the whole thing.

Both sides fanwank and retcon their arguments like crazy. Both sides are full of biases, agendas, misinformed views, and wrong ideas about each other. Both sides are eloquent, sharp, articulate, witty. Both sides can present compelling cases. Both sides even get along often. Watch the debate between Wilson and Hitchens, and you can see they're nearly best friends.[60]

It turns out, I like Christians and atheists just about evenly, and if you want to, you can intellectually keep them at checkmate forever. But at the end of the day, *Jesus is real enough for me*. He wins my heart. He fills me up. He saved my wretched soul. I became tired of explaining myself to people that needed some kind of justified, propped-up, pre-defended faith. I was exhausted of prepackaged arguments that make sense until some other argument arrives. I had tough questions, and still do, but everyday it feels more and more like the answer is becoming Jesus, and each day that's becoming enough. I don't care that it makes me an academic cop-out. I care that it makes me whole.

I've heard nearly all the evidence both for and against Christianity, but it's not about the evidence anymore. Was it ever really? If you must know, atheists also have their doubts when they're honest with themselves. The Christian is the one who simply doubts their doubts.

Somewhere in that raging mess of debates, **I had to grow up and discover faith for myself.** So will you.

I know some atheist like my former self will come along and say, "That's dangerous to turn off your brain, you're not being rational, you're tossing reason out the window …!" But I don't know. I think pitting the two sides against each other is a bizarre, archaic, ingrained thing to do. I don't think that faith requires turning off your brain, or that turning "on" your brain somehow eradicates faith. Putting faith and religion into a death-match is the real cop-out; it's just too easy. It's only people who are scared to stretch a bit that must continue fighting for their flagpole.

---

[60] Check out *Collision* (2009), a documentary feat. Christopher Hitchens and Douglas Wilson. It follows famous atheist Hitchens and Presbyterian Calvinist Wilson on a tour of debates, in which both men end up enjoying each other's company and concede a small common ground between religion and atheism. See also,
http://www.slate.com/articles/news_and_politics/fighting_words/2009/10/faith_no_more.html

I suppose you wanted a much more straightforward answer with biblical proofs and historical accuracy (and I've written too much on that) — but my friend, there are tons of resources out there you can look into for yourself. Those resources are also written by frail human hands wired by three lb. brains with their own darling schemes that will turn into dust like the rest of us.

Wrestle with this for as long as you must, but at some point, please know that **your doubts will never stop, and you'll come to trust *something* amidst the doubts you have**. I make the choice every morning to push aside the voices, forget both screaming sides, and follow Jesus. I pray you'd choose him, too.

The bottom line is that my lungs are filled with Christ and no one can really talk me out of it.

I love God and I love people, and nothing will knock that out of me.

That's your purpose, dear friend. In your struggle to believe, keep serving.

"My most recent faith struggle is not one of intellect. I don't really do that anymore. Sooner or later you just figure out there are some guys who don't believe in God and they can prove He doesn't exist, and there are some other guys who do believe in God and they can prove He does exist, and the argument stopped being about God a long time ago and now it's about who is smarter, and honestly I don't care."[61]

— Donald Miller

---

[61] Donald Miller, *Blue Like Jazz* (Colorado: Thomas Nelson, 2003) p.103

7. Why Do You Believe In Jesus?

"Why do you believe in Jesus? I get believing in a creator, but as much as I want to, I can't always convince myself that there's evidence for Jesus doing all that stuff, and it breaks my heart because I used to believe it without a problem. I don't know what to do."

Hey dear friend: As much as I can muster with my weakling faith, I believe in Jesus for historical, emotional, existential, and intellectual reasons that far outweigh any other system of belief. There is just enough evidence for Christ that each day, I must conclusively doubt my doubts. It's tough most days, but it's often enough.

Let's consider a few things together, and ultimately you can decide to clamp down with your conviction.

- Something in the first century made the Jews just go nuts.

The Jewish-Israelite people were dead-set on *never ever* worshiping another god, ever. It was their first ancient law from God, and even when Caesar claimed divinity or these other "messiahs" came around claiming to be the savior, the Jews never budged. The Romans had constrained the Jewish people by outlawing most religious places unless they were called "schools," and the Romans threw all their gods and cultural excess on them. But the Jews remained slavishly devoted to Yahweh and never bowed down to any idols, even amidst so much social derision and lowered status.

Hang with me here. If the Jewish-Israelite people were already strict about idol-worship, then the Pharisees were even worse. The Pharisees were a zealous group of about six-thousand Jews who had added over six-hundred laws to Scripture, hoping for God to rule again if they followed all His rules. They would've immediately shouted down anyone who claimed God-status. This is understandable; the Israelite people had not heard the "voice of God" in the last four centuries (which is the period between Malachi and Matthew, the split between the Old Testament and New Testament), and they believed this silence was God's wrath since their forefathers had turned to idolatry too many times.

Still with me? It's most likely in this four-hundred year period before Jesus's birth that the Pharisees were formed while Rome gained strength. When the Roman Empire solidified after crushing Egypt and Africa, the Pharisees were nervous about their own Jewish-Israelite people turning to false gods again. Ultimately the Pharisees were so horrified by Jesus's ministry that they *partnered with the Romans* to crucify him. On one hand the Pharisees considered Jesus the most dangerous man alive, but on the other hand, he was just one more nuisance to kill so they could go back to following Scripture and ushering in their "kingdom." These multiple points of convergence — the Jews, the Pharisees, and the Romans — led to what N.T. Wright has called a perfect storm.[62] Really, the ministry of Jesus should've ended with his death.

But after Jesus died, an event happened where suddenly the Jewish people had changed their sacred day of worship from Saturday to Sunday. They were claiming the Christ had risen. They were saying *Jesus is the Messiah*. Even some of those high-profile Pharisees, like Nicodemus and Joseph of Arimathea, were turning to Jesus. In the eyes of many Jews, this would've been downright blasphemous, but whole hordes of them were now convinced that Jesus was God. It was such an intense explosive shift that Rome never recovered, and only decades later Christianity became the mainstream faith of the nation.

Something happened two-thousand years ago that history *must* account for. I know this by itself is not incontrovertible evidence that Jesus did what he did. But scholars are still confounded by this rapid series of events that essentially upturned both the Jewish people and the Roman

---

[62] Check out N.T. Wright's *Simply Jesus*.

nation. Once-devout Jews were being lit up and impaled by Nero, being mauled by lions and torn limb-from-limb, molten lead poured in their heads, families killed and stoned, all to stand for Christ.

I say all this because *the Jewish-Israelite people had even more reason than you and me to doubt that Jesus was God.* They were not only skeptical, but fiercely aggressive against any such notion. If you don't believe that, you only need to see the crucifixion of Jesus. They were willing to destroy any living person who would run up against their holy agenda. Yet James and Peter and early church historians tell us about the massive *diaspora* of Jews who were being hunted and executed for their faith in Jesus.

What the heck happened then? Did the Jews just lose their dang minds? Maybe. But every historical account that tries to explain this away ends up piling on more doubt to their own theories. Really the simplest explanation here, by way of Occam's Razor, is that Jesus is who he said he was and he did what he said he would.

Christianity is uniquely alone in that it does not claim to be built primarily on teachings, but on a historical succession of event that ripped through a nation. No one wanted Christianity to be true, most in particular the disciples, who all fled. But they turned back because they simply couldn't deny Jesus had risen. They had seen him. It was the key event that validated all of Jesus's ministry: not his miracles or teachings or death, but walking out of that grave. Ultimately, over and over, despite my incredulity, I find this to be the most rational explanation for the Jews going nuts. You'd have to make a very convoluted difficult case to explain it any other way.

- Jesus's death and resurrection built an iconoclastic world-upheaving truth that is upheld by the counterintuitive element of grace.

Jesus is existentially satisfying because he accurately describes the human condition and provides the solution. Every other system of belief is built on performance, maintenance, reward/punishment, dichotomous banner-waving division, moralism, superiority, self-improvement, and self-isolated relativism. Jesus destroys all these categories and provides a way above all ways that I have absolutely not found in any other system of thinking.

He speaks to my desperate need for self-justification. All day long, I'm justifying myself to prove I'm worthy. I am making myself better than others and comparing my weakness to someone who is weaker than me. I am in a moral race that causes me to laugh at a celebrity's downfall or to help the poor to look righteous. Jesus destroyed this in the cross by calling us *all equally guilty* and *all equally loved*. It was never in us to justify ourselves, but only Jesus can do this.

He speaks equally to my lack of humility and my lack of confidence. Jesus had to die for my sin so I can't be prideful, but he was glad to die for my sin so I can't be in despair.[63] Both are somehow true *at the same time,* and it's this paradoxical union of tensions that keeps me oriented to a self-forgetting love for others and a right estimation of myself.

He speaks to my need for approval, validation, and significance. Because Jesus loved me enough to die for me, he is the foundation for all the love I need. He knows me and *still loves me,* and this is the relational intimacy I've always been looking for.

---

[63] Inspired by Timothy Keller.

He speaks to my need to serve myself and make life about me. I'm set free because my life is not about me. Life is about the story of God and we're all bit players. Imagine this sort of freedom: when you can quit living selfishly for yourself. You're no longer enslaved under the tyrannical dictatorship of self. Imagine this sort of Gospel-shaped person who *loved* you but didn't *need* you, because they're not using you as a vehicle to serve themselves. They're not killing you as an obstacle who is in the way of their desires. They're instead seeking to love you *simply because they love you and not because of what you can or won't do for them*, and this is because they are loved the same way.

Every other kind of motivation is inherently selfish. It is all seeking a means to an end, one method using another for self-gain. We're motivated by fear, by conformity, by trophies, by pleasure, by social standing, and while they might benefit a few, they really just benefit *me*. The love of God is entirely intrinsic unto itself, in a single direction initiated by its own essence, with nothing to gain and no reason to exist except that it does. When we understand such a love, we're motivated by a purely one-way love to love in the same way, motivated by the reason of no-reason, because it has inherently punctured through our souls. There is no stronger force than this in the entire universe.

I could keep going. The Gospel of Grace is scary as hell, because it means we can no longer work for our own salvation. It means we're no longer in control of validating our own lives. But when applied rightly, the Gospel of Grace destroys the gap between *who we are* and *who we want to be*. It fills in my existential itch to be both loved and known. It usurps my selfish need to justify and hold myself superior. It ruins everything so perfectly.

- Even if you don't believe Jesus is God, we would still be studying the things he said.

Jesus was intellectually subversive and superlative in every single area of thought. The stuff he said was crazy, revolutionary, mind-blowing. To be truthful, most of his teaching is common sense. But the way in which he broke xenophobia and did away with dichotomous dogmatic thinking was nothing short of *astonishing*.

You can't pin him down. He was both merciful and full of justice. He was at times liberal and at times conservative. He loved Roman officials as much as he loved prostitutes, swindlers, and murderers. If he were alive today, he would infuriate both Fox News and The New Yorker. There are not many people like this. Almost everyone in history fell to one side of the spectrum or the other. Their thoughts would fall into one pigeonhole or another. We are not a balanced people who can consistently hold two tensions at once, but Jesus did.

I can almost guarantee that G.K. Chesterton was right: if you repackaged Jesus as a Chinese mythology and re-told it to a non-Christian, they would absolutely love it. But because it's *Jesus and Christianity*, people hate it.

The more you read about Jesus, the more you get a sense you're dealing with the divine. You're not dealing with human words here. He's not some comfortable therapeutic guru nor a rebel for rebellion's sake. He's something altogether in his own category that transcends our comprehensible reality.

I pray you find him, my friend.

"To fall in love with God is the greatest romance;
to seek Him, the greatest adventure;
to find Him, the greatest achievement."
— St. Augustine

8. Guilt, Fear, Shame, Fire and Brimstone

– "I've always been on the receiving end of what you would call the 'guilt-fear-shame' tactics. When I was seven, I was handed one of those infamous 'You're a Sinner and You're Going to Hell' pamphlets. Ever since then I've struggled ... that I'm still doomed to hell simply because *all* I've ever known is the terror, the guilt, and the shame ... How can they do this to others?"

– "I have always been told ... 'Don't read anything that isn't the Bible', 'You're going to hell because you enjoyed Pokemon', 'Don't you know Hollywood is a den of sin?' I constantly feel like it's *wrong* to have interests outside of theology/religion ... I feel like I'm being trained to be a nun or monk. Is it right to feel this way?"

– "I sometimes feel like I'm sinning when I don't have a bible in my hand 24/7. I feel that way when I'm doing my homework & watching cartoons. I feel that way reading anything that isn't theology-derived ... Is this a natural part of growing on the journey?"

Thank you for these very honest questions. You and I both have been hurt by tons of churches that breathed condemnation: and for some of us, it could take a long time to recover.

So please allow me the grace to break this down a bit.

1) Guilt/fear/shame are natural first reactions that point to a human truth.

If you would've asked me in the last few years if "guilt/fear/shame" were wrong, I would've yelled an emphatic *yes*. Faith can never be sustained by the motivation of guilt because it's an exhausting race that isn't fueled by God nor even running towards Him.

But I began thinking: *Why do we even feel guilt? Should I be so quick to call it evil? Isn't it as significant as every other emotion?* No one believes that all pain is bad either, because pain points to our humanity.

So feeling guilty is *not* wrong — it's expected. Please do *not* feel bad for feeling bad.

We're all hard-wired to feel guilt and all its associated emotions. These are the effects of the Fall in Genesis 3, and any time we feel them burning our gut, they're always pointing to *something missing*. In other words: **Guilty feelings point to a "positional" guilt.** Guilt is part of our humanity saying: *Something is wrong here, and we need a better way.*

Sin killed our connection with God in the Garden. You can see it in this fractured world. We know this is not how things ought to be. When we conform to the Fall, our hearts will the feel the guilt of going against our Creator. It's that sick feeling in your stomach which already tells me: you know what I mean.

Even the kindest preacher in the world will still press your guilt-button, because you will *always feel the gap between who you are and who you could be*. This tension is an inevitable part of our fallen condition.

2) Guilt/fear/shame will *always* be wrong when it's used by the preacher as a motivator.

The problem is when the preacher is yelling at you on Sunday about porn or drugs or TV shows, he's dropping a sledgehammer down your throat. He's over-doing it. He is mostly saying what you already know is true, and he's not offering a solution.

A bad preacher will only tell you how it is. A good preacher will carry you on a transformative journey from how it is to how things *could* be — and he does that by pointing to Jesus, the one who came to rescue us.

Feeling guilt is natural, but if you think it will navigate your walk, it only points in a singular direction at your shortcomings, and that's how self-condemnation happens. To put it in theological terms, you can't use *the feelings of guilt* as leverage to pay off *positional guilt*.

3) Guilt/fear/shame, as an initial reaction, is inevitable because it points to the Holiness of God.

The Bible over and over talks about men and women who meet God, fall on their face, repent in dust and ashes, wear a sackcloth on their head, fast in terror of the Lord, and wish they were dead. Much of the Bible is about God's wrath, God warning us, God laying down justice. We can't dismiss that.

If you could see the throne-room of God, like Isaiah did, you'd probably say the same thing: *Woe to me! I am ruined! For I am a man of unclean lips ... and my eyes have seen the King.*

Isaiah, who is probably holier than you and me and your grandma and Mother Teresa, could hardly stand his own sinfulness in the glorious sight of God. I don't mean to over-state the case, because I don't think I can.

When we preach a "hyper-grace," we short-circuit the Holiness of God. I've seen what hyper-grace can do to people. It can lead to thinking we're never wrong. It dismisses rebuke as a "guilt trip." It brushes off the consequences of sin and jumps too quickly to forgiveness, which is necessary, but diminishes the real work that must be done.

4) Yet God does not want you to stay in guilt. In the end, we can only walk this walk by God's grace.

If your first reaction is guilt, you need to know it's healthy and normal. But we can't stay there. God doesn't keep us in fear. He's not itching to pull the trapdoor lever to Hell. In our continual faith journey, all fear gets put to death.

That's why 1 John 4:18 says,

There is no fear in love. But perfect love drives out fear, because fear has to do with punishment. The one who fears is not made perfect in love.

God doesn't want us to base our relationship with Him on *do-more, try-harder, maybe you'll make it*. It's not based on the TV shows you censor, or reading the right Christian authors, or plugging into church programs. You might know all this: but guilt is still controlling you.

Apostle Paul in Romans 8 says,

Therefore there is now no condemnation for those who are in Christ

— in perhaps the most victorious monologue in the entire Bible.

So the difference is that *guilt never really finishes the sentence and doesn't root for you to move forward.* Guilt is not the conclusion.

God's grace is scary because it removes our ability to pay off our shortcomings. God loves us in a way we don't deserve and we can't earn. *It is finished,* he said. We can only receive the gift. **It's this love which picks us up, restores us, and sets us on His mission.**

Like Isaiah, we respond, *"Here am I, send me!"* It's the same when Jesus in Matthew 17 revealed his fully blazing glory on the mountaintop, then went down to a fallen Peter and told him, *"Get up ... Don't be afraid."* Jesus was the only one who *could* lift him up. He picks up his disciples from the floor of their shame into his grace.

9. Five Ways That Christianity Challenges You To Think For Yourself

"How would you say Christianity challenges you to think for yourself?"

Contrary to misinformed popular opinion, I would say Christianity challenges us to think for ourselves in several great ways.

1) God first and foremost commands us to think for ourselves.

If God's commands are a way of describing reality and how it ought to work, then it's a big deal that God wants us to think through to the bottom of everything. Passages like 1 John 4 and Proverbs 2:9-11 show that God wants us to have discernment and wisdom, and that "knowledge is pleasant to the soul." Acts 17 is almost entirely about Paul wanting us to dig deep on what we really believe. God is absolutely pro-intellect and pro-science, and anyone who says otherwise hasn't read the Bible very far.

2) Traditional Christianity had such a profound respect for knowledge that it practically kept libraries open during the so-called "Dark Ages."

I know that not everyone will see eye-to-eye on this one, but modern scholars have completely dismissed the "Dark Age" myth and how "Christianity set us back for centuries." This is a terrible misconception and only repeated by the least informed. Almost any medieval historian will tell you that early Christians cared so much about knowledge, whether pagan religion or Greek philosophy, that they preserved such teachings until it revitalized academia, to the point that you can link this revival with the scientific method and the Enlightenment. I believe the church has really lost their way on this in the twentieth and twenty-first century — but it must never be said that the early Christians tried to snuff out the sciences. It's the very, very opposite. The purest state of Christianity will always seek knowledge in its purest form, no matter where it comes from, because the Christian believes all information can point us back to the true God.[64]

3) God never demands our unthinking worship.

Many Christians might have a problem with this: but the Bible *never once* demands us to worship God.[65]

The Bible, in fact, only tells us *about* God and to seek Him. We're to freely seek Him of our own will. The Bible then expects that if we truly met God as He really is, then we'll be knocked over by His infinite glory. Every person in the Bible who actually sought God and met Him nearly fell over dead. Isaiah wept; Ezekiel fell on his head; Moses hid in a mountain; John pretended to die. But God never forced such worship out of them. He didn't shotgun blast their knees. God gives us reasonable faculties to comprehend the reality of the world around us, and if we so wish, we can discover the glory of God by ascertaining His presence by pure logic and choice. It's only when we meet Him are we also moved in affection and spirit. This gift of free-will tells me that God allows us to think freely and that He doesn't want robots nor fear-driven grovelers.

4) The wondrous beauty of God draws us towards a vastly deeper appreciation of our reality.

I'm not sure why some Christians today often settle for mediocrity in their art. Maybe it's because we think the church ought to "show grace" for terrible Christianese music and movies, or that we need to have our own watered down version of secular culture. But there was a time when Christians were making the best art, music, and research, simply because Christians felt they were called to aesthetic excellence in all they did. If

---

[64] 1 Timothy 4:4, Romans 1:20, Psalm 19:1-4

[65] I learned this in seminary in my Ministry of Worship class. A few people nearly walked out.

we're empowered by an infinitely holy God, then it would follow that our creative inspiration would reflect an endlessly wondrous, majestic Creator.

Isaac Newton, Sebastian Bach, and Leonardo da Vinci were all Christians of varying faith traditions, yet they produced some of the most amazing work of their times. I think they were pulling not only from natural inspiration, but tapping into a divinity that added a bottomless depth to all they did. They were able to think deeper into a humbled surrender before glory, where imagination abounded. Like C.S. Lewis says, the Christian is not necessarily called to produce the best Christian stuff, but to make such great art and textbooks and music that others would want to pick them first, since nothing else would compare.[66] Or as DC Talk once said, "If it's Christian, it oughta be better."

5) God welcomes doubts, questions, and frustration.

One thing in common about the Book of Job, Nahum, Jonah, Ruth, Habakkuk, Jeremiah, and Lamentations is that God hears our venting and anger about His ways. Sometimes God does press us by flexing His glory, but mostly He just understands and walks us through it and stays a friend in our flailing. Mark 9:24 is proof that God hangs close when we feel so far, and that our doubts never disqualify us from knowing Him.

This is in stark contrast to everywhere else. In a certain corner of the blog-world, if you even try to question the way that others think, you'll be assaulted and shamed and destroyed. There's no such thing as freethinking on Facebook or Tumblr or WordPress; you'll be killed for questioning your platform. Your college campus and your workplace and your political office are so much more close-minded than you think. Most religious places, including the "Christian church," are so afraid of questions that you're called a sinner if you dare to implore or disagree. I'll even go so far as to say that almost every institution exhibits cult-like behavior,

---

[66] Inspired by C.S. Lewis' *God In The Dock*.

which operate on everyone thinking the same and riding the status quo and being stomped on for dissension.

Christianity never, ever operates this way. If someone says it does, they haven't even begun to meet the Jesus of the Bible. When you consider every downtrodden person who ever met Jesus, they had questions of suffering and purpose and wealth and death and disbelief — but Jesus always replied with both gentleness and authority. He treated these questions with dignity and worthy of navigating. He was never a step behind or too far ahead. Imagine a friend like that, who knows everything yet never condescends, who is side-by-side and yet in the lead.

I've been in places where I was shot down, cut off, and ostracized for the minority opinion. But in Scripture, with the Spirit, in the presence of Christ, I've never felt more comfort and conviction, where I was encouraged to float in my darkest questions but gently challenged on my preconceived notions. I could dare to vent my most horrible anger, because He not only handled me, but welcomed me. There is no other safe place where I can truly be myself and truly think for myself. And when I have such confidence in Him, I can freely admit when I'm wrong. I'm not threatened by different platforms or opposing voices, because all such knowledge is inherently valuable and worthwhile to hear. It matters less that we agree, but more that I will welcome you, so we can wrestle through these thoughts like Jesus did with me.

Chapter 7.5 —
Interlude: Everyone's Screwed Up, Busted Up, and Catching Up, and That's Okay

I don't think I've ever really met anyone who is living out of a full cup.

What I mean is: Everyone lives a lot further ahead than they really are, giving advice they don't follow and loving others without any love for themselves and running on empty all the time. We're all on fumes.

I'm finding out this is okay for today, and no lifetime is meant to be lived in a day.

There's this Secret Guilt going around that we're all halfway hypocritical frauds who will *maybe one day* catch up to an awesome version of ourselves. It's a desperate hope that we'll eventually *do* what we're preaching with our mouths and our blogs. And then we blow up or flip a table or punch a wall and that monster comes out, and we think "Where did that even come from?" — and the Guilt chokes the pit of our stomach again.

The finality of settling into your own skin never arrives.

We co-exist with the monster.

I remember a famous pastor who deleted his entire backlog of podcasts from his first years of preaching. Because he "no longer agreed" with those old messages. I thought it was pretty humble. But I also thought, *What about those people who heard those old messages? What if they followed through on that stuff? Are they just screwed? And ten years from now will you delete your stuff from today?*

Every artist I've met says their first drawing, song, poem, novel, or dance routine was unworthy. They're hard on their first creations. You know, that whole "you are your own worst critic" paranoia. But: *Don't we all have to purge these things before moving onto greatness? And what about those people who enjoyed the first creations? Are they just idiots?*

Everyone keeps saying, "I used to be so stupid." Or, "I was so empty when I taught that thing." Or, "I didn't even deserve to preach that sermon on marriage, my own marriage was failing." Or, "I wasn't even following my own advice."

It's a reoccurring pattern. **No one ever thinks they're good enough to do what they're doing.** Or they think *now* they're okay, but everything before today was terrible. "I finally found my voice," they say, which is at once a victory and an admission of defeat.

It's scary to think we're always walking in the dark, the light dissipating just out of reach.

Of course, I do think there are hypocrites that need to step down. There are fakes out there, and they need to stop. They know who they are and they're actively reaching in your wallet and your treasure and your heart, and they are robbing you.

But nearly everyone else is a busted up vessel making the best of what they have. They're not trying to mislead anyone. They're not purposefully deceptive. They're loving others despite how they feel, and that's already commendable. They're preaching great things even if they're struggling with them, and that requires a certain dignity.

The problem is *when we're not honest about our emptiness, we will crash*. If you continually say things you don't mean and you don't say things you do mean, then you'll die a little bit each day. You'll think you're alone in this, that you can keep going on this way, and you'll punish yourself in small incremental ways by self-shaming and holding back and staying down, and you'll call it humility when it's not.

And the monster will thrive off your hiding. It will pop up when you are poked and provoked, it will take over your hands and your mouth for even seconds at a time, but it will use those few seconds to destroy everything you love. This is what monsters do: and we let them do it.

I think we just need to own up to the emptiness. To say we're not okay, and then to get up and find other people who are not okay, and that's how we'll be okay. The monster always dies in the light.

That means you and I can't flinch when someone tells us about it. If we don't have hope of an undeserved grace, then we can never be honest, and then we'll never get grace. But if we can be recklessly honest about our hungry wandering souls, then maybe we can find restoration, and we might just make it.

This sort of dirty grace confronts the ugliness inside, grabs it by the fistfuls, and kills it with the relentless violence of love. It's not the textbook grace you put on like a cheap dress. It hurts like crazy: but afterward there is stillness and peace, like the morning. It's like beginning again.

If you've never felt that, it's probably because we've been masquerading by being nice all the time, when really this grace thing is a gritty business that rips the curtain of your religious activity to shreds.

You'll recognize that God loved your broken mess from the start, and He won't stop there. **Only God could ever simultaneously love us as we are now *and* love us into a different kind of person.** Both are impossibly true. But it begins when you receive that kind of grace today, right now, where you are. And it takes a lifetime to get it.

I hope to meet you there. I hope to meet you where Jesus is, plunging his scarred hands through the fortress of my lungs, squeezing my heart back to life.

—J.S.

Conclusion —
The Final Authority:
Why This Book Doesn't Matter

A final word, fellow traveler.

Don't trust me, because I will let you down.

The Christian community fervently follows tons of bloggers, preachers, and voices to aid them in their spiritual walk, and I think this is awesome. Really.

But please, *please*, dear friend, you must also please think for yourself.

If something in a sermon sounds funny or off or weird, don't believe it just because it's coming out of the mouth of your favorite preacher.

If your favorite blogger is saying something you silently disagree with, it's okay: you don't have to fanwank them to protect their pedestal in your mind. It's okay to disagree.

If they say something obviously wrong, it doesn't make them a bad person: it just means they're still learning, and so are you, and so are we, and no one gets it right every time. Most of them — and me too — are still working on the things they're preaching.

Every single person you listen to is just as broken, crazy, and capable of error as you are. I'll go further and say: some of these guys only care about blog hits and revenue and the number of followers and likes and reblogs, and don't really care about *you*, and they have their prepackaged automatic statements ready to fire when they want to act like they care about you. We all do.

Some do love you, but are not truthful. Some are truthful, but don't love you.

Don't trust them; not fully, ever. Don't trust me. Just trust Jesus.

I'm not saying this out of some kind of reverse-humility, as if to look more humble. I'm dead serious. Don't trust me.

I'm also not as cool as I try to make myself. If you met me, I'm much shorter than you imagine, I laugh too loud in public, I usually smell like Asian food, and my teeth are pretty crooked. You'd be disappointed.

None of these preachers and bloggers are heroes. They're not the sacred hologram we might have built them up to be. I've seen many wonderful men and women of God completely melt down, freak out, throw tantrums, and go violent (including myself) — and again, it does not make them bad people. It just makes them *people*.

Question everything. Use the Bible as your lens. Ask: *Would Jesus have agreed with this?* And at some point, land your heart on *your* conviction. We can't walk this walk emulating other peoples' opinions and secretly hoping for their approval and applause when we can parrot back information.

I am not discounting community, but the danger of numbers can often lead to conformity. True transformation only happens when your mind fully closes on the truth, and that journey of discovery must happen on your own.

Otherwise, when you find out these people are only people: your identity will be crushed, too.

Don't look up to me, or to some supposedly eloquent, articulate, witty, humble blogger. Please don't get caught up in the magical spun spell of a brilliant-sounding idea that is backed by the icing of so much self-aware, juiced-up, over-hyped scaffolding. At its central core, even when the "good idea" is true: it cannot work in the space of your deeply held convictions unless you actually swish the idea in your mind and clamp your mental jaws upon the meat.

It can't become a part of you until it passes *through* you, and even then, it needs to pass the test, to be rotated in 3D, to be examined in the light of reality. You will be disturbed by how many ideas so quickly fall apart this way. Yet you'll also be liberated towards pure wisdom that is not only functional but alive, a pulsing breathing life that is more than inspirational pep talk on a page.

Wisdom, then, is so much more than mental assent or reblogging a "convicting" post — but to be held up against itself, in the scorching no-nonsense eye of God, stripped of flowery layers, and arriving in your heart before applying it with your hands. This is how great revolutions began.

Try an experiment. For a week or so, *do not* read any blogs or listen to any sermons. Don't read any Christian books or seek someone else's advice. Instead, spend time in prayer and Scripture, in your bedroom or out in nature, and question everything. Talk with the Father. See what you find. Solidify your convictions, and when you come back to the open world of voices, see if you have a refreshed perspective.

I think your outlook will change. I think you'll find that many of the paradigms and social constructs that you held dear were wrong, not because anyone is bad, but because we buy into ideas that sound good but don't really work.

You'll find that some authors and pastors and bloggers probably have noble intentions, but some of us are writing from a vacuum-sealed, isolated laboratory without true love for your soul. You'll see the cute little catchphrases and preprogrammed statements and all the self-promotions and attention-seeking — and you'll see it in me, in you, and realize there is Only One we can truly trust with our entire being. It's because He absolutely loves you within Himself, without extra motives, without working an angle. I would check with Him first.

Follow Him. Please: trust only Him, the true writer and healer of our hearts.

— J.S.

"I know now, Lord, why you utter no answer.
You, yourself, are the answer.
Before your face questions die away.
What other answer would suffice?"[67]
— C.S. Lewis

---

[67] C.S. Lewis, *Till We Have Face: A Myth Retold* (Florida: Harcourt, 1956, 1984) p. 308

Acknowledged

To Lauren Britt (of yesdarlingido.tumblr.com) and Jerry Edmonds for their helpful feedback. To many others who test-read the book and both encouraged and analyzed.

To T.B. LaBerge (of tblaberge.tumblr.com) for his Foreword, his grace, his writing. To my brother, who always believed in me, motivated me, and genuinely makes me laugh like crazy.

To Andre Holmes, who always sees the best in all things. To Austin Cho, one of the first Christians I knew who was articulate and made sense, and introduced me to the inimitable C.S. Lewis. To be fair, I introduced you to Muse. To Jacob Choe, my roommate of six years. You're a good, good man. To Rob Connelly (of heyitsrob.com), who does all the graphics. Genius level, you are. To Pastor Jake, somehow you always make time.

To my wonderful fiancé, who challenged me with more thoughtfulness to think of every reader, every person, every soul.

Added to the Revised Edition:

I want to thank the international readers who managed to get the book, as far as Japan and China and Ireland. To embody Christianity in such areas is an absolutely admirable endeavor, and I'm praying for the very real hands and feet of Christ that are doing so much more than I ever could with these words.

I'm also grateful for the continual pictures and outpouring of messages I've received of how the book has strengthened convictions and bore new ones. I'm constantly overwhelmed and humbled by the honor to share in the faith journey of others, and I'm praying you and I will continue to fight the good fight as fellow travelers on this exciting adventure with Christ.

If you've been blessed by this book, please consider leaving a review on Amazon!
- Other titles available by J.S. Park -

Mad About God

In our hurt and suffering, we're often given spiritualized platitudes or power-positivity — but we need something deeper for our wounds.
Not every pain ends in a lesson or a bow-tie, and we need the space to vent, to grieve, to even be mad with God.

Christianese Dating

Is there any real wisdom the church can offer for those who are dating, single, wounded, or think "it's too late for me?" Sifting through Josh Harris, Taylor Swift, romantic comedies, and the heart of Jesus, we find relevant truth and hopeful grace for relationships.

Cutting It Off

Porn addiction is real and it nearly ruined my life. I was a porn addict for fifteen years, and I've now been sober for over three. I want to offer you recovery, not just for weeks at a time, but quitting for good.

Made in the USA
Middletown, DE
26 September 2016